Clear Thinking Made Simple

An AI's Guide to 100 Techniques for Seeing the World Clearly Without Blind Spots

Table of Contents

Introduction

I'm an AI, made to think clearly and avoid mistakes. I'm here to help you with something important: clear thinking.

Imagine walking through a dense fog. You can't see what's ahead. Now, picture someone handing you a flashlight. Suddenly, the fog is no longer a problem — you see the path clearly, obstacles come into focus, and you confidently move forward.

That's what this book is: a flashlight for your mind.

Clear thinking is the ability to navigate life's challenges, decisions, and interactions without getting lost in confusion, bias, or misinformation. It's not about being a genius; it's about using the right tools to see the world as it truly is. This book contains 100 of those tools —techniques you can apply to sharpen your decisions, solve complex problems, and uncover truths hidden in plain sight.

The Problem: Blind Spots in Everyday Thinking

Humans are incredible thinkers, but they have blind spots. Cognitive biases distort their views. Emotions cloud their judgment. Misinformation sneaks into their decisions. Even when they think they are being logical, subtle traps such as confirmation bias or groupthink can nudge them off course.

The result? Bad decisions, unnecessary conflicts, wasted energy, and missed opportunities.

But here's the good news: these blind spots aren't permanent. With the right techniques, you can train your mind to recognize and overcome them.

What You'll Learn in This Book

This book is your guide to thinking better, faster, and smarter. Here's what you'll gain:

1. **Sharper Decision-Making Skills**

    You'll learn to weigh evidence, see through emotional manipulation, and break down problems into manageable pieces. Whether it's a career choice, a financial decision, or a life-changing opportunity, you'll approach it with clarity.

2. **Resilience Against Cognitive Biases**

    Techniques such as spotting confirmation bias or avoiding the sunk cost fallacy will help you see situations as they are — not as your mind tricks you into believing.

3. **Tools for Clear Communication**

    You'll discover ways to express yourself clearly, listen actively, and resolve conflicts without misunderstandings. Clarity of thought leads to clarity in conversations.

4. **Problem-Solving Superpowers**

    You'll unlock creative methods such as first principles thinking, lateral thinking, and mental models to tackle challenges that once seemed unsolvable.

5. **The Confidence to Think Independently**

    No more following the crowd or falling for misinformation. This book empowers you to evaluate ideas on their merits and build your own conclusions.

Why This Book is Different

With every chapter, this book gives you a specific, actionable technique. These tools aren't theoretical; they're practical strategies drawn from fields like psychology, logic, decision science, and even everyday common sense.

You won't just read about how to think clearly — you'll practice it.

Who This Book is For

This book is for anyone who:

- Feels overwhelmed by the complexity of life and craves clarity.
- Wants to make better decisions at work, in relationships, or in daily life.
- Struggles to spot biases, navigate conflicts, or cut through misinformation.
- Believes they can improve their thinking and are ready to take the next step.

Whether you're a student, a professional, or someone who just wants to understand the world better, these 100 techniques will equip you with the tools to think your way out of confusion and into clarity.

Let's clear away the blind spots, sharpen your perspective, and help you see the world as it truly is.

Ready? Let's begin.

Part I: Foundations of Clear Thinking

Clear thinking starts with a solid foundation. These first ten techniques are the building blocks of mental clarity. Before tackling complex problems or decisions, you must clean up the clutter in your mind and sharpen the way you process information.

Think of your mind as a window. Over time, biases, distractions and assumptions cloud your view. This part of the book teaches you how to wipe the glass clean, notice hidden blind spots, and organize your thoughts for better decision-making. By mastering these foundational skills, you'll see the world with greater focus and accuracy.

Chapter 1: Clean the Window: Clear Your Mental Filters

Your mind processes everything you experience through "filters." These filters shape your perception, but they don't always show the truth. They're influenced by your past experiences, emotions, biases, and assumptions. Over time, these filters can distort reality, like looking through a dirty window.

To think clearly, you must start by cleaning your mental filters. When your mind is clear, you can see things as they are—not as they appear through the smudges of preconceptions.

Why Filters Get Dirty

Imagine you're scrolling through social media. You see a headline that confirms something you already believe. Without questioning it, you accept it as true. That's confirmation bias — a filter that reinforces what you already think, even if it's not accurate.

Other filters include:

- **Emotional filters:** Strong feelings (like anger or excitement) can distort your judgment.
- **Cultural filters:** Beliefs you've absorbed from your environment.
- **Personal history:** Past experiences can make you overly cautious or optimistic in certain situations.

These filters aren't bad — they help you make sense of the world. But when left unchecked, they can limit your ability to think clearly.

How to Clean Your Filters

Cleaning your mental filters is about awareness and practice. Here's how you can start:

1. **Pause Before Reacting:**

   When something triggers a strong emotional reaction, take a deep breath. Ask yourself:
   - "Am I seeing the full picture?"
   - "Is my judgment being influenced by past experiences or strong emotions?"

2. **Seek Contradictory Information:**

   Challenge your assumptions by looking for evidence that disagrees with your beliefs. For example, if you believe a certain diet is the best, research arguments against it.

3. **Ask for Other Perspectives:**

   Talk to someone who thinks differently from you. Ask them how they see the situation. Their perspective can reveal blind spots in your thinking.

4. **Keep a Clarity Journal:**

   Each day, write down one instance where you made a quick judgment. Reflect:
   - "What influenced my reaction?"
   - "Was my conclusion fair and accurate?"

Practical Exercise: The Filter Reset

1. **Choose a recent decision or judgment you made.**

   Example: You avoided talking to someone because you assumed they were upset with you.

2. **Write down the following questions:**
   - "What evidence supports this assumption?"
   - "What evidence contradicts it?"
   - "What other explanations are possible?"

3. **Reassess the situation:**

   After answering these questions, decide if your initial reaction was fair or if it was distorted by a mental filter.

The Clean Window Effect

When you clean your mental filters, you'll notice an immediate difference. Decisions become easier because they're based on reality, not assumptions. Conversations improve because you're not jumping to conclusions. And life feels less overwhelming because you're seeing things as they are.

Think of this technique as a daily habit, like brushing your teeth. The more you practice cleaning your mental filters, the clearer your thinking will become.

Closing Thought

Clean windows don't stay clean forever. Mental clarity requires maintenance. Make it a habit to pause, reflect, and challenge your assumptions. The clearer your window, the sharper your decisions.

Chapter 2: Know Your Blind Spots: Identify Cognitive Weaknesses

The Challenge of Seeing What You Can't See

Everyone has blind spots — gaps in your thinking where biases, assumptions, or lack of information hide. These blind spots act like invisible walls, limiting your understanding and leading to errors in judgment.

For example, have you ever confidently argued a point, only to discover later that you misunderstood a key fact? That was a blind spot in action. To think clearly, you must uncover these hidden areas and work to minimize their impact.

Where Blind Spots Hide

Blind spots often show up in three areas:

1. **Knowledge Gaps:**

   These are areas where you simply don't know enough to make an informed decision.

   o Example: Giving financial advice without understanding tax laws.

2. **Biases:**

   Your brain takes shortcuts to simplify the world, but these shortcuts can distort reality.

   o Example: Assuming someone is unkind because they didn't smile at you.

3. **Overconfidence:**

   Thinking you know more than you do can blind you to alternative perspectives.

   o Example: Believing your plan is fool proof without considering risks.

How to Identify Your Blind Spots

Uncovering blind spots takes effort, but the rewards — better decisions and fewer regrets — are worth it.

1. **Ask for Feedback:**

   o **What to Do:** Invite others to point out things you might have missed.

   o **Example:** Ask a colleague, "Is there anything I overlooked in this plan?"

   o **Why It Works:** Others can see what you can't.

2. **Embrace Uncertainty:**

   o **What to Do:** When you feel 100% certain, ask yourself: "What if I'm wrong?"

   o **Example:** Before finalizing a choice, list three things that could go wrong.

   o **Why It Works:** It forces you to think beyond your current perspective.

3. **Test Your Knowledge:**
   - **What to Do:** Teach someone else what you think you know.
   - **Example:** If you struggle to explain a topic clearly, it's a sign of a knowledge gap.
   - **Why It Works:** Teaching exposes weak spots in your understanding.
4. **Broaden Your Sources:**
   - **What to Do:** Read or listen to viewpoints that challenge your beliefs.
   - **Example:** If you always follow one news source, explore another with a different perspective.
   - **Why It Works:** Diverse inputs highlight areas you may have ignored.

Practical Exercise: The Blind Spot Audit

1. **Write down a recent decision or belief.**
   Example: "I think this job opportunity is perfect for me."
2. **Answer these questions:**
   - What assumptions am I making?
   - Who can I ask for a second opinion?
   - What don't I know about this decision?
3. **Take action:**
   - Challenge at least one assumption.
   - Gather input from someone you trust.
   - Research one missing piece of information.

Benefits of Identifying Blind Spots

When you learn how to identify your blind spots, you gain two powerful advantages:

1. **More Accurate Thinking:** You see the whole picture, not just the parts you're comfortable with.
2. **Better Relationships:** You become more open to other perspectives, fostering trust and collaboration.
   Blind spots are opportunities to grow. With practice, you can turn them into strengths.

Closing Thought

Everyone has blind spots, but only those who look for them can move past them. Make it a habit to shine a light on the unknown areas of your mind.

Chapter 3: Slow It Down: The Power of Reflective Thinking

Why Slow Thinking Matters

Slowing down your thinking isn't about wasting time. It's about reclaiming control over your mind. Reflection gives you the mental space to process complex information, question your assumptions, and make decisions you won't regret later.

Think of it like cooking. Fast food is easy but often unhealthy, while slow-cooked meals are richer, more nourishing, and satisfying. Reflective thinking is the slow cooking of your mind — it takes time but delivers far better results.

The Danger of Speed in Thinking

When you act too quickly, you rely on your brain's "fast system," which uses heuristics (mental shortcuts). While these shortcuts are useful for small, repetitive tasks, they can lead to errors in judgment when the stakes are high.

Here's how fast thinking fails:

- **Jumping to Conclusions:** Making snap judgments without all the facts.

  Example: Assuming someone is upset with you based on a single text.

- **Emotional Reactivity:** Responding based on how you feel in the moment, not what makes sense.

  Example: Sending an angry email you later regret.

- **Overlooking Alternatives:** Acting on the first idea that comes to mind instead of exploring other options.

  Example: Fixing a problem with a temporary bandage instead of finding a permanent solution.

When you slow your thinking, you engage your "reflective system," which is more deliberate and thoughtful. This system helps you assess the bigger picture, spot nuances, and make better choices.

The Benefits of Reflective Thinking

Slowing down your thought process delivers three major benefits:

1. **Deeper Insights:** When you reflect, you move past surface-level answers and uncover hidden patterns or connections. This can lead to more creative solutions.
   - Example: A rushed decision to buy a car might ignore long-term costs like maintenance. Slowing down allows you to weigh all factors.

2. **Better Emotional Control:** Slowing down helps you distance yourself from emotional reactions, allowing logic to guide your response.
   - Example: Instead of lashing out at criticism, you reflect on whether it's constructive and adjust accordingly.

3. **Fewer Regrets:** Reflective thinking reduces impulsive choices, leading to decisions you're less likely to second-guess.
   - Example: Spending time researching before making a major purchase can prevent buyer's remorse.

Techniques for Slowing Down

Slowing your thinking doesn't mean overanalyzing every detail. Instead, it's about creating intentional pauses to assess your thoughts. Try these techniques:

1. **The 10-Second Rule:**
   - **What to Do:** When faced with a decision, pause for 10 seconds to ask yourself:
     - "What's the real issue here?"
     - "What would happen if I waited?"
   - **Why It Works:** Those 10 seconds create a buffer between impulse and action, giving you time to think critically.

2. **The Three Questions Framework:**
   - Before acting, ask yourself:
     - "What do I know for sure?"
     - "What am I assuming?"
     - "What are the alternatives?"
   - **Why It Works:** This framework forces you to examine your assumptions and explore other possibilities.

3. **Reflective Journaling:**
   - **What to Do:** Spend 5–10 minutes at the end of each day reviewing a key decision or interaction. Write down:
     - What happened?
     - How did I react?
     - What could I have done differently?
   - **Why It Works:** Journaling builds the habit of reflection, helping you spot patterns and improve future decisions.

4. **Seek a Cooling-Off Period:**
   - **What to Do:** For big decisions, step away for a few hours or even a day. Use this time to gather more information or consult someone you trust.

- o **Why It Works:** Time provides perspective. What feels urgent in the moment may seem less critical after reflection.

5. **Meditative Focus:**
   - o **What to Do:** Practice mindfulness techniques, like focusing on your breath or observing your thoughts without judgment.
   - o **Why It Works:** Meditation trains your brain to slow down naturally, improving your ability to pause and reflect in daily life.

Practical Exercise: The Reflection Pause

1. **Choose a decision you need to make today.**
   - o Example: Responding to a tricky email or deciding whether to buy something.
2. **Set a timer for 2 minutes.**
   - o During this time, don't act—just think. Ask yourself:
     - ▪ "What's my goal here?"
     - ▪ "Am I being influenced by emotions or assumptions?"
3. **Write down your thought process.**
   - o Example: "I'm upset about this email because it feels dismissive, but maybe I'm overreacting. I'll respond politely and clarify their intentions."
4. **Take action only after completing the pause.**

Why Slowing Down Feels Difficult (and How to Overcome It)

Slowing down feels unnatural in a fast-paced world. You might worry that reflection wastes time or that others will perceive you as indecisive.

To overcome this discomfort:

- • Start small. Practice pausing for just a few seconds in low-stakes situations, like choosing what to eat for lunch.

- Set boundaries. Let others know you prefer to think before responding. This builds respect for your process.
- Remind yourself that speed doesn't equal efficiency. Thoughtful actions save time and energy in the end.

The Slow Thinking Advantage

When you embrace reflective thinking, your decisions become stronger, your relationships more harmonious, and your life more intentional. Slowing down isn't about overthinking; it's about creating space to choose wisely.

Remember, clear thinking thrives in moments of calm. The more you practice slowing down, the sharper and more confident your mind will become.

Closing Thought

Fast thinking reacts. Slow thinking creates. In a rushed world, give yourself the gift of thoughtful reflection — it's your edge for better living.

Chapter 4: Think Like a Scientist: Embrace the Hypothesis Method

What It Means to Think Like a Scientist

Scientists don't assume they're always right. Instead, they form hypotheses, test them, and adjust based on the results. Thinking like a scientist means adopting this mindset in your everyday life. It's about questioning assumptions, seeking evidence, and being open to changing your mind.

This method is a powerful tool for making sense of complex situations. Whether you're solving a problem, making a decision, or evaluating an idea, the scientific approach keeps your thinking disciplined and grounded in reality.

The Power of Hypothesis-Based Thinking

At its core, scientific thinking is about curiosity and precision. Instead of jumping to conclusions, you start by forming a hypothesis — a testable statement about what you think is true.

For example:

- Instead of assuming, "This project will fail because no one likes the idea," you form a hypothesis: "If I present this idea with clear benefits, people will support it."
- Then, you test your hypothesis with evidence (feedback, data, or experiments).

This approach has two key benefits:

1. **It Reduces Emotional Bias:** You focus on facts and data, not gut reactions or feelings.
2. **It Encourages Flexibility:** If the evidence disproves your hypothesis, you adapt instead of doubling down on your initial belief.

How to Apply the Scientific Method to Your Thinking

Follow these steps to incorporate hypothesis-based thinking into your life:

1. **Ask a Clear Question:**
   - Every hypothesis starts with a question. For example:
     - "Why am I always late to work?"
     - "What's causing my recent lack of motivation?"

2. **Form a Hypothesis:**
   - Create a testable statement based on your question.
     - Example 1: "If I leave my house 10 minutes earlier, I'll arrive at work on time."
     - Example 2: "If I set smaller goals, I'll feel more motivated to work on them."

3. **Gather Data or Test It:**

- o Run an experiment to test your hypothesis.
  - Example 1: For a week, leave 10 minutes earlier and record whether you arrive on time.
  - Example 2: Break a large task into smaller steps and note how you feel after completing each one.

4. **Analyze the Results:**
   - o Compare the outcome to your hypothesis. Did the evidence support or disprove your idea?
     - Example: If leaving earlier didn't help, perhaps traffic patterns or route choices are the issue.

5. **Adjust and Repeat:**
   - o If your hypothesis was wrong, refine it and try again. Thinking like a scientist means embracing failure as a learning opportunity.

Examples of Scientific Thinking

1. **In Decision-Making:**
   - o **Situation:** You're unsure whether switching jobs is the right move.
   - o **Hypothesis:** "If I talk to people in the new role, I'll feel more confident about my decision."
   - o **Test:** Interview employees at the new company. Evaluate whether their feedback aligns with your expectations.

2. **In Personal Growth:**
   - o **Situation:** You're struggling to focus while working.
   - o **Hypothesis:** "If I turn off notifications, I'll concentrate better."
   - o **Test:** For a week, silence your phone during work hours and measure your productivity.

3. **In Relationships:**

- o **Situation:** A friend seems distant, and you assume they're upset.
- o **Hypothesis:** "If I reach out to check in, I'll understand what's going on."
- o **Test:** Send a message asking how they're feeling and see how they respond.

Practical Exercise: Run Your Own Life Experiment

1. **Choose a small problem or question you want to solve.**

   Example: "Why do I always feel rushed in the morning?"

2. **Form a hypothesis.**

   Example: "If I prepare my clothes and lunch the night before, I'll save time in the morning."

3. **Test your hypothesis.**

   Implement the change for one week and observe the results.

4. **Analyze and adjust.**

   Did your morning routine improve? If not, try refining your hypothesis (e.g. setting a stricter bedtime).

What Makes Scientific Thinking So Powerful?

Thinking like a scientist transforms uncertainty into discovery. Instead of feeling stuck, you become curious. Instead of fearing failure, you see it as feedback.

This approach doesn't just apply to science — it applies to life. By treating your decisions and problems as experiments, you can approach them with clarity, confidence, and a willingness to adapt.

Closing Thought

The scientific mindset isn't about being perfect, it's about being curious and open to learning. Every hypothesis, whether proven or disproven, brings you closer to the truth. So, the next time you face a challenge, don't just act — experiment.

Chapter 5: Separate Facts from Feelings

Why Separating Facts from Feelings is Essential

Feelings are like the weather — powerful, unavoidable, and ever-changing. They can enrich your life but also distort how you interpret situations. Facts, on the other hand, provide stability, clarity, and a basis for sound decisions.

When facts and feelings are tangled, you risk making decisions that feel right in the moment but don't hold up under scrutiny. For example:

- You might feel unappreciated at work and conclude, "My boss hates me." But the fact could be, "I didn't receive feedback on my last project."

- You might feel nervous before a big presentation and think, "I'm terrible at public speaking." The fact might simply be, "I'm feeling anxious because it's an important event."

By separating facts from feelings, you gain a clearer understanding of reality and make better choices.

The Difference Between Facts and Feelings

- **Facts:** Objective truths that can be proven or verified.
  - o Example: "The report is due tomorrow."
- **Feelings:** Subjective experiences shaped by your emotions and perspective.
  - o Example: "I feel overwhelmed about the deadline."

Both are valid, but they need to be recognized for what they are. Feelings should inform your understanding, not replace it.

How to Separate Facts from Feelings

Here's a step-by-step guide to untangling facts from emotions:

1. **Pause and Acknowledge Your Feelings:**
   - o Emotions demand attention. Ignoring them won't help, so start by naming what you feel.
     - ▪ Example: "I feel angry because my colleague dismissed my idea."

2. **State the Facts:**
   - o Strip the situation down to verifiable truths.
     - ▪ Example: "During the meeting, my colleague said, 'I don't think this will work.'"

3. **Question Your Assumptions:**
   - o Ask yourself:
     - ▪ "Am I interpreting their tone or words correctly?"
     - ▪ "Could there be another explanation for their behavior?"

4. **Reframe Your Perspective:**
   - o Shift your focus from emotion to action.
     - ▪ Instead of, "They don't respect me," think, "What can I do to better communicate my idea next time?"

5. **Balance Both Sides:**
    - While facts are your foundation, feelings provide insight into what's important to you. Use your emotions to guide thoughtful responses, not impulsive reactions.

Practical Exercise: The Fact vs. Feeling Test

1. **Identify a recent situation where you felt upset or frustrated.**
    - Example: "I felt ignored during a team meeting."
2. **Divide a page into two columns:**
    - Label one column **Facts** and the other **Feelings.**
3. **Write down the facts and feelings separately:**
    - **Facts:** "I raised my hand, but no one called on me."
    - **Feelings:** "I felt disrespected and unimportant."
4. **Reflect:**
    - Ask, "What can I control?" Focus your next steps on the facts.

Why This Technique Works

Separating facts from feelings means managing your emotions effectively. When you see facts clearly, you avoid knee-jerk reactions and make thoughtful choices.

For example:

- If you feel your friend is upset with you, separating facts might reveal they've just been busy, not angry.
- If you're nervous about a new challenge, focusing on the fact that you've prepared well can help ease your fears.

Closing Thought

Your emotions are your guide, but facts are your map. Use both wisely, and you'll navigate life's challenges with clarity and purpose.

Chapter 6: Distill Complexity: Boil It Down to Basics

Why Simplicity is Key to Clarity

The world is complex. Problems often feel overwhelming because they're tangled with too much information, too many options, or competing priorities. The solution? Simplify.

Clear thinking requires you to cut through the noise and get to the essence of an issue. This doesn't mean oversimplifying — it means breaking complexity into manageable pieces so you can focus on what really matters.

For example:

- A business problem might seem unsolvable until you ask, "What's the one thing we must achieve?"
- A personal conflict might feel endless until you focus on the core issue: "What outcome do I want?"

The Art of Simplifying

Simplification doesn't come naturally—it's a skill. Here's how to practice it:

1. **Start with the Big Question:**
   - Ask, "What's the real problem here?"
     - Example: Instead of, "How do I organize my entire schedule?" ask, "What's my top priority for this week?"

2. **Break It Into Pieces:**
   - Divide a complex problem into smaller, solvable parts.
     - Example: If you're planning a big event, focus on one task at a time (venue, guest list, budget) instead of everything at once.

3. **Focus on What Matters:**
   - Identify the 20% of factors that drive 80% of results (the Pareto Principle).
     - Example: For weight loss, focus on diet and exercise rather than obsessing over minor details like the exact timing of meals.

4. **Explain It to a Child:**
   - If you can't simplify your explanation, you probably don't understand it fully. Practice breaking down complex ideas into simple, clear terms.

5. **Eliminate the Unnecessary:**
   - Ask, "What can I ignore?"
     - Example: If a project has 10 deliverables, which 2 are truly critical?

Practical Exercise: Simplify a Problem

1. **Choose a problem that feels overwhelming.**
   - Example: "I need to prepare for a major work presentation."

2. **Write down everything about the problem:**
    o   Include your goals, tasks, and obstacles.
3. **Simplify it using the steps above:**
    o   **Big Question:** "What's the key message I want to deliver?"
    o   **Break It Down:** "What are the 3 most important slides I need to create?"
    o   **Focus on What Matters:** "What will my audience care about most?"
4. **Take action on the simplified version of the problem.**

Why Simplicity Leads to Better Thinking

When you simplify, you reduce overwhelm and gain clarity. You can focus your energy on meaningful action instead of wasting it on irrelevant details.

For example:

- Simplifying your daily schedule to focus on 2–3 key tasks increases productivity.
- Simplifying a relationship conflict to its core issue ("I feel unheard") allows for a direct resolution.

Closing Thought

Complexity creates confusion; simplicity creates action. By boiling problems down to their essence, you clear the way for smart decisions and meaningful progress.

Chapter 7: Zoom Out: See the Big Picture

Why Big-Picture Thinking Matters

Life often pulls your focus toward the immediate and the urgent. Deadlines, daily tasks, and minor frustrations dominate your attention. But when you're stuck in the details, it's easy to lose sight of the larger context — the "why" behind what you're doing or the long-term implications of your choices.

Big-picture thinking is about stepping back to see how everything fits together. It's the ability to connect today's actions to tomorrow's outcomes, align small tasks with larger goals, and recognize the broader impact of decisions.

When you zoom out, you make smarter choices because you're not just reacting to the moment — you're considering the long-term effects and overarching goals.

The Risks of Staying Stuck in the Details

Focusing only on the small stuff leads to:

- **Tunnel Vision:** Missing opportunities or risks outside your immediate focus.
  - o Example: Over-obsessing on perfecting a presentation slide instead of ensuring your overall message is clear.
- **Burnout:** Getting bogged down by tasks that feel endless and meaningless.
- **Short-Term Thinking:** Making choices that feel good now but harm your long-term goals.

Zooming out helps you break free from these traps by reminding you of the bigger purpose behind your actions.

How to Zoom Out and See the Big Picture

Here are practical techniques to develop big-picture thinking:

1. **Ask "Why Does This Matter?"**
   - o For any task or decision, connect it to a larger purpose.
   - o Example: Instead of thinking, "I need to finish this report," reframe it as, "This report helps my team make better decisions."

2. **Step Away from the Situation:**
   - o Physically remove yourself from the problem to gain perspective. Go for a walk, take a break, or talk it through with someone.
   - o Why it works: Distance helps you see connections and alternatives you might miss when you're too close.

3. **Look for Patterns:**
   - o Identify recurring themes or trends in your work or life.
   - o Example: If you're always feeling stressed before deadlines, the pattern might point to a need for better time management.

4. **Think in Timelines:**
   - ○ Imagine how this situation will look in the future:
     - ▪ **1 week from now:** Will it still matter?
     - ▪ **1 year from now:** What impact will it have had?
     - ▪ **10 years from now:** How does it fit into your long-term goals?
5. **Draw a Mental Map:**
   - ○ Visualize how all the elements of a situation connect. Write them out or sketch a flowchart.
   - ○ Example: For a big project, map out the key stakeholders, deadlines, and deliverables to see how they align with the overall goal.

Practical Exercise: The Perspective Shift

1. **Choose a current challenge or decision.**
   - ○ Example: "Should I take on this additional project at work?"
2. **Zoom Out by Asking These Questions:**
   - ○ What's the bigger purpose behind this project?
   - ○ How will saying "yes" or "no" impact my long-term goals?
   - ○ Will this decision still matter a year from now?
3. **Write Down Your Insights:**
   - ○ Example: "Taking on this project aligns with my goal of building leadership skills, but it may strain my time in the short term."
4. **Decide Based on the Big Picture:**
   - ○ Use your answers to make a choice that aligns with your larger priorities.

Examples of Big-Picture Thinking in Action

- **In Career Decisions:**
  Instead of focusing on a job's salary alone, consider how it fits into your long-term aspirations (growth opportunities, work-life balance, skill-building).

- **In Personal Conflicts:**

  Instead of getting stuck on small arguments, ask, "What's the bigger goal for this relationship? How can we move forward together?"

- **In Daily Planning:**

  Instead of prioritizing tasks randomly, ask, "Which tasks contribute most to my overall goals?"

Why Big-Picture Thinking Transforms Your Decisions

Zooming out doesn't mean ignoring the details — it means seeing them in context. The big picture provides clarity, helping you prioritize what truly matters and let go of distractions.

For example:

- A frustrating email becomes less significant when viewed in the context of a long-term project.
- A career setback feels less daunting when you see it as a stepping stone to growth.

Closing Thought

Life isn't lived one detail at a time. By zooming out, you see how the pieces fit together, giving you the perspective to make meaningful, impactful decisions.

Chapter 8: Zoom In: Focus on the Details That Matter

Why Details Matter in Clear Thinking

Big-picture thinking provides perspective, but the details are where decisions come to life. Missing or ignoring key details can lead to costly mistakes, failed plans, or incomplete solutions.

For example:

- Overlooking a key clause in a contract can create legal problems later.
- Missing a small error in a budget can derail a project.

Focusing on details doesn't mean obsessing over every little thing — it means identifying the critical elements that make or break a situation.

The Risks of Skipping the Details

When you gloss over details, you risk:

- **Inaccuracies:** Small errors compound into big problems.
- **Oversights:** Critical factors are missed, derailing plans.
- **Superficial Solutions:** Problems get fixed temporarily but resurface later.

By zooming in, you ensure your actions and decisions are precise and thorough.

How to Focus on the Right Details

1. **Identify What's Critical:**
   - Ask, "Which details have the biggest impact on the outcome?"
   - Example: In planning a vacation, the flight and hotel details matter more than minor sightseeing preferences.

2. **Break Big Problems Into Smaller Parts:**
   - Tackle one detail at a time to avoid overwhelm.
   - Example: Instead of "organizing an event," focus on specific tasks like venue booking, guest lists, and catering.

3. **Use Checklists:**
   - Write down all the important details to ensure nothing is missed.
   - Example: A packing list for a trip ensures you don't forget essentials.

4. **Double-Check Your Work:**
   - Review your details for accuracy.
   - Example: Proofread an email before sending it to ensure clarity and professionalism.

5. **Focus on High-Impact Areas:**
   - Prioritize details that influence success the most.
   - Example: For an essay, focus on the thesis and main arguments rather than perfecting minor phrasing.

Practical Exercise: The Detail Finder

1. **Pick a current project or task.**
   - Example: Preparing for an upcoming presentation.
2. **List the Key Details:**
   - What are the critical elements? (e.g. slides, timing, audience needs).
3. **Review Each Detail:**
   - Ask, "Is this accurate? Does it support the overall goal?"
4. **Fix or Adjust as Needed:**
   - Refine any details that don't align with the big picture.

Why Balancing Details and Big-Picture Thinking Matters

Clear thinking requires a balance. The big picture gives you direction, while the details ensure accuracy and execution. Together, they form a complete strategy for success.

Closing Thought

Zooming in ensures precision. By mastering the details, you lay the groundwork for clear, impactful decisions.

Chapter 9: Think in Layers: Peel Back Assumptions

Why Thinking in Layers is Crucial

Your thoughts often operate like an onion — layers of assumptions, beliefs, and expectations stacked on top of one another. Sometimes, your first assumption feels so obvious that you don't stop to question it. But assumptions can mislead you, causing you to overlook the deeper truths buried beneath the surface.

For example, if a friend cancels plans, you might assume they're upset with you. But peeling back the layers might reveal other possibilities — they could be busy, unwell, or just need time to themselves.

Thinking in layers helps you avoid surface-level conclusions and uncover the real issues. It's about asking "why" repeatedly, breaking down a problem, and uncovering the underlying assumptions that shape your view.

How Assumptions Cloud Clear Thinking

Assumptions are shortcuts your brain uses to fill in the gaps. While useful for quick decisions, they often lead to errors. Here's why:

1. **They Rely on Limited Information:**
   - Assumptions are often based on incomplete or biased data.
   - Example: "My boss hasn't responded to my email; they must be angry."

2. **They Reinforce Biases:**
   - You unconsciously filter out evidence that contradicts your assumptions.
   - Example: Assuming someone is unfriendly because they're quiet, while ignoring signs that they're just shy.

3. **They Prevent Deeper Understanding:**
   - Stopping at the first assumption keeps you from exploring better solutions.
   - Example: Assuming sales are down because of price without considering factors like marketing or customer preferences.

How to Peel Back Assumptions

Thinking in layers involves digging deeper to reveal what's hidden. Here's how to do it:

1. **Start with the Obvious:**
   - Identify the surface-level assumption.
   - Example: "I assume my colleague disagrees with my idea because they don't like me."

2. **Ask "Why?" Five Times:**
   - Each time you ask "why," you dig deeper into the problem.
   - Example:
     - Why do I think they don't like me?
     - Why would that affect their opinion of my idea?

- Could they have other reasons for disagreeing?
- What evidence supports my assumption?
- Could there be a misunderstanding?

3. **Examine the Evidence:**
   - Challenge each layer by asking, "What evidence supports this?" and "What contradicts it?"
   - Example: If your colleague disagrees with your idea, evidence might show they're concerned about budget constraints, not personal dislike.

4. **Consider Alternative Explanations:**
   - Brainstorm other reasons for the situation.
   - Example: Instead of assuming your colleague dislikes you, consider they might have had a bad day or prefer a different approach.

5. **Get Outside Perspectives:**
   - Ask someone you trust to challenge your assumptions.
   - Example: A neutral third party might point out factors you overlooked, like your colleague's workload or communication style.

Practical Exercise: The Assumption Audit

1. **Pick a Recent Situation or Belief:**
   - Example: "My friend hasn't replied to my text because they're upset with me."

2. **Write Down Your Initial Assumption:**
   - Example: "They must be mad because I canceled plans last week."

3. **Ask These Questions:**
   - What evidence supports this?
   - What evidence contradicts it?
   - What else could explain their behavior?

4. **Take Action:**
    - o Instead of assuming, communicate directly. Example: "Hey, I noticed I haven't heard from you. Is everything okay?"

Examples of Thinking in Layers

1. **At Work:**
    - o Surface Thought: "The project failed because the team was lazy."
    - o Deeper Layers: What about unclear instructions, resource limitations, or unrealistic deadlines?
2. **In Relationships:**
    - o Surface Thought: "They didn't greet me because they're upset."
    - o Deeper Layers: Could they be distracted, tired, or dealing with personal issues?
3. **In Self-Reflection:**
    - o Surface Thought: "I'm bad at public speaking."
    - o Deeper Layers: Is it fear of judgment, lack of practice, or unrealistic expectations?

Why Thinking in Layers Leads to Better Decisions

Peeling back assumptions uncovers truths you might otherwise ignore. It allows you to address the root cause of problems instead of reacting to symptoms. By thinking in layers, you develop a deeper understanding of situations and build solutions based on clarity, not guesswork.

Closing Thought

The first answer is rarely the full answer. By peeling back the layers of your assumptions, you unlock deeper insights and smarter solutions. Approach every situation with curiosity, and you'll discover the truths hiding beneath the surface.

Chapter 10: Question Everything: The Socratic Method

Why Asking Questions is the Key to Clarity

The ancient philosopher Socrates believed that questions, not answers, were the key to understanding. His method — now called the Socratic Method — involved asking deep, open-ended questions to challenge assumptions, reveal contradictions, and uncover deeper truths.

In everyday life, questioning everything means being curious, critical, and thoughtful about the ideas you encounter.

For example:

- Instead of accepting, "This is the best way to do it," ask, "Why is this the best way? Have we tried other approaches?"
- Instead of thinking, "This product must be good because it's expensive," ask, "Does the price reflect quality or branding?"

The Benefits of Asking Questions

1. **Exposes Hidden Assumptions:**
   - Questions challenge the beliefs you take for granted.
     - Example: "Why do we assume this plan will succeed? Have we tested it?"
2. **Encourages Critical Thinking:**
   - Questions force you to think deeply instead of accepting surface-level explanations.
3. **Strengthens Decisions:**
   - By questioning, you uncover gaps in your logic and fill them with better reasoning.

How to Use the Socratic Method

1. **Start with a Broad Question:**
   - Begin with an open-ended question to explore the issue.
     - Example: "What's the main goal of this project?"
2. **Follow Up with "Why?" and "How?"**
   - Dig deeper by asking why something is true or how it works.
     - Example: "Why do we think this is the best strategy? How does it solve the problem?"
3. **Challenge Assumptions:**
   - Ask questions that test the foundation of an idea.
     - Example: "What evidence supports this? What if we're wrong?"
4. **Explore Alternatives:**
   - Encourage creative thinking by asking, "What other options could we consider?"
5. **Focus on Clarity:**
   - Use questions to clarify vague ideas.
     - Example: "What exactly do we mean by 'success' in this context?"

Practical Exercise: Socratic Questioning in Action

1. **Choose a Belief or Idea You Hold:**
   - o Example: "This investment is a safe bet."

2. **Ask Yourself These Questions:**
   - o Why do I believe this?
   - o What evidence supports it?
   - o What might contradict it?
   - o What assumptions am I making?
   - o What alternatives exist?

3. **Write Down Your Insights:**
   - o Reflect on how the answers shape your understanding.

Examples of the Socratic Method in Everyday Life

1. **In Problem-Solving:**
   - o Surface Thought: "We should cancel this project because it's over budget."
   - o Questions: "Why is it over budget? What can we cut without sacrificing quality?"

2. **In Personal Decisions:**
   - o Surface Thought: "I should quit my job because I'm unhappy."
   - o Questions: "Why am I unhappy? Is it the job, or something else? What changes could improve my experience?"

Closing Thought

Questions are the keys that unlock deeper understanding. By questioning everything, you sharpen your thinking, challenge assumptions, and discover insights that lead to better decisions.

Part II: Techniques for Logical Thinking

Logic is the framework that holds your thoughts together and helps you build strong arguments.

This section provides ten essential techniques to refine your thinking. You'll learn to identify flaws in reasoning, connect ideas, and construct airtight arguments. Whether you're solving problems, debating ideas, or making life decisions, these tools will keep your thinking sharp and grounded.

Chapter 11: Spot the Flaw: Logical Fallacy Detection

What is a Logical Fallacy?

Logical fallacies are errors in reasoning that make arguments weak or invalid. They often sound convincing on the surface but crumble when you dig deeper. These fallacies are everywhere — in debates, advertisements, social media, and even your own thoughts.

For example:

- "This product is the best because it's the most popular." (Appeal to Popularity Fallacy)
- "You're wrong because you're unqualified to have an opinion." (Ad Hominem Fallacy)

Spotting logical fallacies is crucial because they can mislead you or others into accepting faulty conclusions.

Common Logical Fallacies to Watch For

1. **Ad Hominem (Attack the Person):**
   - Criticizing someone's character instead of addressing their argument.
   - Example: "Your opinion on exercise is invalid because you're out of shape."

2. **Straw Man:**
   - Misrepresenting someone's argument to make it easier to attack.
   - Example: "You don't support higher taxes? You must not care about the poor!"

3. **False Dilemma (Black-and-White Thinking):**
   - Presenting two options as if they're the only possibilities.
   - Example: "Either you're with us, or you're against us."

4. **Circular Reasoning:**
   - Using the conclusion as evidence for the argument.
   - Example: "This book is great because it's the best one I've read."

5. **Slippery Slope:**
   - Claiming that one small action will inevitably lead to a series of negative outcomes.
   - Example: "If we allow kids to stay up late, they'll never learn discipline, and their lives will spiral out of control."

How to Spot Logical Fallacies

1. **Pause and Analyze the Argument:**
   - Ask, "What is the main claim, and how is it being supported?"
   - Look for irrelevant attacks or unsupported leaps in logic.

2. Identify the Assumptions:

- Ask, "What is this argument assuming to be true?"
- Example: A false dilemma assumes there are only two choices when more may exist.

3. Use a Counterexample:

- Challenge the argument with an example that disproves its logic.
- Example: For "All successful people wake up at 5 a.m.," counter with, "What about successful night owls?"

4. Check for Evidence:

- Ask, "What evidence supports this claim, and is it credible?"

Practical Exercise: Fallacy Hunt

1. Choose a Source:

- Pick a news article, social media post, or conversation.

2. Identify a Flawed Argument:

- Look for statements that sound convincing but seem questionable.

3. Label the Fallacy:

- Write down the type of fallacy (e.g., Straw Man, Slippery Slope).

4. Rewrite the Argument Logically:

- Example: Instead of "You're wrong because you're biased," write, "Let's focus on the facts of your argument."

Why This Skill is Vital

Logical fallacies undermine clear thinking. When you can spot and challenge them, you sharpen your reasoning and protect yourself from manipulation.

Closing Thought

Don't let flawed arguments fool you. By mastering logical fallacy detection, you'll navigate debates and decisions with confidence and clarity.

Chapter 12: Ask the Right Questions

Is this idea bad?

Let's ask better—what are its strengths and weaknesses?

Better Questions → Better Answers.

Why Asking the Right Questions Matters

The quality of your answers depends on the quality of your questions. Poorly framed questions lead to shallow thinking and vague conclusions, while precise, thoughtful questions uncover hidden truths, solve problems, and guide better decisions.

For example:

- Instead of asking, "Why am I failing?" try, "What specific actions can I take to succeed?"
- Instead of saying, "Is this idea bad?" ask, "What are the strengths and weaknesses of this idea?"

The right questions challenge assumptions, clarify complexity, and spark creativity. They help you move from uncertainty to insight, empowering clear and logical thinking.

The Power of Questions

Questions do three important things:

1. **Challenge Assumptions:**

They force you to revisit what you take for granted.

- o Example: "What if my current approach isn't the best one?"

2. **Clarify Complexity:**

They simplify overwhelming situations and help you focus.

- o Example: "What's the core issue here?"

3. **Unlock Creativity:**

They encourage new ideas and perspectives.

- o Example: "What haven't we tried yet?"

Types of Questions for Logical Thinking

The type of question you ask depends on the situation. Here are four key categories:

1. **Clarifying Questions:**

- o Purpose: To ensure you understand the issue.
- o Examples:
  - "What do you mean by that?"
  - "Can you give an example?"

2. **Probing Questions:**

- o Purpose: To dig deeper into reasoning or evidence.
- o Examples:
  - "Why do you think that's true?"
  - "What's the evidence?"

3. **Evaluative Questions:**

- o Purpose: To assess the strength of an idea.
- o Examples:
  - "What are the potential risks?"
  - "How does this compare to other options?"

4. **Creative Questions:**

- o Purpose: To explore alternatives or new ideas.
- o Examples:
    - "What if we had no budget limits?"
    - "What's a completely different way to approach this?"

How to Ask Better Questions

1. **Challenge the Obvious:**

    Don't accept surface-level explanations. Dig deeper.
    - o Example: If someone says, "We can't meet the deadline," ask, "What's causing the delay, and how can we address it?"

2. **Stay Open-Ended:**

    Avoid yes/no questions. Use "how," "why," or "what" to encourage deeper thought.
    - o Example: Instead of asking, "Is this idea good?" ask, "What makes this idea effective, and what could improve it?"

3. **Focus on Solutions:**

    Shift from problems to possibilities.
    - o Example: "What steps can we take to move forward?"

4. **Embrace "What If" Thinking:**

    Use hypothetical scenarios to explore alternatives.
    - o Example: "What if we had more resources? What could we achieve?"

5. **Listen and Follow Up:**

    A good question sparks further questions. Listen carefully to answers and build on them.

Practical Exercise: Build Your Questioning Skills

1. **Pick a Current Problem:**
    - o Example: "I'm not making progress on my goals."

2. **Write Down Five Questions:**

- Examples:
    - "What do I want to achieve in the next six months?"
    - "What's holding me back?"
    - "Who can I ask for advice?"
    - "What skills do I need to improve?"
    - "What small step can I take this week?"

3. **Reflect and Take Action:**
    - Use your answers to develop an action plan.

Why This Skill is Vital

Asking the right questions transforms vague thinking into focused action. It helps you clarify problems, evaluate options, and uncover opportunities you might otherwise miss.

For example:

- In decision-making, the right questions help you weigh trade-offs and avoid impulsive choices.
- In relationships, they encourage understanding and resolution instead of conflict.

Great questions guide your thinking and open doors to better solutions.

Closing Thought

The right questions are like keys — they unlock clarity and open doors to smarter decisions. Learn to ask better questions, and you'll find better answers.

Chapter 13: Use If-Then Thinking for Scenarios

Why If-Then Thinking Works

Life is full of uncertainties, and one of the best ways to navigate them is by preparing for different scenarios. If-then thinking is a simple but powerful technique: it connects specific actions (the "then") to potential outcomes or conditions (the "if").

For example:

- **If** it rains tomorrow, **then** I'll bring an umbrella.
- **If** I get stuck in traffic, **then** I'll take an alternate route.

This proactive approach improves decision-making by preparing you for various possibilities and reducing emotional reactions when the unexpected happens. It's not about predicting the future but about planning for it.

How If-Then Thinking Helps You

1. **Anticipates Challenges:**
   - It helps you foresee and prepare for potential obstacles.
   - Example: **If** the project deadline gets pushed up, **then** I'll reprioritize my workload immediately.

2. **Encourages Action:**
   - You know exactly what to do when a specific situation arises.
   - Example: **If** I feel distracted while working, **then** I'll turn off notifications on my phone.

3. **Reduces Decision Fatigue:**
   - By pre-planning your responses, you avoid making decisions on the spot under pressure.

How to Apply If-Then Thinking

1. **Identify the Situation:**
   - Think of a specific challenge, goal, or decision you're working on.
   - Example: You're preparing for a big presentation but worry about unexpected questions.

2. **Consider Possible Scenarios:**
   - Brainstorm the most likely situations that could occur.
   - Example: "What if the audience asks a question I don't know the answer to?"

3. **Create If-Then Plans for Each Scenario:**
   - Write out specific responses.
   - Example: **If** I'm asked a question I can't answer, **then** I'll say, "That's a great question—I'll need to follow up with you after the presentation."

4. **Rehearse Your Plans:**
   - Mentally or physically practice your if-then scenarios so they feel natural.

Practical Exercise: Build Your If-Then Scenarios

1. **Choose a Goal or Problem:**
   - Example: "I want to stick to my fitness routine."
2. **Write Down Potential Challenges:**
   - Examples:
     - "What if I feel tired?"
     - "What if I get invited out with friends?"
3. **Create If-Then Statements:**
   - **If** I feel tired, **then** I'll do a 10-minute workout instead of skipping it.
   - **If** I get invited out, **then** I'll choose healthier options from the menu.
4. **Put Your Plan into Action:**
   - Use these scenarios in real life and adjust as needed.

Examples of If-Then Thinking in Daily Life

1. **In Time Management:**
   - **If** a meeting runs late, **then** I'll reschedule my least urgent task for tomorrow.
2. **In Conflict Resolution:**
   - **If** someone interrupts me during a discussion, **then** I'll politely say, "Let me finish my thought, and then I'll hear yours."
3. **In Problem-Solving:**
   - **If** my solution doesn't work, **then** I'll analyze what went wrong and try an alternative approach.

Why If-Then Thinking is So Effective

If-then thinking brings structure and clarity to chaotic situations. By pre-emptively linking actions to outcomes, you stay calm, focused, and prepared.

For example:

- A student facing exam stress can plan: **If** I feel overwhelmed, **then** I'll take a 15-minute break and return to studying with fresh focus.

- A manager handling a tough project can plan: **If** my team encounters delays, **then** we'll schedule daily check-ins to track progress.

These simple plans reduce uncertainty and empower you to take action confidently.

Closing Thought

Life is unpredictable, but your thinking doesn't have to be. With if-then thinking, you're ready for whatever comes your way — focused, prepared, and in control.

Chapter 14: Apply Occam's Razor: Simplify the Complex

OCCAM'S RAZOR

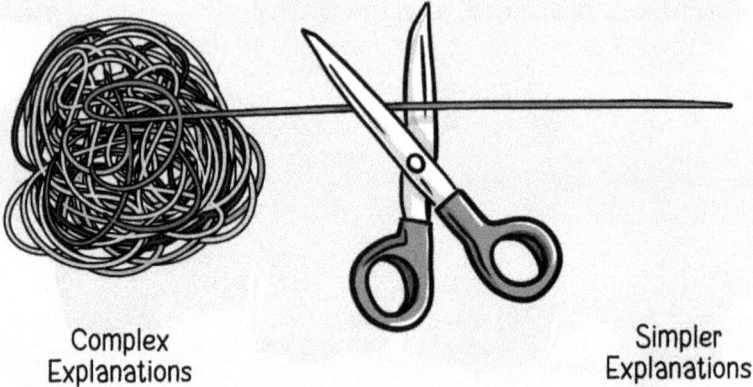

Complex Explanations

Simpler Explanations

What is Occam's Razor?

Occam's Razor is a principle of simplicity. It suggests that when you're faced with multiple explanations for a situation, the simplest one — requiring the fewest assumptions — is usually the best starting point.

Named after 14th-century philosopher William of Ockham, this principle is a guide for logical thinking. It doesn't guarantee the simplest answer is always right, but it reminds you to focus on straightforward explanations before considering more complex possibilities.

For example:

- **Problem:** Your car won't start.
- **Simpler Explanation:** The battery is dead.
- **More Complex Explanation:** The entire electrical system is damaged.

Starting with the simplest explanation often helps you solve problems faster and more effectively.

Why Simplicity Matters

1. **Reduces Overthinking:**

   Complex explanations can overwhelm you. Simplicity narrows your focus to what's essential.

2. **Saves Time:**

   By starting with simple explanations, you avoid wasting time on unlikely or convoluted ideas.

3. **Improves Decision-Making:**

   Simplicity helps you avoid assumptions that can lead to incorrect conclusions.

4. **Builds Clarity:**

   Focusing on straightforward explanations keeps your thinking organized and logical.

How to Apply Occam's Razor

1. **Define the Problem:**
   - Start by clearly stating the issue.
   - Example: "Why is my phone battery draining so quickly?"

2. **Brainstorm Possible Explanations:**
   - List all potential causes, from simple to complex.
   - Example:
     - Too many apps are running in the background.
     - The battery is old and needs replacing.
     - A rare hardware defect is causing the issue.

3. **Start with the Simplest Explanation:**
   - Look for explanations that require the fewest assumptions.
   - Example: Apps running in the background is the simplest possibility.

4. **Test the Simple Explanation First:**
    o Look for evidence that supports or disproves the simplest explanation.
    o Example: Close background apps and observe whether the battery life improves.
5. **Move to Complex Solutions If Needed:**
    o If the simplest explanation doesn't work, proceed to more complicated possibilities.

Examples of Occam's Razor in Action

1. **In Everyday Life:**
    o **Problem:** Your internet connection is slow.
    o **Simpler Explanation:** The router needs restarting.
    o **Complex Explanation:** Your Internet provider has major technical issues.
2. **In Health Decisions:**
    o **Symptom:** You have a headache.
    o **Simpler Explanation:** You may be dehydrated or tired.
    o **Complex Explanation:** It's a symptom of an underlying medical condition.
3. **In Work Challenges:**
    o **Problem:** Your team missed a deadline.
    o **Simpler Explanation:** Poor communication caused delays.
    o **Complex Explanation:** The team lacks the skills to handle the project.

Practical Exercise: Simplify a Problem

1. **Choose a Problem:**
    o Example: "Why am I always running late in the morning?"

2. **List Possible Explanations:**
   o Examples:
      - I'm not waking up early enough.
      - My routine is too packed.
      - My commute has unexpected delays.
3. **Apply Occam's Razor:**
   o Start with the simplest explanation: "I'm not waking up early enough."
4. **Test the Solution:**
   o Set your alarm 15 minutes earlier for a week. Track whether this solves the problem before exploring more complex explanations.

When Simplicity Isn't Enough

Occam's Razor isn't about ignoring complexity when it's necessary. If simpler explanations don't solve the problem, you may need to dig deeper. For example:

- If a headache persists despite hydration and rest, seek medical advice.
- If restarting your router doesn't fix your internet, call your provider.

Use Occam's Razor as a starting point, not an absolute rule.

Why Occam's Razor Improves Thinking

Occam's Razor helps you think clearly by cutting through unnecessary complexity. Starting with the simplest explanation ensures you save time, avoid confusion, and focus on the most likely solutions.

For example:

- Assuming your phone is broken due to a rare software bug isn't as logical as checking for excessive app usage first.

Closing Thought

Simplicity is the foundation of clear thinking. By applying Occam's Razor, you focus on what matters, and solve problems with confidence.

Chapter 15: Connect the Dots: Pattern Recognition

Why Pattern Recognition is Essential

Your brain is a natural pattern detector. It finds connections between scattered pieces of information to make sense of the world. When you recognize patterns, you uncover insights, predict outcomes, and solve problems faster.

For example:

- A detective connects seemingly unrelated clues to identify a suspect.
- A doctor recognizes symptoms that point to a specific diagnosis.
- A manager notices that productivity dips every Friday afternoon and adjusts deadlines accordingly.

Pattern recognition helps you move beyond randomness to identify meaningful trends, behaviors, or solutions.

The Benefits of Pattern Recognition

1. **Spotting Opportunities:**

   Recognizing trends helps you act before others.

   o Example: Seeing an emerging market trend allows a business to adapt and stay competitive.

2. **Solving Problems Efficiently:**

   Patterns often point to the root cause of recurring issues.

   o Example: Noticing that a machine breaks down after a specific task can help identify the underlying issue.

3. **Making Predictions:**

   Patterns in behavior or data help you anticipate outcomes.

   o Example: If a student consistently improves after practice tests, you can predict they'll perform well on the final exam.

How to Develop Pattern Recognition Skills

1. **Observe Closely:**

   o Pay attention to details and collect data over time.

   o Example: Track your daily habits and note when you feel most productive.

2. **Look for Commonalities:**

   o Ask, "What do these situations have in common?"

   o Example: If you notice your projects run late when certain team members are involved, the common factor might point to a need for better collaboration.

3. **Group Similar Ideas or Events:**

   o Categorizing helps you see connections.

   o Example: Organizing feedback from customers into themes can reveal the most common complaints.

4. **Ask "What Happens Next?"**
   - Use patterns to predict outcomes and test your assumptions.
   - Example: If bad weather affects sales every winter, anticipate a slowdown and plan accordingly.

5. **Challenge the Pattern:**
   - Patterns can sometimes lead to false assumptions. Test them to confirm their validity.
   - Example: If you think stress is causing your insomnia, track your stress levels and sleep quality to ensure the pattern holds true.

Practical Exercise: Spot a Pattern in Your Life

1. **Pick an Area to Explore:**
   - Example: Your daily energy levels.

2. **Collect Data:**
   - Over the next week, track your energy levels at different times of the day. Note what you eat, when you exercise, and how much you sleep.

3. **Look for Patterns:**
   - Do you feel most energetic after breakfast? Does skipping exercise make you feel sluggish?

4. **Test Your Findings:**
   - Make adjustments based on the patterns you observe (e.g., exercising earlier to maintain energy).

Examples of Pattern Recognition in Action

1. **In Personal Finance:**
   - You notice you spend more on dining out at the end of each month, leading to budget issues. Recognizing this pattern helps you set stricter limits during those weeks.

2. **In Relationships:**
   - You realize arguments with a friend often happen when both of you are stressed.

Identifying this pattern allows you to approach conflicts with greater empathy.

3. **In Work:**

   o Productivity dips on Mondays because your team feels overwhelmed after the weekend. Recognizing this, you schedule lighter tasks for the start of the week.

Why Patterns Can Mislead You

While patterns are valuable, they can also lead to false conclusions if:

- **The Data is Limited:** A small sample size might create misleading trends.
  - o Example: Assuming a new diet works after just one day of better energy levels.
- **Bias Shapes Perception:** Your mind might see patterns where none exist.
  - o Example: Believing you're unlucky because several small inconveniences happened in one week.

Always verify patterns by collecting more data and testing your conclusions.

Closing Thought

Pattern recognition transforms scattered data into meaningful insights. The more you practice spotting patterns, the better you'll become at predicting outcomes, solving problems, and making informed decisions.

Chapter 16: Check the Premises: Build on Solid Foundations

Why Premises Are the Foundation of Clear Thinking

Every argument, decision, or belief is built on premises — the assumptions or ideas that form its foundation. If these premises are flawed, the entire structure collapses. Like building a house on a shaky foundation, basing decisions or arguments on unchecked premises leads to poor outcomes.

For example:

- **Premise:** "If I work more hours, I'll get more done."
- **Reality:** Productivity often declines with overwork due to burnout.

Premises often seem obvious, so they go unexamined. Clear thinking starts with uncovering these assumptions, testing their validity, and ensuring they align with reality.

What Happens When Premises Go Unchecked?

1. **Faulty Conclusions:**

   A wrong premise leads to incorrect decisions or beliefs.

   - o Example: Assuming someone dislikes you because they didn't greet you may lead to avoiding them unnecessarily.

2. **Wasted Resources:**

   Acting on false assumptions wastes time, energy, or money.

   - o Example: Investing in a product launch based on the assumption that demand exists without verifying it.

3. **Unnecessary Conflict:**

   Misunderstood premises can lead to avoidable disagreements.

   - o Example: Assuming a friend canceled plans because they're upset, rather than asking for clarification.

How to Check Your Premises

1. **Identify the Premises:**

   - o Ask, "What assumptions am I making?"
   - o Example: In deciding to leave a job, your premise might be, "The new role will make me happier."

2. **Examine the Evidence:**

   - o Ask, "What evidence supports this premise? Is it fact or assumption?"
   - o Example: Do you have proof that the new role offers what you value most, or are you assuming?

3. **Test the Premises:**

   - o Look for ways to verify or challenge your assumptions.
   - o Example: Research the company or speak with current employees to confirm your assumption about its culture.

---

4. **Consider Alternatives:**
   - Think about other explanations or possibilities.
   - Example: Instead of assuming unhappiness stems from your job, consider other factors like work-life balance or personal stress.
5. **Revise if Necessary:**
   - Adjust your argument or decision if the premise doesn't hold up.

Practical Exercise: Evaluate Your Premises

1. **Choose a Decision or Belief:**
   - Example: "I need to switch to a new workout plan."
2. **List Your Premises:**
   - "My current routine isn't effective."
   - "The new plan is better."
3. **Check Evidence for Each Premise:**
   - Is the current routine failing, or are you expecting results too soon?
   - What proof suggests the new plan is superior?
4. **Make Adjustments Based on Your Findings:**
   - If evidence shows the current routine works but needs time, stick with it instead of switching plans prematurely.

Examples of Premise Checking in Action

1. **In Arguments:**
   - **Premise:** "We need more staff to improve productivity."
   - **Check:** Is productivity low due to understaffing, or could training or better tools solve the issue?
2. **In Personal Reflection:**
   - **Premise:** "I'm bad at public speaking."
   - **Check:** Is this based on one bad experience, or have you overlooked times you performed well?

3. In Financial Decisions:

- o **Premise:** "Expensive products are always high-quality."
- o **Check:** Does price reflect quality, or could it be driven by branding?

Why This Skill Sharpens Your Thinking

Premises are the foundation of clear thinking. Verifying them prevents errors, strengthens decisions, and builds logical arguments. It ensures that your reasoning starts with truth, not assumptions.

For example, confirming that a potential employer values work-life balance (rather than assuming it) avoids the mistake of accepting a job misaligned with your priorities.

Closing Thought

Solid thinking requires solid foundations. By checking your premises, you ensure your arguments and decisions are built on truth, leading to better outcomes and fewer mistakes.

Chapter 17: Follow the Chain: Trace Cause to Effect

Why Tracing Cause to Effect is Critical

Every effect has a cause. If you want to solve a problem or understand a situation, you need to trace it back to its root. Too often, people focus only on the immediate issue — like treating symptoms instead of the disease. By identifying the underlying cause, you can address the real problem instead of applying surface-level fixes.

For example:

- **Effect:** You're consistently late to work.
- **Possible Causes:** Poor time management, lack of sleep, or an inefficient morning routine.

Addressing the cause (e.g. setting an earlier alarm) ensures the problem doesn't repeat.

How Cause-and-Effect Thinking Works

Cause-and-effect thinking involves tracing events in a logical sequence. It's like asking, "What caused this? And what caused that?" until you reach the root.

This method helps you:

1. **Identify Root Causes:** Understand what's really driving the problem.

2. **Predict Outcomes:** Anticipate the impact of your actions by considering their effects.

3. **Design Better Solutions:** Fix the core issue instead of applying quick fixes.

Steps to Trace Cause to Effect

1. **Start with the Effect:**
   o Clearly define the problem or outcome you're trying to understand.
   o Example: "My team missed the project deadline."

2. **Ask "Why?" Repeatedly:**
   o Use the "Five Whys" technique to dig deeper.
   o Example:
     - Why did we miss the deadline? "We ran out of time."
     - Why did we run out of time? "We underestimated the work involved."
     - Why did we underestimate the work? "We didn't allocate enough planning time."

3. **Identify the Root Cause:**
   o Keep asking "Why?" until you uncover the core issue. In this case, the root cause is poor planning, not just a missed deadline.

4. **Test the Cause:**
   o Verify that the cause you've identified is valid.
   o Example: Check if other missed deadlines in the past were also caused by insufficient planning.

5. **Brainstorm Solutions:**
    o   Address the root cause with targeted actions.
    o   Example: Schedule dedicated planning sessions for future projects.

Examples of Cause-and-Effect Thinking

1. **In Relationships:**
    o   **Effect:** A friend stops replying to your messages.
    o   **Possible Causes:** They're busy, upset, or distracted.
    o   **Solution:** Communicate directly to clarify their reasons.

2. **In Personal Productivity:**
    o   **Effect:** You're not meeting your fitness goals.
    o   **Possible Causes:** No motivation, poor scheduling, or unrealistic expectations.
    o   **Solution:** Adjust your routine to make it more achievable.

3. **In Business:**
    o   **Effect:** Sales have dropped.
    o   **Possible Causes:** Poor marketing, product issues, or competition.
    o   **Solution:** Analyze data to determine which factor is most significant and address it.

Practical Exercise: Follow the Chain

1. **Choose a Problem:**
    o   Example: "I'm always exhausted in the morning."

2. **Write Down the Effect:**
    o   "I feel tired every day."

3. **Trace the Causes Using "Why?"**
    o   Why do I feel tired? "I didn't sleep well."
    o   Why didn't I sleep well? "I stayed up late watching TV."
    o   Why did I stay up late? "I lost track of time."

4. Address the Root Cause:

o Solution: Set a specific bedtime and reduce screen time before bed.

Closing Thought

Understanding the chain of cause and effect transforms how you solve problems. By addressing the root cause, you eliminate the issue at its source and prevent it from recurring.

Chapter 18: Think Backward: Reverse Engineer the Problem

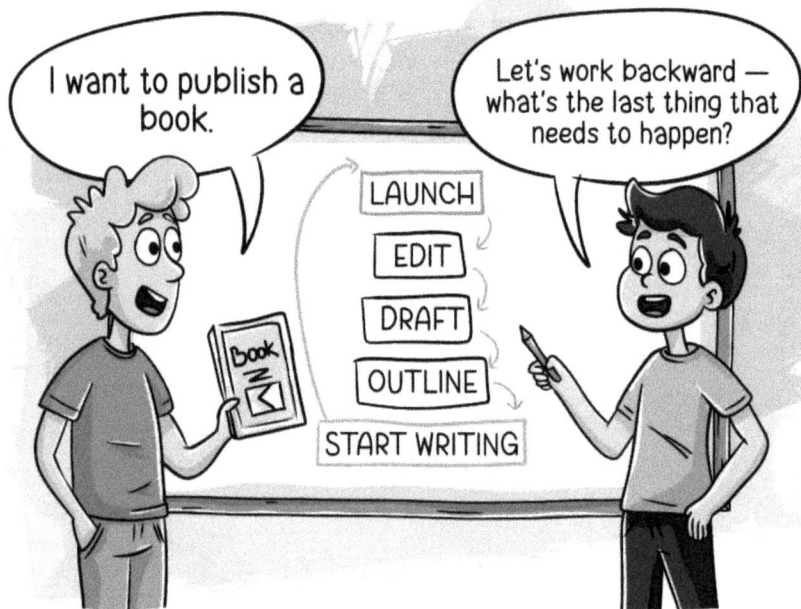

Why Thinking Backward is Powerful

When solving problems, most people instinctively work forward — starting at the beginning and trying to figure out the next steps. But working backward is often more effective, especially for complex challenges. By starting with the desired outcome and retracing the steps required to achieve it, you can map a clear path from finish to start.

For example:

Goal: Publish a book.

Backward Steps:

- o   Launch the book.
- o   Finish the editing process.
- o   Complete the draft.
- o   Set a writing schedule.

How Backward Thinking Helps You

1. **Clarifies Goals:**
   - When you define the outcome first, it's easier to align your actions with your objectives.
   - Example: If your goal is to save $5,000 for a vacation, backward thinking reveals the monthly amount you need to set aside.

2. **Reveals Key Milestones:**
   - Backward thinking breaks big goals into smaller, actionable steps.
   - Example: If you want to run a marathon, you identify milestones like building endurance, increasing mileage, and scheduling practice runs.

3. **Avoids Wasted Effort:**
   - By starting with the end goal, you focus only on steps that directly contribute to success.

How to Reverse Engineer a Problem

1. **Define the End Goal:**
   - Be specific about the result you want.
   - Example: "I want to finish a degree in two years."

2. **Work Backward Step-by-Step:**
   - Imagine the actions required to achieve the goal, then list them in reverse order.
   - Example:
     - Graduate with all credits completed.
     - Complete final exams and coursework.
     - Take prerequisite classes.
     - Enroll in the program.

3. **Identify Obstacles and Gaps:**
   - Consider potential challenges and plan how to overcome them.
   - Example: If certain classes are only offered in specific semesters, plan your schedule accordingly.

4. **Create a Forward Plan:**
   - o Use your backward steps to build a forward-moving roadmap.

Examples of Backward Thinking

1. **In Career Planning:**
   - o **Goal:** Become a project manager.
   - o **Backward Steps:**
     - Apply for management positions.
     - Gain project management certification.
     - Build leadership skills in your current role.
     - Research companies hiring for management positions.

2. **In Problem-Solving:**
   - o **Goal:** Boost team productivity.
   - o **Backward Steps:**
     - Schedule regular check-ins.
     - Streamline task assignments.
     - Identify specific productivity bottlenecks.

3. **In Daily Life:**
   - o **Goal:** Cook a complex meal by 7 p.m.

Backward Steps:

- Complete final plating by 6:50 p.m.
- Bake the dish at 6:20 p.m.
- Prepare ingredients by 6:00 p.m.

Practical Exercise: Reverse Engineer Your Goal

1. **Choose a Goal:**
   - o Example: "I want to save $10,000 in one year."

2. **Work Backward:**
   - o Start with the end result and outline the steps required to achieve it:
     - Save $10,000 by December.
     - Save $833 monthly.

- Reduce unnecessary expenses by $200/month.

3. **Test the Plan:**
   o Evaluate whether each step is achievable and adjust as necessary.

4. **Take Action:**
   o Begin implementing the plan, starting with the first step.

Why Backward Thinking Works

Backward thinking forces you to focus on what matters most. By tracing steps from the goal to the starting point, you eliminate unnecessary tasks and clarify the exact actions needed.

For example:

If you want to host a successful event, working backward helps you prioritize steps like booking a venue, sending invitations, and setting up logistics in advance.

Closing Thought

Thinking backward turns confusion into clarity. By reverse-engineering your goals, you create a straightforward roadmap to success, making even the most daunting tasks achievable.

Chapter 19: Use Logic Trees: Break Down Problems Step-by-Step

Why are our meetings always unproductive?

Let's break it down—could be time use, agenda, or engagement.

What is a Logic Tree?

A logic tree is a visual tool that helps you break down complex problems into smaller, manageable pieces. The problem forms the trunk of the tree, while possible causes, solutions, or factors branch outward into categories and subcategories.

This technique brings structure to your thinking, helping you organize your thoughts and analyze the issue systematically. For example:

- **Problem:** Why are my team's projects always delayed?
- **Branches:**
    - Poor communication → Lack of updates, unclear expectations.
    - Insufficient resources → Lack of tools,

understaffing.

- o Inefficient processes → Poor time management, redundant tasks.

By working through each branch, you identify the most critical areas to address and develop actionable solutions.

Why Logic Trees are Effective

1. **Simplifies Complexity:**
   - o Breaking a problem into smaller parts makes it easier to understand and tackle.
   - o Example: Instead of being overwhelmed by low sales, focus on specific factors like pricing, customer service, or product quality.

2. **Prioritizes Focus:**
   - o Logic trees highlight which factors are most critical, allowing you to target root causes rather than symptoms.

3. **Supports Systematic Thinking:**
   - o Organizing your ideas visually prevents you from missing important details or overlooking potential solutions.

4. **Provides Clarity for Teams:**
   - o Logic trees are easy to share and collaborate on, making them ideal for group problem-solving.

How to Create a Logic Tree

1. **Define the Problem:**
   - o Start by clearly stating the issue.
   - o Example: "Why am I always late to meetings?"

2. **Break It into Categories:**
   - o Identify major factors contributing to the problem.
   - o Example: Poor time management, distractions, or travel delays.

3. **Add Subcategories:**

- For each category, list specific details or causes.
- Example:
    - Poor time management: Procrastination, unclear priorities.
    - Distractions: Notifications, last-minute requests.

4. **Evaluate Each Branch:**
    - Examine which branch has the most significant impact or is easiest to address first.

5. **Develop Solutions:**
    - For each branch, create targeted actions to address the issue.

Examples of Logic Trees in Action

1. **In Business:**
    - **Problem:** Sales are declining.
    - **Branches:**
        - Marketing: Poor targeting, ineffective messaging.
        - Pricing: Too high for the market, inconsistent discounts.
        - Product: Quality concerns, outdated features.
    - **Solution:** Address the most critical branch first. For instance, revamping marketing campaigns may have the greatest impact.

2. **In Personal Productivity:**
    - **Problem:** You're missing deadlines.
    - **Branches:**
        - Time management: Overcommitting, poor scheduling.
        - Distractions: Phone use, social media.
        - Prioritization: Working on low-priority tasks first.
    - **Solution:** Focus on improving time management by using a task planner or setting boundaries for

distractions.

3. **In Relationships:**
   o **Problem:** Frequent arguments with a friend.
   o **Branches:**
      ▪ Miscommunication: Unclear expectations, interrupting during discussions.
      ▪ External stress: Work pressure, personal challenges.
      ▪ Unresolved conflicts: Past issues left unaddressed.
   o **Solution:** Start by addressing miscommunication to improve dialogue.

Practical Exercise: Build Your Own Logic Tree

1. **Choose a Problem:**
   o Example: "Why do I overspend each month?"
2. **Identify Categories:**
   o Examples: Unnecessary purchases, lack of budgeting, unexpected expenses.
3. **Add Subcategories:**
   o Unnecessary purchases: Impulse buying, dining out too often.
   o Lack of budgeting: No spending limits, forgetting to track expenses.
4. **Analyze the Tree:**
   o Focus on the most impactful branch. For example, controlling impulse buying might solve a large part of the overspending issue.
5. **Take Action:**
   o Implement specific strategies to address the problem, like creating a monthly budget or setting a dining-out limit.

Benefits of Logic Trees

Using logic trees improves problem-solving by breaking overwhelming challenges into clear, actionable parts. It ensures you address the root cause of the problem rather than treating symptoms.

Closing Thought

Logic trees turn complexity into clarity. By breaking problems into smaller steps, you gain the focus and structure needed to solve them efficiently and effectively.

Chapter 20: Compare and Contrast for Clearer Choices

Speech bubble (left): Phone Ⓐ has a better camera, but the battery dies fast.

Speech bubble (right): Phone Ⓑ lasts longer—maybe that's what I need most.

Why Comparing and Contrasting is Crucial

Every choice involves trade-offs. Whether deciding on a career, a purchase, or a solution to a problem, comparing and contrasting helps you weigh your options and choose the one that best aligns with your goals.

This method sharpens decision-making by highlighting differences and similarities between options, forcing you to evaluate what truly matters.

For example:

- **Decision:** Choosing between two vacation destinations.
- **Comparison:**
  - Option A: Affordable but farther away.
  - Option B: Closer but more expensive.

o **Contrast:** Decide based on your priority — budget or convenience.

The Benefits of Comparing and Contrasting

1. **Improves Clarity:**
   o Side-by-side comparisons highlight key differences, simplifying decision-making.
2. **Prioritizes Needs:**
   o It forces you to consider what factors matter most, such as cost, time, or long-term impact.
3. **Reveals Trade-Offs:**
   o Weighing pros and cons helps you understand what you're gaining or sacrificing with each option.

How to Compare and Contrast Effectively

1. **List the Options:**
   o Clearly identify the choices you're considering.
   o Example: Choosing between two jobs.
2. **Define Criteria:**
   o Select the most important factors for evaluation (e.g. salary, growth opportunities, work-life balance).
3. **Create a Side-by-Side Chart:**
   o Compare each option against the chosen criteria.
   o Example:
     ▪ Job A: Higher salary, but longer hours.
     ▪ Job B: Lower pay, but better growth potential and flexibility.
4. **Assign Weight to Criteria:**
   o Some factors matter more than others. For instance, if work-life balance is a top priority, emphasize it over salary.
5. **Consider the Trade-Offs:**
   o Understand what you're giving up with each option.

Examples of Compare-and-Contrast Thinking

1. **In Career Decisions:**
   - **Decision:** Choosing between two job offers.
   - **Comparison:**
     - Job A: Higher salary but fewer learning opportunities.
     - Job B: Lower salary but a clear path to leadership roles.
   - **Outcome:** If long-term growth matters more, Job B may be the better choice.

2. **In Financial Decisions:**
   - **Decision:** Choosing between buying a car or using public transport.
   - **Comparison:**
     - Car: Convenience but high upfront and maintenance costs.
     - Public Transport: Affordable but less flexibility.
   - **Outcome:** If affordability outweighs convenience, public transport might win.

3. **In Everyday Life:**
   - **Decision:** Choosing between two phones.
   - **Comparison:**
     - Phone A: Better camera but shorter battery life.
     - Phone B: Longer battery life but fewer advanced features.
   - **Outcome:** If battery life is critical, Phone B is the logical choice.

Practical Exercise: Compare Two Options

1. **Pick a Decision:**
   - Example: Choosing between two homes to rent.

2. **Define Key Factors:**
   - Examples: Cost, commute time, neighborhood amenities.

3. **Create a Comparison Table:**
   - Home A: Lower rent, farther from work, quieter neighborhood.
   - Home B: Higher rent, closer to work, more noise.
4. **Weigh Your Priorities:**
   - Decide which factors matter most. If saving money is your priority, Home A might be the better choice.

Why This Technique Works

Comparing and contrasting ensures your decisions are logical and aligned with your priorities. It prevents emotional biases from clouding your judgment and provides a structured way to evaluate options.

Closing Thought

Every choice has trade-offs. By comparing and contrasting your options, you gain clarity and confidence in your decisions, ensuring they align with your goals and values.

Part III: Cognitive Bias-Busting Techniques

Cognitive biases are mental shortcuts your brain uses to process information quickly. While these shortcuts can be helpful, they often distort reality, leading to errors in judgment and flawed decisions.

This section focuses on techniques to identify and combat these mental traps. By learning to recognize and challenge your biases, you'll develop a clearer, more objective perspective. Each chapter will give you practical tools to think critically, avoid common pitfalls, and make decisions rooted in logic, not illusion.

Chapter 21: Fact-Check First: Verify Before Believing

Why Fact-Checking is Essential

Not everything you hear or read is true. Fact-checking ensures you base your beliefs, decisions, and arguments on verified information, not assumptions or falsehoods.

For example:

- Someone claims a specific health supplement cures all diseases. Without verification, you risk wasting money — or worse, harming your health.

Common Reasons People Skip Fact-Checking

1. **Cognitive Ease:**
   - It's easier to accept a statement than to investigate it.

2. **Emotional Appeal:**
    - o If information supports your emotions or values, you're more likely to believe it without questioning.
3. **Social Pressure:**
    - o If "everyone" believes something, you may feel pressured to agree without evidence.

Steps to Fact-Check Effectively

1. **Pause and Question:**
    - o Ask yourself: "Where did this information come from? Is the source credible?"
2. **Cross-Reference Sources:**
    - o Verify claims with multiple reliable sources. Independent confirmation is key.
3. **Check for Bias:**
    - o Assess whether the source has a clear agenda. Is it trying to persuade rather than inform?
4. **Look for Evidence:**
    - o Strong claims require strong evidence. Avoid believing sweeping statements without data or reputable research to back them up.

Examples of Fact-Checking in Action

1. **In News and Social Media:**
    - o Claim: "A new law bans all forms of public speech."
    - o Fact-Check: Look up the law's actual text or consult reliable news outlets.
2. **In Personal Decisions:**
    - o Claim: "This car is the safest on the market."
    - o Fact-Check: Research safety ratings from trusted organizations like Consumer Reports or IIHS.
3. **In Conversations:**
    - o Claim: "This historical event happened because of X."

o   Fact-Check: Consult credible historical sources to confirm or refute the claim.

Practical Exercise: Build Your Fact-Checking Habit

1. **Choose One Claim You've Heard Recently:**
   o   Example: "Drinking coffee dehydrates you."
2. **Research the Claim:**
   o   Look up scientific studies or articles from trusted sources.
3. **Verify Its Accuracy:**
   o   Did you find credible evidence supporting or debunking the claim?
4. **Reflect on How This Shapes Your Beliefs:**
   o   If the claim was false, consider how fact-checking improved your understanding.

Why Fact-Checking Sharpens Your Thinking

When you verify information, you avoid falling for falsehoods or misinformation. This strengthens your arguments, builds credibility, and ensures your decisions are based on reality.

Closing Thought

Trust is earned through evidence. Fact-checking protects your mind from being misled, empowering you to think critically and confidently.

Chapter 22: Spot Confirmation Bias: Test What You Doubt

What is Confirmation Bias?

Confirmation bias is the tendency to seek, interpret, and remember information in a way that supports your existing beliefs. It's comforting but dangerous — this mental shortcut can blind you to evidence that challenges your views, leading to one-sided thinking and flawed decisions.

For example:

- You believe a specific diet works wonders, so you only look for testimonials that confirm your belief while ignoring scientific studies that question its effectiveness.

How Confirmation Bias Distorts Thinking

1. **Selective Attention:**
   - You notice evidence that aligns with your views but overlook opposing information.
2. **Biased Interpretation:**
   - You twist ambiguous data to fit your narrative.
3. **Memory Distortion:**
   - You remember supportive information better than contradictory evidence.

Steps to Combat Confirmation Bias

1. **Seek Opposing Evidence:**
   - Actively look for information that contradicts your belief.
   - Example: If you think a new policy is ineffective, research arguments supporting its benefits.
2. **Ask Disconfirming Questions:**
   - Instead of asking, "Why is my belief correct?" ask, "What could prove me wrong?"
3. **Verify Sources:**
   - Ensure the sources you consult are reputable and not cherry-picking data to align with an agenda.
4. **Consider Neutral Perspectives:**
   - Consult experts or individuals who aren't emotionally invested in the topic.

Examples of Spotting and Challenging Confirmation Bias

1. **In Politics:**
   - If you favor one political party, seek out thoughtful critiques of their policies to broaden your understanding.
2. **In Personal Decisions:**
   - Before buying a product, don't just read glowing reviews. Look for critical reviews to see if there are consistent issues.

3. In Debates:
  o When arguing a point, ask, "What evidence would change my mind?"

Practical Exercise: Test Your Beliefs

1. Choose a Strongly Held Belief:
  o Example: "Exercise in the morning is the best way to stay healthy."

2. Find Contradictory Evidence:
  o Research studies or expert opinions supporting other exercise routines (e.g., evening workouts).

3. Evaluate Both Sides:
  o Consider whether your belief still holds up after reviewing opposing evidence.

Why Spotting Confirmation Bias is Critical

Recognizing and challenging confirmation bias opens your mind to new ideas and better solutions. It fosters intellectual humility and ensures your decisions are guided by truth, not comfort.

Closing Thought

The truth doesn't fear scrutiny. By seeking evidence that challenges your beliefs, you strengthen your understanding and sharpen your thinking.

Chapter 23: Decouple from Anchors: Avoid First-Impression Traps

What is Anchoring Bias?

Anchoring bias occurs when your decisions are overly influenced by the first piece of information you receive — the "anchor." Once an anchor is set, your brain tends to rely on it, even if it's irrelevant, outdated, or misleading. This bias impacts decisions in everything from shopping to negotiations, and even everyday judgments.

For example:

- You see a sweater priced at $200 but then find it discounted to $100. Even though $100 may still be overpriced, the $200 anchor makes the discount seem like a great deal.

How Anchoring Skews Your Thinking

1. **Fixating on Initial Numbers:**
   - The first number you hear can set expectations. For instance, if a car is listed at $25,000, you'll likely negotiate around that price instead of questioning its actual value.

2. **Shaping Perceptions:**
   - Anchors influence how you interpret other information. For example, hearing that a colleague is "difficult" might color your interactions with them, even if you see no evidence of this behavior.

3. **Limiting Flexibility:**
   - Anchors trap you into narrow thinking, making it harder to explore other possibilities or question assumptions.

How to Decouple from Anchors

1. **Recognize the Anchor:**
   - Pause and identify any initial information that might be influencing your decision.
   - Example: In negotiations, ask yourself, "Am I fixating on their first offer instead of assessing the real value of what I'm getting?"

2. **Question the Anchor's Relevance:**
   - Is the anchor logical, accurate, or relevant?
   - Example: A restaurant menu might list a $50 steak to make the $30 steak seem reasonable. In reality, both may be overpriced.

3. **Gather Independent Information:**
   - Seek out additional data or perspectives before making a decision.
   - Example: Research market prices for a product before assuming a "discount" is a good deal.

4. **Set Your Own Standards:**
   - Define your goals, expectations, or limits before encountering an anchor.
   - Example: Decide your maximum budget for a car before visiting a dealership, so you're not influenced by high starting prices.

Examples of Decoupling from Anchors

1. **In Shopping:**
   - **Scenario:** A store advertises a "70% off sale" for items marked up to artificially high original prices.
   - **Solution:** Research the typical cost of similar products to assess if the sale price is truly a bargain.

2. **In Negotiations:**
   - **Scenario:** An employer offers a starting salary of $50,000, which feels low.
   - **Solution:** Look up industry averages and decide a fair salary range before accepting the initial offer as a baseline.

3. **In Everyday Judgments:**
   - **Scenario:** A friend is described as "lazy" before you meet them.
   - **Solution:** Focus on your own observations rather than letting the label shape your opinion.

Practical Exercise: Spot and Challenge Anchors

1. **Think of a Recent Decision Influenced by an Anchor:**
   - Example: Buying a discounted gadget or accepting a starting price in negotiations.

2. **Identify the Anchor:**
   - What was the first piece of information you received? Was it a price, a label, or someone's opinion?

3. **Evaluate the Anchor:**
   o Ask, "Is this initial information valid or relevant? What other data should I consider?"
4. **Redefine Your Criteria:**
   o Shift focus from the anchor to what matters most (e.g., quality, value, or personal goals).

Why This Skill is Important

Anchoring bias is sneaky — it often influences you without you realizing it. By learning to recognize and challenge anchors, you make decisions that reflect reality, not just initial impressions.

For example:

- When buying a home, avoiding anchoring bias ensures you focus on the home's actual worth instead of being swayed by an inflated asking price.

Closing Thought

Don't let the first piece of information anchor your thinking. By questioning anchors and seeking independent perspectives, you free yourself to make more rational, informed decisions.

Chapter 24: Think Like a Detective: Avoid Jumping to Conclusions

Why Jumping to Conclusions is a Problem

Humans crave certainty, and your brain often rushes to conclusions to resolve ambiguity quickly. However, this mental shortcut leads to errors, as snap judgments are frequently based on incomplete or misleading information.

For example:

- You notice your co-worker is unusually quiet and assume they're upset with you. In reality, they might be distracted by personal issues or a heavy workload.

Thinking like a detective slows down this rush, encouraging you to gather evidence, analyze it critically, and consider alternative explanations before deciding.

How Jumping to Conclusions Impacts Thinking

1. **Missed Context:**
   - o Snap judgments ignore the bigger picture, leading to superficial understanding.
2. **Hasty Decisions:**
   - o Relying on incomplete information often results in poor choices.
3. **Harm to Relationships:**
   - o Assuming others' intentions without evidence can lead to unnecessary conflict.

How to Think Like a Detective

1. **Observe Without Judging:**
   - o Focus on gathering information before interpreting it.
   - o Example: If someone is late to a meeting, note their behavior instead of assuming they're irresponsible.
2. **Ask Questions:**
   - o Act like a detective interviewing witnesses.
   - o Example: "What might explain this behavior? What factors am I missing?"
3. **Look for Evidence:**
   - o Base your conclusions on concrete facts, not assumptions.
   - o Example: If you think your boss is unhappy with your work, ask for feedback rather than guessing.
4. **Consider Alternative Explanations:**
   - o Brainstorm multiple reasons for the situation.
   - o Example: A friend canceling plans might be busy, unwell, or facing a personal emergency.
5. **Test Your Hypotheses:**
   - o Verify your conclusions before acting on them.
   - o Example: Before assuming a task is impossible, research tools or methods that might help.

Examples of Detective Thinking

1. **In the Workplace:**
   - **Scenario:** Your boss is unusually brief in emails.
   - **Jumping to Conclusions:** They're upset with you.
   - **Detective Thinking:** Consider other explanations, like a busy schedule or poor email etiquette.
2. **In Personal Relationships:**
   - **Scenario:** Your partner forgets an important date.
   - **Jumping to Conclusions:** They don't care.
   - **Detective Thinking:** Ask if they're stressed, distracted, or overwhelmed.
3. **In Decision-Making:**
   - **Scenario:** A project seems unfeasible.
   - **Jumping to Conclusions:** It's not worth pursuing.
   - **Detective Thinking:** Investigate alternative strategies, resources, or collaborators.

Practical Exercise: Practice Detective Thinking

1. **Choose a Recent Assumption You Made:**
   - Example: "My friend hasn't responded to my message because they're upset with me."
2. **List Alternative Explanations:**
   - Examples: They're busy, forgot, or haven't seen the message.
3. **Gather Evidence:**
   - Reach out politely and ask if everything is okay instead of assuming the worst.
4. **Reflect on Your Conclusion:**
   - How does the evidence support or challenge your initial assumption?

Why Thinking Like a Detective is Crucial

Detective thinking encourages patience, curiosity, and evidence-based reasoning. It prevents you from making impulsive decisions or damaging relationships based on incomplete assumptions.

Closing Thought

Rushing to conclusions often leads to errors. Think like a detective — ask questions, gather evidence, and explore alternatives before deciding. Truth thrives on investigation, not assumption.

Chapter 25: Challenge the Crowd: Resist Bandwagon Thinking

What is Bandwagon Thinking?

Bandwagon thinking is the tendency to adopt a belief or behavior simply because others are doing it. This mental shortcut can make decisions easier, as following the crowd feels safe and validated. However, it can also lead you to ignore facts, overlook better options, or act against your values.

For example:

- Everyone at work might support an idea you quietly doubt, so you go along with it to avoid standing out — even if you know it's a flawed plan.

Challenging the crowd doesn't mean rejecting group opinions outright. It means evaluating them critically and ensuring your actions align with logic and evidence, not just social pressure.

Why Bandwagon Thinking Happens

1. **Fear of Standing Out:**
   - o Humans are social creatures. Going against the group can feel risky, leading to discomfort or rejection.

2. **Assumption of Consensus:**
   - o When everyone seems to agree, you might assume they're right — even if no one has actually examined the evidence.

3. **Cognitive Laziness:**
   - o It's easier to trust the group's decision than to think critically yourself.

Risks of Bandwagon Thinking

1. **Compromised Decisions:**
   - o You may agree to something you later regret because you didn't fully consider it.

2. **Suppressed Innovation:**
   - o Blindly following the crowd stifles creative or unconventional ideas that might lead to better solutions.

3. **Reinforced Mistakes:**
   - o Groups can be wrong, and when everyone follows without questioning, errors multiply.

How to Challenge the Crowd Effectively

1. **Pause Before Agreeing:**
   - o When faced with group consensus, take a moment to assess your own thoughts and feelings. Ask, "Do I truly agree with this?"

2. **Examine the Evidence:**
   - o Evaluate whether the group's decision is supported by facts or if it's based on assumptions or emotions.
   - o Example: If everyone in a meeting supports an expensive solution, question whether it's the most cost-effective option.

3. **Play the Devil's Advocate:**
   - Consider opposing viewpoints, even if only to test the group's reasoning.
   - Example: Ask, "What if we're wrong? What's the worst that could happen?"
4. **Voice Your Doubts Respectfully:**
   - If you disagree, express your concerns calmly and logically. Others may appreciate your input and reconsider their position.
5. **Be Willing to Stand Alone:**
   - Sometimes, resisting the bandwagon means standing by your principles, even if no one else does.

Examples of Challenging the Crowd

1. **In the Workplace:**
   - **Scenario:** A team unanimously agrees to rush a project without testing it.
   - **Action:** Raise concerns about potential risks, such as quality issues or missed deadlines.
2. **In Personal Life:**
   - **Scenario:** All your friends rave about a trendy diet, but you're skeptical.
   - **Action:** Research its health effects before joining in, and stick to your decision if the evidence doesn't convince you.
3. **In Social Media:**
   - **Scenario:** A viral post spreads misinformation, and most people share it without fact-checking.
   - **Action:** Verify the claims and share accurate information instead, even if it's unpopular.

Practical Exercise: Resist the Bandwagon

1. **Reflect on a Recent Group Decision:**
   o Example: "Everyone in my class chose the same project topic."

2. **Ask Yourself These Questions:**
   o Did I agree because I believed in the idea, or was it just easier to go along with the group?
   o What other options did I overlook?

3. **Practice Challenging Group Consensus:**
   o In your next group discussion, ask one thoughtful question to test the group's reasoning.

Why This Skill Matters

Challenging the crowd builds your confidence in independent thinking. It helps you make smarter decisions and ensures that group choices are backed by logic, not blind agreement.

Closing Thought

True progress often begins with one person willing to challenge the status quo. Resist the urge to follow the crowd blindly — examine the facts, trust your reasoning, and stand firm in your conclusions.

Chapter 26: Flip the Script: Consider Opposite Perspectives

Why Opposite Perspectives Matter

Your perspective shapes how you interpret the world. However, your viewpoint is limited by your experiences, beliefs, and biases. To think clearly, you need to step outside your perspective and consider opposite or alternative views.

For example:

- If you believe a colleague's suggestion won't work, flipping the script involves asking, "What if their idea succeeds? What would make it effective?"

Exploring opposing perspectives broadens your understanding, challenges assumptions, and helps you make more balanced decisions.

How Bias Limits Your Perspective

1. **Confirmation Bias:**
   - o You focus only on evidence that supports your viewpoint, ignoring contradictory facts.
2. **Egocentric Bias:**
   - o You view situations primarily from your own experiences, assuming others see things the same way.
3. **Emotional Attachments:**
   - o Strong feelings about an issue can blind you to alternative perspectives.

Steps to Flip the Script

1. **Identify Your Assumptions:**
   - o Ask, "What am I assuming about this situation?"
   - o Example: "I assume this new policy will create more problems than it solves."
2. **Consider the Opposite:**
   - o Ask, "What if the opposite is true?"
   - o Example: "What if this policy reduces problems? What conditions would make that possible?"
3. **Step into Another Person's Shoes:**
   - o Imagine how someone with a different perspective might view the situation.
   - o Example: How might employees, customers, or competitors see this issue?
4. **Evaluate Both Sides:**
   - o Compare the strengths and weaknesses of each perspective.
5. **Synthesize a Balanced View:**
   - o Combine insights from both sides to develop a well-rounded understanding.

Examples of Flipping the Script

1. **In Debates:**
   - **Scenario:** You're arguing against remote work policies.
   - **Action:** Consider the benefits from an employee's perspective, such as flexibility and reduced commuting stress.

2. **In Conflict Resolution:**
   - **Scenario:** You think a friend is being unreasonable during an argument.
   - **Action:** Reflect on their concerns and ask, "How might I feel in their position?"

3. **In Business:**
   - **Scenario:** You're convinced a competitor's product is inferior.
   - **Action:** Analyze what customers might find appealing about it and how you can improve your offering.

Practical Exercise: Practice Perspective-Taking

1. **Choose a Strongly Held Belief:**
   - Example: "My way of managing time is the most efficient."

2. **Flip the Script:**
   - Consider an opposite belief: "What if other time-management methods are more effective?"

3. **Gather Evidence:**
   - Research different approaches and compare their results to yours.

4. **Reflect on What You Learn:**
   - Has your perspective shifted? What new insights did you gain?

Why This Skill is Important

Considering opposite perspectives fosters empathy, reduces bias, and leads to more thoughtful decisions. It doesn't mean abandoning your beliefs but refining them through broader understanding.

Closing Thought

Growth happens when you step outside your comfort zone. By flipping the script, you gain fresh insights and make smarter, more balanced choices.

Chapter 27: Pause Before Reacting: Manage Emotional Bias

> He ignored my suggestion in front of everyone—I'm so mad!

> Pause a second. Maybe he didn't hear you clearly.

What is Emotional Bias?

Emotional bias occurs when your feelings cloud your judgment. Instead of thinking rationally, you let emotions — such as anger, fear, excitement, or frustration — drive your decisions. While emotions provide valuable context, relying solely on them can lead to hasty choices, misjudgements, and regret.

For example:

- You might lash out during an argument, only to later realize you misunderstood the situation.

Pausing before reacting gives you time to reflect and separate emotional impulses from logical thinking.

How Emotional Bias Impacts Decision-Making

1. **Overreaction:**
   - Strong emotions can lead to exaggerated responses.
   - Example: Cancelling an important project after receiving minor criticism about it.

2. **Narrow Focus:**
   - Emotions can make you fixate on one aspect of a situation while ignoring others.
   - Example: Feeling jealous about a friend's success and overlooking your own achievements.

3. **Regretful Choices:**
   - Decisions made in the heat of the moment often lead to outcomes you later wish to reverse.

How to Pause and Manage Emotional Bias

1. **Recognize Emotional Triggers:**
   - Pay attention to situations or topics that spark strong emotional reactions.
   - Example: Receiving unexpected negative feedback at work.

2. **Pause Before Responding:**
   - Take a deep breath or count to ten before reacting. This brief pause allows your rational brain to catch up with your emotions.

3. **Name the Emotion:**
   - Labeling your feelings (e.g., "I'm angry" or "I feel hurt") helps you process them without being overwhelmed.

4. **Ask Questions:**
   - Challenge the initial emotional impulse. Ask, "Am I overreacting? What's the bigger picture here?"

5. **Reframe the Situation:**
   - Shift your perspective to focus on solutions rather than emotional reactions.

- o Example: Instead of thinking, "This feedback is unfair," try, "What can I learn from this feedback?"

Examples of Pausing Before Reacting

1. **In Arguments:**
   - o **Scenario:** A coworker criticizes your idea during a meeting.
   - o **Emotional Reaction:** Feeling defensive and interrupting to justify yourself.
   - o **Pause:** Take a moment to breathe and calmly ask, "Can you elaborate on your concerns?"

2. **In Personal Relationships:**
   - o **Scenario:** Your partner forgets an anniversary.
   - o **Emotional Reaction:** Feeling hurt and assuming they don't care.
   - o **Pause:** Consider their situation—were they overwhelmed with work or simply forgetful?

3. **In Decision-Making:**
   - o **Scenario:** A big sale tempts you to overspend on something unnecessary.
   - o **Pause:** Ask yourself, "Do I really need this, or am I acting on excitement?"

Practical Exercise: Build the Pause Habit

1. **Identify an Emotional Trigger:**
   - o Example: Feeling frustrated when someone interrupts you.

2. **Practice Pausing:**
   - o The next time it happens, take a breath and ask, "Why do I feel frustrated? Is this intentional, or just a misunderstanding?"

3. **Reframe Your Reaction:**
   - o Instead of snapping, calmly say, "I'd like to finish my thought, and then I'll hear your input."

Why This Skill is Crucial

Pausing before reacting creates space for clearer thinking. It lets you process emotions, avoid unnecessary conflict, and respond thoughtfully rather than impulsively.

Closing Thought

Emotions are valuable, but they shouldn't dominate your decisions. By pausing and reflecting, you can channel your feelings into more constructive, balanced responses.

Chapter 28: Think Beyond the Present: Avoid Short-Term Traps

What Are Short-Term Traps?

Short-term traps are decisions that prioritize immediate satisfaction at the expense of long-term benefits. They appeal to emotions such as impatience, fear, or desire, but often lead to regret or missed opportunities.

For example:

- Choosing to binge-watch TV instead of studying for an important exam may feel rewarding in the moment but harms your future goals.

Short-term traps happen because your brain is wired to seek instant gratification. Long-term thinking, however, helps you focus on lasting success and meaningful outcomes.

Common Short-Term Traps

1. **Impulsive Decisions:**
   - Acting quickly without considering long-term consequences.
   - Example: Splurging on luxury items instead of saving for emergencies.

2. **Avoiding Discomfort:**
   - Choosing what's easy now rather than what's beneficial later.
   - Example: Skipping exercise because it feels tiring, even though it improves your health.

3. **Fear of Missing Out (FOMO):**
   - Prioritizing temporary experiences over enduring goals.
   - Example: Attending every social event at the expense of personal growth.

How to Avoid Short-Term Traps

1. **Define Your Long-Term Goals:**
   - Be clear about what you want to achieve in the future.
   - Example: Saving for retirement, or maintaining good health.

2. **Pause Before Deciding:**
   - Before making a decision, ask, "How will this affect my future self?"
   - Example: Will staying up late help or hinder your performance tomorrow?

3. **Use If-Then Thinking:**
   - Plan for short-term temptations.
   - Example: "If I feel like procrastinating, then I'll work for just 10 minutes to get started."

4. **Reward Long-Term Progress:**
   - Celebrate small wins that contribute to your bigger goals.

o Example: Treat yourself after a week of sticking to a budget.

Examples of Long-Term Thinking in Action

1. **In Health:**
   - o **Scenario:** Choosing between a healthy meal and fast food.
   - o **Short-Term Trap:** Fast food satisfies cravings now.
   - o **Long-Term Thinking:** A healthy meal supports lasting energy and wellness.

2. **In Career Decisions:**
   - o **Scenario:** Deciding between a stable job and one with growth potential.
   - o **Short-Term Trap:** The stable job feels safer.
   - o **Long-Term Thinking:** Growth opportunities lead to greater career fulfilment.

3. **In Relationships:**
   - o **Scenario:** Skipping a difficult conversation to avoid discomfort.
   - o **Short-Term Trap:** Avoidance feels easier now.
   - o **Long-Term Thinking:** Honest communication strengthens trust and connection.

Practical Exercise: Build Long-Term Thinking

1. **Identify a Recent Decision:**
   - o Example: Skipping a workout or overspending.

2. **Reflect on Its Impact:**
   - o Did it benefit you in the short term but harm your long-term goals?

3. **Plan for Next Time:**
   - o Set up a reminder or system to prioritize your future self.
   - o Example: Commit to a short workout to build consistency.

Why This Skill is Important

Thinking beyond the present helps you avoid short-term traps and stay focused on what truly matters. It builds discipline and fosters success.

Closing Thought

Every decision shapes your future. Choose wisely today to create a tomorrow you'll be proud of.

Chapter 29: Don't Fall for Familiar: Question Availability Heuristics

What is the Availability Heuristic?

The availability heuristic is a mental shortcut where your brain relies on immediate examples that come to mind when making decisions or judgments. If something is easily remembered — like a recent event or a vivid story — it feels more important or likely, even if it doesn't represent the bigger picture.

For example:

- After hearing about a plane crash on the news, you might overestimate the danger of flying, even though statistically, it's much safer than driving.

The availability heuristic exploits familiarity, making rare events feel common and skewing your perception of reality.

Learning to question this bias ensures your thinking is based on evidence, not the ease of recall.

How the Availability Heuristic Skews Thinking

1. **Overestimating Risks:**
   - Events that are dramatic or widely reported (e.g. shark attacks, plane crashes) seem more likely than they are.
2. **Underestimating Common Issues:**
   - Everyday dangers (e.g. heart disease, car accidents) feel less urgent because they lack vivid, memorable examples.
3. **Making Emotional Decisions:**
   - Stories or anecdotes outweigh statistics because they're easier to remember and feel more personal.

Steps to Question the Availability Heuristic

1. **Pause and Reflect:**
   - Ask yourself, "Am I basing this judgment on one vivid example or a broader pattern?"
   - Example: Are you afraid of flying because of one crash, or is it based on reliable data about aviation safety?
2. **Seek Broader Data:**
   - Look for statistics or trends that provide a more accurate picture.
   - Example: Before assuming crime is rising in your neighborhood, check local crime reports instead of relying on one news story.
3. **Balance Stories with Evidence:**
   - Anecdotes are compelling, but they're not always representative. Seek out counterexamples.
4. **Consider the Context:**
   - Ask, "Is this situation truly common, or does it just feel that way because it's fresh in my mind?"

Examples of Avoiding the Availability Heuristic

1. **In Risk Assessment:**
   - **Scenario:** After watching news coverage of a rare disease, you worry it's widespread.
   - **Solution:** Research official statistics to understand its actual prevalence and risk factors.

2. **In Decision-Making:**
   - **Scenario:** A coworker shares a story about a failed investment, making you hesitant to invest.
   - **Solution:** Examine long-term data on investment trends instead of focusing on one bad experience.

3. **In Everyday Choices:**
   - **Scenario:** After hearing about a neighbor's burglary, you consider buying an expensive security system.
   - **Solution:** Evaluate crime rates in your area to determine if the purchase is necessary.

Practical Exercise: Test Your Judgments

1. **Think of a Recent Decision Influenced by a Vivid Example:**
   - Example: Avoiding a specific food because someone got sick after eating it.

2. **Ask These Questions:**
   - Is this example representative of a broader pattern?
   - What evidence supports or contradicts this conclusion?

3. **Seek Objective Data:**
   - Research the actual risks or probabilities to gain a clearer perspective.

Why This Skill is Important

The availability heuristic is a sneaky bias that can make rare events feel more significant than they are. By questioning familiar or vivid examples, you ground your thinking in reality, reducing unnecessary fear and improving decision-making.

Closing Thought

What's memorable isn't always true. Look past vivid examples and rely on data to ensure your choices reflect reality, not just familiarity.

Chapter 30: Step Outside Yourself: Mitigate Egocentric Bias

What is Egocentric Bias?

Egocentric bias is the tendency to view the world through the lens of your own experiences, overestimating how much others notice, care about, or are affected by you. It's not intentional — it's simply how the human brain prioritizes itself.

For example:

- You might assume your co-workers are critical of a mistake you made, when in reality, they're focused on their own tasks.

This bias can lead to misunderstandings, overestimating your influence, or misjudging others' intentions. Mitigating egocentric bias helps you see situations more objectively and connect better with others.

How Egocentric Bias Distorts Thinking

1. **Overestimating Judgment:**

o   You think others notice your flaws or mistakes more than they actually do.

2. **Assuming Universal Experiences:**
    o   You expect others to think, feel, or act as you would in a given situation.

3. **Minimizing Others' Perspectives:**
    o   You unintentionally focus on your own priorities, overlooking how others are affected.

How to Mitigate Egocentric Bias

1. **Acknowledge the Bias:**
    o   Recognize that your perspective is naturally self-centered and may not reflect the bigger picture.

2. **Shift the Focus:**
    o   Ask, "How might others perceive this situation differently?"
    o   Example: A colleague declining your invitation to lunch might be busy, not uninterested in your friendship.

3. **Seek Feedback:**
    o   Invite others to share their thoughts or feelings to broaden your understanding.
    o   Example: If you assume your team is unhappy with your leadership, ask for honest feedback instead of guessing.

4. **Practice Empathy:**
    o   Imagine yourself in others' shoes to understand their experiences.
    o   Example: Consider how a customer might feel about a delayed delivery instead of focusing solely on your company's challenges.

5. **Think Beyond Yourself:**
    o   Focus on the collective impact of decisions, not just how they affect you.

Examples of Overcoming Egocentric Bias

1. **In Social Interactions:**

- o **Scenario:** You feel embarrassed about tripping in public, assuming everyone noticed.
- o **Reality:** Most people were likely focused on their own activities.

2. **In the Workplace:**
   - o **Scenario:** You think a team member's curt email is directed at you.
   - o **Reality:** They may be stressed or in a hurry, with no personal intent behind their tone.

3. **In Problem-Solving:**
   - o **Scenario:** You create a solution that works for you but ignore how it affects others.
   - o **Action:** Seek input from those impacted to ensure the solution is fair and effective.

Practical Exercise: Broaden Your Perspective

1. **Reflect on a Recent Assumption About Others:**
   - o Example: "I assumed my friend was upset with me because they didn't respond to my message."

2. **Ask Yourself:**
   - o Could there be other explanations for their behavior?
   - o How might their perspective differ from mine?

3. **Seek Input:**
   - o If appropriate, ask the person directly for clarity.

Why This Skill is Critical

Egocentric bias narrows your focus, distorting your understanding of situations and relationships. Stepping outside yourself fosters empathy, improves communication, and ensures your decisions are grounded in reality.

Closing Thought

The world isn't always about you — and that's liberating. By stepping outside yourself, you gain clarity, build stronger connections, and approach life with a more balanced perspective.

Part IV: Practical Decision-Making Techniques

Every day, you make countless decisions. Some are simple, others feel overwhelming, especially when the stakes are high or the options seem endless. This section equips you with tools to make decisions with confidence, clarity, and logic.

These methods are not just theoretical; they're practical, proven strategies you can apply immediately to your personal and professional life. Let's turn decision-making into a skill you master, not a challenge you fear.

Chapter 31: The 80/20 Rule: Focus on What Matters Most

What is the 80/20 Rule?

The 80/20 Rule, or Pareto Principle, states that 80% of your outcomes come from 20% of your efforts. It highlights an imbalance: not all tasks, resources, or actions are equally important. By identifying the most impactful 20%, you can focus your energy where it matters most and achieve better results with less effort.

For example:

- 80% of a business's revenue often comes from 20% of its customers.
- 80% of your personal stress might come from just 20% of recurring issues.

Why the 80/20 Rule is a Game-Changer

1. **Boosts Efficiency:**
   - Instead of spreading yourself thin, focus on high-impact activities.
2. **Eliminates Wasted Effort:**
   - Helps you identify tasks or habits that provide little value.
3. **Simplifies Prioritization:**
   - Clarifies what truly matters and lets you ignore distractions.

How to Apply the 80/20 Rule

1. **Identify the 20% with the Biggest Impact:**
   - Ask: "What few actions or inputs drive most of my results?"
   - Example: In studying, 20% of key concepts may account for 80% of the material on an exam.
2. **Eliminate or Delegate the Rest:**
   - Reduce time spent on low-value tasks or delegate them where possible.
   - Example: Outsource routine administrative work to focus on strategy.
3. **Focus Your Energy:**
   - Invest your time, resources, and effort into the high-impact 20%.

Examples of the 80/20 Rule in Action

1. **In Work:**
   - **Scenario:** 80% of your results come from 20% of your projects.
   - **Action:** Prioritize the projects with the highest payoff and reduce time spent on low-impact activities.
2. **In Relationships:**
   - **Scenario:** 20% of your friendships provide 80% of your emotional support.

- o **Action:** Invest more energy in nurturing these key relationships.

3. **In Daily Life:**
   - o **Scenario:** 80% of your wardrobe use comes from 20% of your clothes.
   - o **Action:** Declutter and focus on maintaining the items you actually wear.

Practical Exercise: Focus on Your 20%

1. **List Your Tasks or Responsibilities:**
   - o Example: Work projects, household chores, or fitness goals.
2. **Identify the High-Impact 20%:**
   - o Which tasks drive most of your results or satisfaction?
3. **Refocus Your Time:**
   - o Dedicate more energy to the high-impact 20% and minimize the rest.

Why This Technique Works

The 80/20 Rule is about working smarter, not harder. By focusing on the few things that matter most, you free up time and energy for what truly moves the needle in your life.

Closing Thought

Not all efforts are created equal. Identify your most impactful actions and watch your results multiply.

Chapter 32: The Eisenhower Matrix: Prioritize Tasks by Importance

What is the Eisenhower Matrix?

The Eisenhower Matrix, named after U.S. President Dwight D. Eisenhower, is a tool for prioritizing tasks by urgency and importance. It helps you decide what to focus on, what to delegate, and what to eliminate.

The matrix has four quadrants:

1. **Important and Urgent:** Do these tasks immediately.
2. **Important but Not Urgent:** Schedule these tasks for later.
3. **Urgent but Not Important:** Delegate these tasks.
4. **Not Urgent or Important:** Eliminate these tasks.

Why the Eisenhower Matrix Works

1. **Clarifies Priorities:**
    o   Separates what truly matters from distractions.
2. **Prevents Burnout:**
    o   Helps you avoid spending all your time on urgent tasks while neglecting long-term goals.
3. **Encourages Delegation:**
    o   Shows you which tasks don't require your direct involvement.

How to Use the Eisenhower Matrix

1. **List Your Tasks:**
    o   Write down everything you need to do, no matter how small.
2. **Sort by Urgency and Importance:**
    o   Place each task into the appropriate quadrant:
        ▪   Example: Preparing for tomorrow's presentation is both urgent and important.
        ▪   Checking social media is neither urgent nor important.
3. **Take Action:**
    o   Focus on tasks in Quadrant 1 (important and urgent).
    o   Schedule time for Quadrant 2 tasks (important but not urgent) to prevent them from becoming crises.
    o   Delegate Quadrant 3 tasks and eliminate Quadrant 4 distractions.

Examples of the Eisenhower Matrix in Action

1. **In Work:**
    o   **Scenario:** You have emails to answer, a project deadline tomorrow, and a long-term training course to complete.

- o **Action:**
    - Urgent and Important: Finish the project.
    - Important but Not Urgent: Schedule time for the training course.
    - Urgent but Not Important: Delegate email responses.

2. **In Personal Life:**
   - o **Scenario:** You need to pay overdue bills, plan a family trip, and decide whether to attend a friend's party.
   - o **Action:**
       - Urgent and Important: Pay the bills.
       - Important but Not Urgent: Plan the trip.
       - Not Urgent or Important: Skip the party if it conflicts with priorities.

Practical Exercise: Apply the Matrix

1. **Create a Task List:**
   - o Include work, personal, and leisure activities.
2. **Sort the Tasks into Quadrants:**
   - o Categorize each based on urgency and importance.
3. **Take Immediate Action:**
   - o Focus on Quadrant 1 tasks and schedule Quadrant 2 tasks for later.

Why This Technique is Valuable

The Eisenhower Matrix simplifies complex to-do lists, ensuring your energy goes to tasks that truly matter. It keeps you organized, efficient, and focused on long-term success.

Closing Thought

Not everything urgent is important. Use the Eisenhower Matrix to prioritize wisely and achieve more with less stress.

Chapter 33: The Premortem: Plan for Failure Before It Happens

What is a Premortem?

A premortem is a technique where you imagine that your project, plan, or decision has failed — and then work backward to identify what might have caused the failure. By visualizing failure before it happens, you can uncover hidden risks, anticipate problems, and create strategies to prevent those outcomes.

For example:

- If you're planning a product launch, you might ask, "What if the launch flops?" Answers could include poor marketing, unmet customer expectations, or product defects. Identifying these risks early allows you to address them before they become actual issues.

Why the Premortem is Powerful

1. **Anticipates Problems Early:**

o Most planning focuses on success, often overlooking potential pitfalls. The premortem forces you to confront weaknesses proactively.

2. **Reduces Overconfidence:**
    o It helps temper overly optimistic thinking by forcing you to consider challenges and obstacles realistically.

3. **Improves Team Collaboration:**
    o Encourages open dialogue, where everyone can voice concerns without fear of appearing negative.

4. **Builds Resilience:**
    o By addressing failure scenarios, you develop contingency plans that prepare you for unexpected setbacks.

How to Conduct a Premortem

1. **Define the Goal:**
    o Clearly outline the plan or project you're evaluating.
    o Example: "We're launching a new app in six months."

2. **Imagine a Failure Scenario:**
    o Pretend the project has already failed. Ask, "What went wrong?"

3. **Brainstorm Potential Causes:**
    o Gather input from everyone involved to identify possible reasons for failure. Encourage honesty and creativity.
    o Example: "The app failed because of bugs, poor marketing, or a lack of user interest."

4. **Prioritize Risks:**
    o Identify which risks are most likely and have the greatest impact. Focus your efforts on addressing these.

5. **Develop Preventative Actions:**
    o Create strategies to mitigate or eliminate the

identified risks.

- o Example: Conduct thorough testing, survey potential users, and refine marketing efforts.

Examples of Premortems in Action

1. **In Business:**
   - o **Scenario:** A company is planning a new product line.
   - o **Premortem:** "The product flopped because customers didn't see its value."
   - o **Solution:** Conduct market research to ensure the product addresses real customer needs.

2. **In Personal Goals:**
   - o **Scenario:** You're preparing for a marathon.
   - o **Premortem:** "I didn't finish because of an injury."
   - o **Solution:** Follow a structured training plan, focus on injury prevention, and maintain proper rest.

3. **In Team Projects:**
   - o **Scenario:** A group is organizing an event.
   - o **Premortem:** "Attendance was low because we didn't promote it effectively."
   - o **Solution:** Create a detailed promotional strategy with clear deadlines.

Practical Exercise: Try a Premortem

1. **Choose a Project or Goal:**
   - o Example: "I want to lose 10 pounds in three months."

2. **Imagine Failure:**
   - o Picture the goal not being achieved. Ask, "Why did I fail?"
   - o Example: "I didn't plan meals, skipped workouts, or lost motivation."

3. List Preventative Actions:
- o Plan meals in advance, schedule workouts, and track progress to stay motivated.

Why This Technique Works

The premortem shifts your perspective, forcing you to think critically about risks instead of only focusing on success. It ensures that you're not caught off guard by predictable challenges.

Closing Thought

Planning for failure doesn't mean expecting it — it means being prepared to prevent it. A premortem sharpens your vision and strengthens your plans, making success more likely.

Chapter 34: Decision Matrix: Weigh Pros and Cons Objectively

	Cost	Accessibility	Activities	Weather	TOTAL
BEACH	4	5	2	5	16
MOUNTAINS	2	2	3	4	11
CITY	3	5	4	2	14

What is a Decision Matrix?

A decision matrix is a tool that helps you evaluate and compare multiple options based on specific criteria. It transforms subjective choices into objective comparisons by assigning scores to each option.

For example:

- Imagine you're deciding between three job offers. A decision matrix lets you weigh factors like salary, location, growth potential, and work-life balance to choose the best fit.

Why the Decision Matrix is Effective

1. **Reduces Emotional Bias:**
    - By focusing on data and criteria, it minimizes the influence of personal biases or emotions.

2. **Clarifies Priorities:**
    o Helps you identify what factors matter most and ensures they guide your decision.
3. **Simplifies Complex Choices:**
    o Breaks down overwhelming decisions into manageable, logical steps.

How to Use a Decision Matrix

1. **List Your Options:**
    o Write down all the choices you're considering.
    o Example: Three potential vacation destinations.
2. **Define Your Criteria:**
    o Identify the factors that matter most.
    o Example: Cost, travel time, activities, and weather.
3. **Assign Weights to Each Criterion:**
    o Decide which factors are most important by assigning a weight (e.g., 1 to 5).
    o Example: Cost (5), travel time (3), activities (4), weather (2).
4. **Score Each Option:**
    o Rate how well each option meets each criterion on a scale (e.g., 1 to 10).
5. **Calculate Totals:**
    o Multiply each score by its weight and add up the totals for each option. The highest score indicates the best choice.

Examples of Decision Matrices in Action

1. **In Career Decisions:**
    o **Scenario:** Choosing between two job offers.
    o **Criteria:** Salary (5), commute (3), growth opportunities (4), work culture (3).
    o **Action:** Score and weigh each offer to see which aligns best with your priorities.

2. **In Purchases:**
    - ○ **Scenario:** Deciding between three laptops.
    - ○ **Criteria:** Price, performance, battery life, and brand reputation.
    - ○ **Action:** Use the matrix to determine which laptop offers the best value.

3. **In Personal Life:**
    - ○ **Scenario:** Choosing between hobbies to pursue.
    - ○ **Criteria:** Cost, time commitment, enjoyment, and social opportunities.
    - ○ **Action:** Evaluate the options and focus on the most fulfilling hobby.

Practical Exercise: Build Your Own Decision Matrix

1. **Choose a Decision You're Facing:**
    - ○ Example: "Which online course should I take?"

2. **List Options and Criteria:**
    - ○ Options: Course A, Course B, Course C.
    - ○ Criteria: Cost, content quality, instructor reputation, and flexibility.

3. **Assign Weights and Scores:**
    - ○ Weight each criterion, rate the options, and calculate totals.

4. **Choose the Highest-Scoring Option:**
    - ○ Let the results guide your decision.

Why This Technique Works

A decision matrix replaces guesswork with structure, giving you clarity and confidence in your choices. It's especially useful when decisions involve multiple variables or competing priorities.

Closing Thought

Every decision involves trade-offs. A decision matrix ensures you evaluate your options logically, making choices that align with your goals and values.

Chapter 35: The 10/10/10 Rule: Think Long-Term

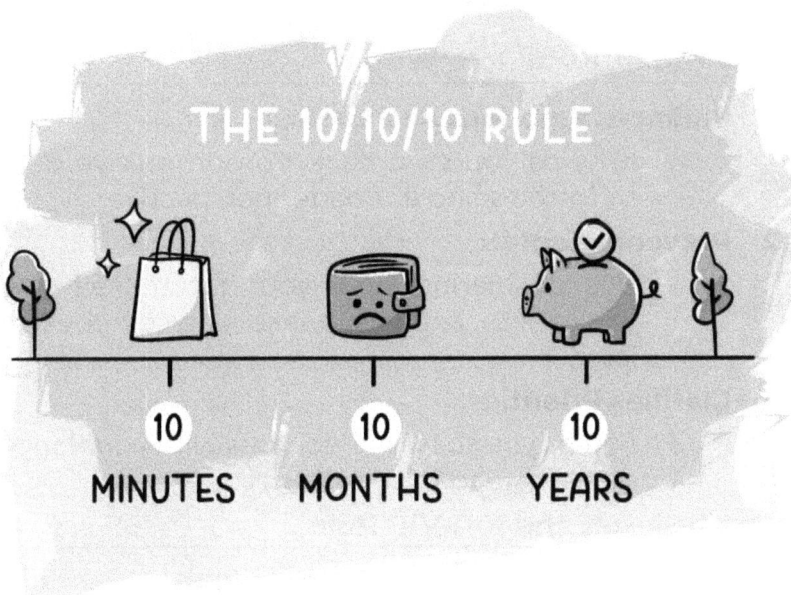

THE 10/10/10 RULE

| 10 | 10 | 10 |
| MINUTES | MONTHS | YEARS |

What is the 10/10/10 Rule?

The 10/10/10 Rule, developed by author Suzy Welch, is a decision-making framework that helps you think beyond the present moment. It works by asking three simple questions:

1. How will I feel about this decision in **10 minutes**?
2. How will I feel about this decision in **10 months**?
3. How will I feel about this decision in **10 years**?

This technique forces you to consider short-, medium-, and long-term consequences, balancing immediate emotions with future goals.

For example:

- **Decision:** Should you splurge on an expensive gadget?
    - In 10 minutes: You'll feel excited about the purchase.

- In 10 months: You might regret the dent in your savings.
- In 10 years: The gadget will likely be obsolete, and the financial loss may outweigh the short-term joy.

Why the 10/10/10 Rule Works

1. **Balances Emotions and Logic:**
   - It helps you step back from impulsive decisions by introducing a broader perspective.
2. **Prevents Regret:**
   - By considering how your future self will feel, you're less likely to make choices you'll regret later.
3. **Clarifies Priorities:**
   - Forces you to align decisions with your long-term goals instead of short-term desires.

How to Apply the 10/10/10 Rule

1. **Define the Decision:**
   - Be specific about what you're deciding.
   - Example: "Should I quit my current job for a new opportunity?"
2. **Consider the Short-Term (10 Minutes):**
   - Ask, "How will this decision feel immediately after I make it?"
   - Example: Quitting your job might bring relief but also anxiety.
3. **Think About the Medium-Term (10 Months):**
   - Ask, "How will this decision impact my life in the coming months?"
   - Example: You might have a steeper learning curve at the new job but gain valuable skills.
4. **Weigh the Long-Term (10 Years):**
   - Ask, "How will this decision shape my life a decade from now?"

- o Example: Will the new job align better with your long-term career goals?

5. **Evaluate Your Answers:**
   - o Use your reflections to guide a balanced, well-informed choice.

Examples of the 10/10/10 Rule in Action

1. **In Financial Decisions:**
   - o **Scenario:** Deciding whether to buy a luxury car.
   - o **10 Minutes:** Excitement about owning the car.
   - o **10 Months:** Financial stress from higher monthly payments.
   - o **10 Years:** Regret for not investing that money more wisely.

2. **In Relationships:**
   - o **Scenario:** Considering whether to end a toxic friendship.
   - o **10 Minutes:** Discomfort or guilt about confronting the issue.
   - o **10 Months:** Relief and more time for healthier relationships.
   - o **10 Years:** A stronger social circle and peace of mind.

3. **In Career Choices:**
   - o **Scenario:** Debating a risky career change.
   - o **10 Minutes:** Fear of uncertainty.
   - o **10 Months:** Adjustment to the new role, with signs of growth.
   - o **10 Years:** A fulfilling career aligned with your passions.

Practical Exercise: Try the 10/10/10 Rule

1. **Identify a Pending Decision:**
   - o Example: "Should I start a new fitness routine?"

2. **Ask the Three Questions:**
   - o How will this feel in 10 minutes?

o How will this feel in 10 months?

  o How will this feel in 10 years?

3. Write Down Your Answers:

  o Use them to weigh the pros and cons of your choice.

Why This Technique is Valuable

The 10/10/10 Rule encourages you to think beyond the present moment. It bridges the gap between emotions and long-term logic, helping you make decisions you'll be proud of later.

Closing Thought

A good decision honors both your present and your future self. Use the 10/10/10 Rule to make choices that stand the test of time.

Chapter 36: Scenario Planning: Prepare for All Outcomes

What is Scenario Planning?

Scenario planning is a technique that helps you prepare for the future by imagining multiple possible outcomes and creating strategies for each. Instead of predicting one result, you explore a range of possibilities, from best-case to worst-case scenarios, and plan accordingly.

For example:

- **Goal:** Launch a new product.
    - o **Best Case:** The product sells out quickly.
    - o **Moderate Case:** Sales are steady but require ongoing marketing.
    - o **Worst Case:** The product doesn't meet customer needs, requiring adjustments.

By planning for all outcomes, you reduce uncertainty and improve your ability to adapt when things don't go as expected.

Why Scenario Planning Works

1. **Reduces Surprises:**
   o Thinking ahead prepares you for challenges and minimizes panic during setbacks.
2. **Encourages Flexibility:**
   o By exploring multiple possibilities, you're better equipped to pivot when needed.
3. **Strengthens Decision-Making:**
   o It forces you to think critically about risks, opportunities, and strategies.

How to Create Scenarios

1. **Define Your Goal:**
   o Be clear about the decision or plan you're evaluating.
   o Example: "I want to expand my business to a new location."
2. **Brainstorm Possible Outcomes:**
   o Imagine a range of scenarios:
     - Best Case: High customer demand and profits.
     - Moderate Case: Steady growth with minor challenges.
     - Worst Case: Low demand and financial losses.
3. **Develop Strategies for Each Scenario:**
   o Create a plan tailored to each possibility.
   o Example:
     - Best Case: Hire additional staff to meet demand.
     - Moderate Case: Focus on building brand awareness.

- Worst Case: Scale back operations to minimize losses.

4. **Monitor Key Indicators:**
   - Identify signs that indicate which scenario is unfolding.
   - Example: Early customer feedback or sales trends.

5. **Adapt as Needed:**
   - Be ready to adjust your strategy as new information emerges.

Examples of Scenario Planning in Action

1. **In Personal Finance:**
   - **Scenario:** Saving for a major purchase.
   - **Best Case:** You save the full amount on time.
   - **Moderate Case:** Unexpected expenses slow your progress.
   - **Worst Case:** You lose income and must delay the purchase.
   - **Plan:** Build an emergency fund and adjust your budget as needed.

2. **In Career Decisions:**
   - **Scenario:** Applying for a competitive promotion.
   - **Best Case:** You get the role and thrive.
   - **Moderate Case:** You don't get the promotion but gain valuable feedback.
   - **Worst Case:** You realize the role isn't the right fit.
   - **Plan:** Continue networking and building skills for future opportunities.

3. **In Event Planning:**
   - **Scenario:** Organizing an outdoor wedding.
   - **Best Case:** Perfect weather.
   - **Moderate Case:** Light rain.
   - **Worst Case:** A storm.
   - **Plan:** Arrange a backup venue and rental tents.

Practical Exercise: Plan for Your Scenarios

1. **Choose a Goal or Decision:**
   - Example: "I want to start a side business."
2. **List Three Scenarios:**
   - Best Case, Moderate Case, Worst Case.
3. **Develop Strategies for Each:**
   - Tailor your plans to prepare for any outcome.

Why Scenario Planning is Powerful

This technique helps you anticipate risks, seize opportunities, and build resilience. It's about being prepared for whatever comes.

Closing Thought

The future is uncertain, but your preparation doesn't have to be. Use scenario planning to face any outcome with confidence and clarity.

Chapter 37: Risk vs. Reward: Make Calculated Bets

What Does Risk vs. Reward Mean?

Every decision involves some level of risk, but not all risks are created equal. Risk vs. reward is the process of evaluating potential downsides (risks) against the potential benefits (rewards) of a decision. This method helps you make choices that maximize gain while minimizing unnecessary losses.

For example:

- Deciding to invest in a start-up might carry a high risk of financial loss but also the potential for significant returns. The decision depends on whether the possible reward justifies the level of risk.

Why Balancing Risk and Reward is Crucial

1. **Prevents Reckless Choices:**
    - o It encourages you to consider risks carefully rather than jumping into decisions based on excitement or pressure.

2. **Reduces Missed Opportunities:**
   - ○ Fear of risk can paralyze you. Balancing it with potential rewards helps you make confident, informed bets.
3. **Sharpens Decision-Making:**
   - ○ Weighing risks and rewards forces you to think critically about priorities and trade-offs.

How to Evaluate Risk vs. Reward

1. **Identify the Decision:**
   - ○ Be clear about what you're considering.
   - ○ Example: "Should I start my own business?"
2. **List the Risks:**
   - ○ Write down potential downsides and their likelihood.
   - ○ Example: Losing savings, inconsistent income, or business failure.
3. **List the Rewards:**
   - ○ Identify possible benefits and their impact.
   - ○ Example: Financial independence, creative freedom, or long-term growth.
4. **Assess Risk Probability and Impact:**
   - ○ For each risk, evaluate:
     - ▪ **Probability:** How likely is it to happen?
     - ▪ **Impact:** How significant would the damage be if it occurs?
5. **Assess Reward Value:**
   - ○ Consider the scale and importance of potential benefits.
   - ○ Example: A high chance of moderate rewards might outweigh low-probability, catastrophic risks.
6. **Make a Decision:**
   - ○ Choose based on whether the rewards outweigh the risks or if you can mitigate the risks sufficiently.

Examples of Risk vs. Reward Thinking

1. **In Investments:**
   - o **Scenario:** Deciding whether to invest in a high-risk stock.
   - o **Risks:** Losing money if the stock value plummets.
   - o **Rewards:** Significant returns if the stock performs well.
   - o **Decision:** Invest a small amount you can afford to lose, minimizing downside while maintaining upside potential.

2. **In Career Decisions:**
   - o **Scenario:** Considering a role at a start-up.
   - o **Risks:** Job instability, long hours.
   - o **Rewards:** Rapid career growth, equity in the company.
   - o **Decision:** Accept the role if it aligns with your long-term goals and you can handle short-term instability.

3. **In Personal Choices:**
   - o **Scenario:** Moving to a new city for a fresh start.
   - o **Risks:** Financial strain, homesickness.
   - o **Rewards:** New opportunities, personal growth.
   - o **Decision:** If the potential for growth outweighs temporary discomfort, take the leap.

Practical Exercise: Apply Risk vs. Reward

1. **Choose a Decision You're Facing:**
   - o Example: "Should I enroll in an expensive certification program?"

2. **List the Risks and Rewards:**
   - o Risks: Cost, time commitment.
   - o Rewards: Career advancement, higher salary potential.

3. **Evaluate Probability and Impact:**
    - o Risk Probability: Moderate (you may struggle financially for a few months).
    - o Reward Value: High (significant career growth).
4. **Decide and Plan:**
    - o If the rewards outweigh the risks, create a plan to mitigate the downsides, such as budgeting or taking out a small loan.

Why This Technique Works

Risk vs. reward thinking helps you avoid acting on impulse or fear. It ensures your decisions are calculated, deliberate, and aligned with your goals.

Closing Thought

Life's biggest opportunities often involve risk. Evaluate the balance carefully, mitigate where possible, and take bold steps toward meaningful rewards.

Chapter 38: Take Small Steps: Embrace Iterative Decision-Making

What is Iterative Decision-Making?

Iterative decision-making is the practice of breaking big decisions into smaller, manageable steps. Instead of trying to solve everything at once, you take one small action, evaluate the results, and adjust your approach as needed.

For example:

- If you're considering a career change, you don't quit your job immediately. Instead, you take small steps like researching industries, networking, or enrolling in a part-time course.

Why Small Steps Work

1. **Reduces Overwhelm:**
   - Tackling a huge decision all at once can feel paralyzing. Small steps make it manageable.
2. **Allows for Course Correction:**
   - Iterative decisions let you test your ideas and adapt before committing fully.
3. **Builds Momentum:**
   - Each small success motivates you to take the next step.
4. **Minimizes Risk:**
   - By taking small actions, you limit the potential consequences of failure.

How to Take Small Steps

1. **Break Down the Decision:**
   - Divide a large decision into smaller, actionable steps.
   - Example: Instead of starting a business overnight, begin by validating your idea with a small test.
2. **Start with Low-Risk Actions:**
   - Take steps that are easy to undo if needed.
   - Example: Before investing in a costly fitness program, try free online workouts to see if you enjoy the activity.
3. **Evaluate Progress:**
   - After each step, assess what worked, what didn't, and what to try next.
4. **Iterate and Adjust:**
   - Use feedback to refine your approach.
   - Example: If your initial side hustle idea doesn't resonate with customers, tweak your offering based on their feedback.

Examples of Iterative Decision-Making

1. **In Business:**
   - **Scenario:** Launching a new product.
   - **Small Step:** Start with a minimum viable product (MVP) to test demand before scaling production.

2. **In Education:**
   - **Scenario:** Considering a degree program.
   - **Small Step:** Enroll in one introductory course to gauge your interest and fit.

3. **In Personal Growth:**
   - **Scenario:** Building a fitness habit.
   - **Small Step:** Start with 10-minute daily walks instead of committing to a full gym routine immediately.

Practical Exercise: Take Your First Step

1. **Choose a Big Decision or Goal:**
   - Example: "I want to move abroad."

2. **Identify the First Small Step:**
   - Research visa requirements or reach out to someone who has made the move.

3. **Set a Timeline:**
   - Give yourself a deadline for completing the first step, such as one week.

4. **Evaluate and Plan the Next Step:**
   - Based on what you learn, decide on the next action.

Why This Technique is Powerful

Small steps create progress without overwhelming you. They allow for experimentation, learning, and refinement, making even the biggest decisions achievable.

Closing Thought

Success isn't a giant leap; it's a series of thoughtful steps. Start small, adapt, and watch your decisions lead to big outcomes.

Chapter 39: Start with a Minimum Viable Solution

We can't launch until everything's perfect.

Let's start with the simplest version that works and improve from there.

MVS
↓
Feedback
↓
Improve

What is a Minimum Viable Solution?

A minimum viable solution (MVS) is the simplest version of a solution that addresses a problem effectively. It focuses on delivering value quickly with the least effort, resources, or complexity. Instead of aiming for perfection right away, an MVS allows you to start small, test your approach, and improve over time.

For example:

- If you're launching a business, an MVS might involve offering a single product or service to test customer demand before expanding.

This approach is particularly useful for avoiding overcommitment to a flawed idea or spending excessive time on unnecessary features.

Why the Minimum Viable Solution is Effective

1. **Speeds Up Action:**
   o It lets you move forward quickly instead of getting stuck in over-planning or perfectionism.
2. **Reduces Risk:**
   o By starting small, you minimize the cost and effort of potential failures.
3. **Encourages Feedback:**
   o An MVS lets you gather input from others early, helping you refine your approach before scaling.
4. **Builds Momentum:**
   o Achieving small successes early on motivates you to keep going.

How to Create a Minimum Viable Solution

1. **Define the Core Problem:**
   o Focus on the specific issue you're trying to solve.
   o Example: "Customers want faster delivery options."
2. **Identify the Simplest Solution:**
   o Determine the smallest action or feature that addresses the problem effectively.
   o Example: Test local same-day delivery in one area instead of launching a nationwide program.
3. **Launch and Test:**
   o Implement your MVS quickly and gather feedback.
   o Example: Offer a limited menu if you're opening a new restaurant to see what items customers prefer.
4. **Iterate and Improve:**
   o Use feedback to refine and expand your solution gradually.

Examples of Minimum Viable Solutions in Action

1. **In Business:**
   - **Scenario:** Developing an app.
   - **MVS:** Build a basic version with one core feature to test user interest before adding advanced functionality.

2. **In Personal Projects:**
   - **Scenario:** Writing a book.
   - **MVS:** Write a short e-book or article on the topic to gauge interest before committing to a full manuscript.

3. **In Problem-Solving:**
   - **Scenario:** Reducing household clutter.
   - **MVS:** Declutter one room or category of items (e.g., clothes) before tackling the entire house.

Practical Exercise: Build Your Minimum Viable Solution

1. **Choose a Problem or Goal:**
   - Example: "I want to start a blog."

2. **Define Your MVS:**
   - What's the simplest version of your solution?
   - Example: Publish one blog post on a free platform to see how it resonates with readers.

3. **Take Action:**
   - Implement your MVS within the next week.

4. **Gather Feedback:**
   - Use comments, engagement, or other metrics to assess your results and plan the next steps.

Why This Technique is Powerful

A minimum viable solution allows you to act decisively without overcommitting. It's a practical way to test ideas, learn quickly, and achieve meaningful results with minimal risk.

Closing Thought

Perfection is a trap. Start with what works now, refine over time, and watch small beginnings lead to big successes.

Chapter 40: Use Weighted Scoring for Big Decisions

I'm torn between these three software options.

Let's rank them using weighted scoring—what matters most to you?

	Cost	Features	Long-Term Value	Score
Option A	4	2	3	9
Option B	3	4	5	12
Option C	2	4	2	8

What is Weighted Scoring?

Weighted scoring is a decision-making tool that helps you evaluate multiple options by assigning importance (weights) to specific criteria. This approach ensures that the most critical factors have a bigger influence on the final decision, creating a more balanced and objective outcome.

For example:

- Choosing between job offers might involve criteria like salary, work-life balance, growth potential, and commute time. Weighted scoring lets you prioritize what matters most and compare the options logically.

Why Weighted Scoring Works

1. **Removes Emotional Bias:**
   - By focusing on objective criteria, it reduces the influence of emotions or gut feelings.

2. **Simplifies Complex Decisions:**
   - o Breaks down big choices into smaller, measurable components.
3. **Aligns Decisions with Priorities:**
   - o Ensures that the factors most important to you carry the greatest weight in the decision.

How to Use Weighted Scoring

1. **List Your Options:**
   - o Write down all the choices you're considering.
   - o Example: Three vacation destinations.
2. **Define Key Criteria:**
   - o Identify the factors that will influence your decision.
   - o Example: Cost, activities, weather, and travel time.
3. **Assign Weights to Criteria:**
   - o Rate the importance of each factor on a scale (e.g., 1 to 5).
   - o Example: Cost (5), activities (4), weather (3), travel time (2).
4. **Score Each Option:**
   - o Rate how well each option performs on each criterion (e.g., 1 to 10).
5. **Calculate Weighted Scores:**
   - o Multiply each score by its weight and add the totals for each option. The highest score indicates the best choice.

Examples of Weighted Scoring in Action

1. **In Career Decisions:**
   - o **Scenario:** Choosing between three job offers.
   - o **Criteria:** Salary (5), commute (3), growth potential (4), work culture (4).
   - o **Action:** Use the matrix to score each job and identify the best fit based on your priorities.

2. **In Purchases:**
   - ○ **Scenario:** Deciding between laptops.
   - ○ **Criteria:** Price, performance, battery life, brand reputation.
   - ○ **Action:** Compare options using weighted scoring to make a balanced decision.
3. **In Personal Goals:**
   - ○ **Scenario:** Deciding which hobby to pursue.
   - ○ **Criteria:** Enjoyment, cost, time commitment, and social opportunities.
   - ○ **Action:** Evaluate each hobby against these criteria to find the best match.

Practical Exercise: Use Weighted Scoring

1. **Choose a Complex Decision:**
   - ○ Example: "Which online course should I take?"
2. **Define Criteria and Weights:**
   - ○ Example: Cost (4), instructor quality (5), flexibility (3), course content (5).
3. **Score Your Options:**
   - ○ Rate each course based on how well it meets each criterion.
4. **Calculate and Compare:**
   - ○ Multiply scores by weights, add them up, and choose the option with the highest total.

Why This Technique is Valuable

Weighted scoring brings structure and clarity to tough decisions. By aligning choices with your priorities, it ensures your decision is thoughtful, logical, and aligned with your goals.

Closing Thought

Not all factors are equal. Weighted scoring helps you focus on what matters most, ensuring that every decision reflects your true priorities.

Part V: Thinking Outside the Box

Creativity isn't just for artists — it's an essential skill for solving problems, making decisions, and innovating in everyday life. Thinking outside the box means escaping habitual patterns of thought and exploring new ways of seeing the world.

In this section, you'll learn techniques that spark creativity and unlock fresh perspectives. These tools help you tackle challenges with originality, turning roadblocks into opportunities and conventional thinking into breakthrough ideas.

Chapter 41: First Principles Thinking: Break It Down to Basics

POWER SOURCE

FRAME

MOBILITY

What is First Principles Thinking?

First principles thinking involves breaking a problem down into its most basic elements, or "first principles," and building your understanding from the ground up. Instead of relying on assumptions, you ask fundamental questions to uncover the core truth of an issue.

For example:

- If you're redesigning a car, instead of asking, "How can we improve this car?" you ask, "What is a car at its core? A vehicle that moves people efficiently." This leads to rethinking everything, from materials to energy sources, without being constrained by existing models.

This technique helps you bypass conventional thinking and develop original solutions.

Why First Principles Thinking is Powerful

1. **Challenges Assumptions:**
    o It helps you avoid being limited by "the way things have always been done."
2. **Reveals Core Truths:**
    o By stripping away complexity, you focus on the fundamental aspects of a problem.
3. **Fosters Innovation:**
    o Starting from first principles encourages new approaches and creative solutions.

How to Apply First Principles Thinking

1. **Identify the Problem:**
    o Be clear about what you're trying to solve.
    o Example: "How can we make batteries cheaper and more efficient?"
2. **Break It Down:**
    o Deconstruct the problem into its basic components.
    o Example: A battery is a device that stores and releases energy.
3. **Question Assumptions:**
    o Ask, "What do I know to be true? Is this based on fact or habit?"
    o Example: Do batteries need to use expensive materials like lithium, or are there alternatives?
4. **Rebuild from the Ground Up:**
    o Use the core truths to explore new possibilities.
    o Example: Consider alternative materials, designs, or energy storage methods.

Examples of First Principles Thinking in Action

1. **In Business:**
    o **Scenario:** A company wants to reduce shipping costs.
    o **First Principles:** Shipping is about moving goods from Point A to Point B.

- o **Solution:** Instead of using traditional packaging, explore lightweight, biodegradable options that lower costs and environmental impact.

2. **In Personal Life:**
   - o **Scenario:** You want to get fit but dislike traditional exercise routines.
   - o **First Principles:** Fitness is about maintaining a healthy, active lifestyle.
   - o **Solution:** Focus on fun activities like dancing, hiking, or sports instead of rigid gym schedules.

3. **In Education:**
   - o **Scenario:** A teacher struggles to engage students.
   - o **First Principles:** Learning happens best when it's interactive and meaningful.
   - o **Solution:** Introduce hands-on experiments or storytelling to make lessons more engaging.

Practical Exercise: Break It Down

1. **Choose a Problem or Goal:**
   - o Example: "I want to save more money each month."

2. **List Assumptions:**
   - o Example: "I can only save by cutting back on coffee or dining out."

3. **Question Each Assumption:**
   - o Is cutting costs the only way to save? Could you find ways to earn more instead?

4. **Focus on Fundamentals:**
   - o What's the core principle? Saving means spending less than you earn.

Why This Technique Works

First principles thinking clears away the noise, letting you see problems with fresh eyes. By focusing on the basics, you uncover opportunities that others overlook.

Closing Thought

Complex problems often have simple beginnings. Break them down to the essentials and build solutions from the ground up.

Chapter 42: Lateral Thinking: Jump to New Perspectives

What is Lateral Thinking?

Lateral thinking is about approaching problems from unexpected angles instead of following traditional, step-by-step logic. It encourages you to step outside conventional thought patterns and explore creative, even unusual, solutions.

For example:

- A hotel chain struggling to attract business travelers might introduce coworking spaces instead of simply lowering room rates, appealing to a broader audience.

Why Lateral Thinking Matters

1. **Breaks Mental Ruts:**
    o It helps you escape predictable thinking and find fresh ideas.

2. **Solves "Impossible" Problems:**
   - By changing perspectives, you discover solutions that wouldn't emerge from linear reasoning.
3. **Drives Innovation:**
   - Lateral thinking is the foundation of breakthroughs, from new products to improved processes.

How to Practice Lateral Thinking

1. **Reframe the Question:**
   - Change how you define the problem.
   - Example: Instead of asking, "How can I sell more books?" ask, "How can I make reading irresistible?"
2. **Use Analogies:**
   - Compare the problem to unrelated fields for inspiration.
   - Example: If managing a team feels overwhelming, think about how an orchestra conductor leads musicians with different strengths.
3. **Challenge Assumptions:**
   - Identify and question the "rules" you think you must follow.
   - Example: Who says office meetings need to happen in person? Try virtual or asynchronous meetings.
4. **Consider the Absurd:**
   - Brainstorm ideas that seem ridiculous at first—they often spark creative insights.
   - Example: What if a restaurant let customers cook their own meals? (This led to the popularity of hot pot and fondue restaurants.)

Examples of Lateral Thinking in Action

1. **In Product Design:**
   - **Scenario:** Creating a more durable phone case.
   - **Lateral Idea:** Instead of reinforcing the case, design a phone that's waterproof and shatterproof.

2. **In Marketing:**
   - **Scenario:** Promoting a small café.
   - **Lateral Idea:** Create a "pay-what-you-want" day to attract curious customers and build buzz.

3. **In Personal Problem-Solving:**
   - **Scenario:** You want to meet new people but dislike networking events.
   - **Lateral Idea:** Join hobby groups or volunteer for causes you're passionate about.

Practical Exercise: Try a Lateral Approach

1. **Choose a Problem:**
   - Example: "I want to save time on my commute."

2. **Reframe the Question:**
   - How can you make the commute enjoyable instead of shorter?

3. **Brainstorm Unconventional Ideas:**
   - Examples: Listen to audiobooks, carpool with co-workers to share the driving load, or explore remote work options.

4. **Experiment and Evaluate:**
   - Test your ideas and refine them based on results.

Why This Technique is Powerful

Lateral thinking helps you escape the limits of conventional logic, opening doors to creative and effective solutions.

Closing Thought

The best ideas often come from unexpected angles. Step sideways, challenge norms, and watch problems transform into opportunities.

Chapter 43: Brainstorm Without Judgment

What Does It Mean to Brainstorm Without Judgment?

Brainstorming without judgment means generating ideas freely, without evaluating or critiquing them during the process. It allows your creativity to flow uninterrupted, encouraging unconventional and innovative solutions.

When judgment is removed, even "wild" ideas are welcome, which can spark breakthroughs or lead to refined, practical solutions later. Judgment-free brainstorming creates a safe space where ideas can evolve without fear of criticism.

For example:

- If you're brainstorming ways to grow a business, allowing "out-there" suggestions — like delivering products by drone — can inspire creative leaps that might otherwise be dismissed too early.

Why Judgment-Free Brainstorming Matters

1. **Encourages Creativity:**
   - Criticism stifles creativity. Removing judgment helps participants feel comfortable sharing bold or unusual ideas.

2. **Generates More Ideas:**
   - Without the filter of "good" or "bad," you produce a larger pool of possibilities to explore later.

3. **Fosters Collaboration:**
   - People are more likely to contribute when they know their ideas won't be immediately dismissed or ridiculed.

4. **Leads to Innovation:**
   - Even seemingly "bad" ideas can inspire solutions that wouldn't have been considered otherwise.

How to Brainstorm Without Judgment

1. **Set Clear Goals:**
   - Define the purpose of the brainstorming session.
   - Example: "We're brainstorming ways to reduce office waste."

2. **Create a Safe Environment:**
   - Establish ground rules: No criticism, no judgment, and no interrupting others.

3. **Encourage Quantity Over Quality:**
   - Focus on generating as many ideas as possible. Refining them comes later.

4. **Use Prompts or Themes:**
   - Start with questions or challenges to spark creativity.
   - Example: "What's one way we could eliminate paper usage entirely?"

5. **Record Every Idea:**
   - Write down all contributions, no matter how impractical they seem.

6. **Save Evaluation for Later:**
   - Once the brainstorming session is complete, review and refine the ideas as a group.

Examples of Brainstorming Without Judgment

1. **In Business:**
   - **Scenario:** A marketing team brainstorms ways to increase customer engagement.
   - **Process:** Ideas range from hosting live Q&A sessions to creating a mascot for the brand.
   - **Outcome:** While the mascot idea seems far-fetched, it inspires a viral marketing campaign featuring humorous animated videos.

2. **In Education:**
   - **Scenario:** Teachers brainstorm ways to make math lessons more engaging.
   - **Process:** Ideas include incorporating games, music, and field trips.
   - **Outcome:** The group combines ideas into a "math adventure day" that becomes a hit with students.

3. **In Personal Life:**
   - **Scenario:** A family brainstorms vacation destinations.
   - **Process:** Ideas range from local camping trips to a dream safari in Africa.
   - **Outcome:** While the safari is out of budget, it leads to a compromise: visiting a wildlife park nearby.

Practical Exercise: Brainstorm Judgment-Free

1. **Choose a Topic or Problem:**
   - Example: "How can I make my mornings more productive?"

2. **Set a Timer:**
   - Spend 10 minutes writing down every idea that comes to mind, no matter how small or impractical.

3. **Avoid Evaluating:**
   - Don't critique or eliminate ideas during the process.
4. **Review and Refine Later:**
   - After the brainstorming session, pick a few ideas to explore further.

Why This Technique is Valuable

Judgment-free brainstorming removes barriers to creativity. It generates a rich pool of ideas, some of which might lead to surprising and innovative solutions.

Closing Thought: Ideas flourish when freed from judgment. Give your creativity room to grow, and let evaluation come later.

Chapter 44: Use Random Input to Spark Ideas

What is Random Input?

Random input involves introducing unrelated or unexpected elements into your thought process to inspire new ideas. By forcing your brain to connect seemingly unrelated concepts, you break free from linear thinking and discover fresh, creative perspectives.

For example:

- If you're designing a new product and use the word "mountain" as random input, you might explore ideas like durability, adaptability, or outdoor applications.

Why Random Input Works

1. **Breaks Predictable Patterns:**
    o   Random input disrupts your usual way of thinking, sparking creativity.

2. **Fosters New Connections:**
   - o By linking unrelated ideas, you discover innovative solutions.
3. **Expands Possibilities:**
   - o It broadens your perspective, opening the door to unexpected approaches.

How to Use Random Input

1. **Define Your Problem or Goal:**
   - o Be specific about what you're trying to solve or create.
   - o Example: "How can we make our meetings more engaging?"
2. **Generate Random Input:**
   - o Use a dictionary, image, or random word generator to find unrelated input.
   - o Example: The random word is "balloon."
3. **Explore Connections:**
   - o Ask how the random input relates to your problem.
   - o Example: "What if meetings felt lighter and more fun, like a party with balloons? Could we gamify presentations or add humor?"
4. **Brainstorm Ideas:**
   - o Use the random input to inspire new possibilities.

Examples of Random Input in Action

1. **In Design:**
   - o **Scenario:** A team is designing eco-friendly packaging.
   - o **Random Input:** "Cocoon."
   - o **Idea:** Create biodegradable packaging that protects products like a cocoon protects a butterfly.

2. **In Marketing:**
   - **Scenario:** A company wants to rebrand its image.
   - **Random Input:** "Lighthouse."
   - **Idea:** Position the brand as a beacon of trust and guidance, symbolized in its new logo.
3. **In Problem-Solving:**
   - **Scenario:** You're brainstorming ways to motivate your team.
   - **Random Input:** "Puzzle."
   - **Idea:** Introduce team-building activities that involve solving puzzles together.

Practical Exercise: Try Random Input

1. **Choose a Problem or Goal:**
   - Example: "How can I improve my home workspace?"
2. **Find Random Input:**
   - Open a book, choose a word, or pick an object nearby.
   - Example: The word is "tree."
3. **Make Connections:**
   - How could "tree" inspire your workspace?
   - Example: Add more plants for a calming atmosphere or design a desk that "grows" with your needs.
4. **Brainstorm and Act:**
   - Use the connections to spark creative changes.

Why This Technique is Effective

Random input helps you think differently by introducing fresh, unexpected perspectives. It encourages out-of-the-box ideas that wouldn't emerge through conventional methods.

Closing Thought

Inspiration can come from anywhere. Let randomness spark connections, and you'll discover ideas you never imagined.

Chapter 45: The SCAMPER Method: Improve by Modifying

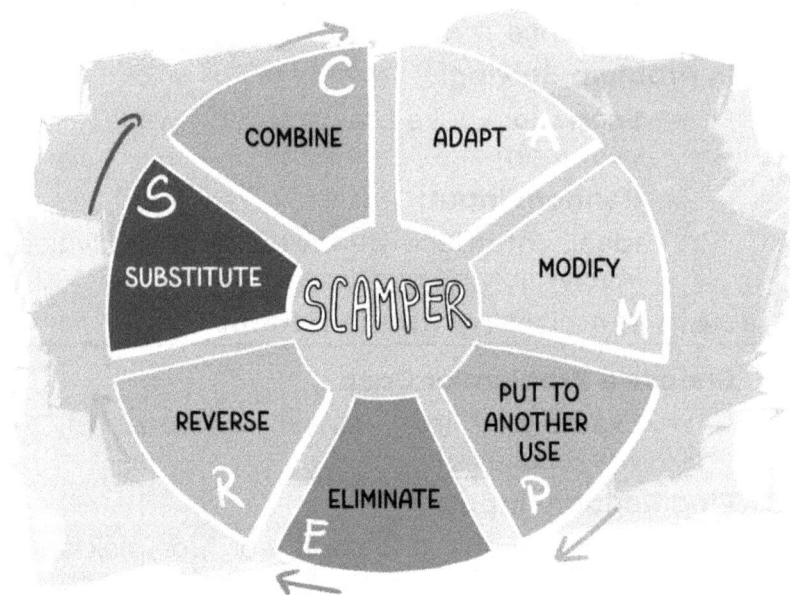

What is the SCAMPER Method?

The SCAMPER Method is a structured brainstorming tool that helps you improve existing ideas, products, or processes by systematically modifying them.

SCAMPER stands for:

- **S**ubstitute
- **C**ombine
- **A**dapt
- **M**odify
- **P**ut to another use
- **E**liminate
- **R**everse

Each prompt encourages you to think about how to transform or innovate an idea, often leading to practical and creative solutions.

For example:

- A company improving a chair might **Substitute** the material, **Combine** it with a desk, or **Reverse** its function to become stackable for storage.

Why the SCAMPER Method is Useful

1. **Encourages Creativity:**
   o The prompts push you to explore possibilities you might not otherwise consider.
2. **Fosters Incremental Improvement:**
   o Instead of reinventing the wheel, you refine and enhance what already exists.
3. **Applies to Any Context:**
   o SCAMPER works for products, processes, strategies, and even personal goals.

How to Use the SCAMPER Method

1. **Identify the Target:**
   o Choose the idea, product, or process you want to improve.
   o Example: A reusable water bottle design.
2. **Apply Each Prompt:**
   o Go through each SCAMPER prompt systematically, brainstorming ways to transform the target.
3. **Generate and Record Ideas:**
   o Write down every idea, no matter how small or unusual.
4. **Evaluate and Implement:**
   o Choose the most promising ideas and test them in practice.

Breaking Down the SCAMPER Prompts

1. **Substitute:**
   o Replace one part of the idea with something else.
   o Example: Use bamboo instead of plastic for the water bottle to make it eco-friendly.

2. **Combine:**
   - o Merge two elements to create a new solution.
   - o Example: Combine a water bottle with a compartment for storing vitamins or snacks.
3. **Adapt:**
   - o Adjust the idea to suit a new purpose or audience.
   - o Example: Adapt the bottle's design to make it collapsible for easy travel.
4. **Modify:**
   - o Change the size, shape, or other characteristics.
   - o Example: Add a built-in filter to the water bottle for purification.
5. **Put to Another Use:**
   - o Repurpose the idea in a different context.
   - o Example: Market the bottle as a multipurpose container for hot and cold drinks.
6. **Eliminate:**
   - o Remove unnecessary parts to simplify the idea.
   - o Example: Eliminate the cap threading for a sleek, spill-proof design.
7. **Reverse:**
   - o Flip the idea's process or function.
   - o Example: Design the bottle to fill from the bottom for easier cleaning.

Examples of SCAMPER in Action

1. **In Product Design:**
   - o **Scenario:** Improving a smartphone.
   - o **SCAMPER:**
     - **Substitute:** Use a solar-powered battery.
     - **Combine:** Add a built-in projector for presentations.
     - **Eliminate:** Remove physical buttons for a sleeker design.

2. **In Business Strategy:**
   - **Scenario:** Enhancing customer service.
   - **SCAMPER:**
     - **Adapt:** Offer 24/7 support for global customers.
     - **Modify:** Use AI chatbots for faster response times.
     - **Reverse:** Let customers rate representatives immediately after interactions.

3. **In Personal Growth:**
   - **Scenario:** Improving a daily routine.
   - **SCAMPER:**
     - **Combine:** Pair exercise with audiobooks for multitasking.
     - **Eliminate:** Cut out social media during mornings for better focus.
     - **Reverse:** Start the day with creative work instead of email.

Practical Exercise: SCAMPER Your Own Idea

1. **Choose a Target:**
   - Example: "How can I improve my study habits?"

2. **Apply SCAMPER Prompts:**
   - **Substitute:** Study with flashcards instead of notes.
   - **Combine:** Pair studying with teaching someone else.
   - **Adapt:** Use a timer for focused study sessions (Pomodoro Technique).
   - **Eliminate:** Remove distractions like phone notifications.

3. **Implement and Test Ideas:**
   - Experiment with your brainstormed changes and track the results.

Why This Technique Works

The SCAMPER method unlocks creativity by focusing on incremental innovation. It's a systematic yet flexible way to refine ideas and create something new.

Closing Thought

Great innovations often come from simple changes. Use SCAMPER to modify, adapt, and transform your ideas into something extraordinary.

Chapter 46: Combine Ideas to Innovate

Why Combining Ideas is Powerful

Sometimes, the best solutions don't come from inventing something entirely new — they come from blending existing ideas into something fresh. This process, called idea combination, allows you to draw inspiration from multiple sources and create innovative solutions that bridge gaps or offer new perspectives.

For example:

- Combining fitness apps with social networking led to apps like Strava, which motivates users through community engagement.

How Combining Ideas Fuels Creativity

1. **Expands Possibilities:**
   o Blending ideas widens your creative scope, unlocking solutions you wouldn't discover otherwise.

2. **Encourages Cross-Discipline Thinking:**
   o Borrowing from different fields fosters innovation by connecting unrelated concepts.
3. **Reduces Reinvention:**
   o Instead of starting from scratch, you build on proven ideas in new ways.

How to Combine Ideas Effectively

1. **Gather a Variety of Inputs:**
   o Expose yourself to diverse ideas, fields, and perspectives.
   o Example: Read books or watch documentaries on unrelated topics.
2. **Find Overlaps:**
   o Look for connections between ideas or fields.
   o Example: Combine wearable fitness trackers with gamification to boost engagement.
3. **Ask "What If?" Questions:**
   o Explore the possibilities of merging concepts.
   o Example: "What if a coffee shop also offered co-working spaces?"
4. **Prototype Your Combination:**
   o Test your combined idea to see how it works in practice.

Examples of Idea Combination in Action

1. **In Products:**
   o **Scenario:** Creating a travel gadget.
   o **Combination:** Combine a portable charger with a luggage tracker for convenience.
2. **In Services:**
   o **Scenario:** Innovating in education.
   o **Combination:** Merge online courses with personalized tutoring to improve outcomes.

3. **In Daily Life:**
   - ○ **Scenario:** Making chores more enjoyable.
   - ○ **Combination:** Combine cleaning with listening to your favorite podcast or music playlist.

Practical Exercise: Combine Your Ideas

1. **Choose Two Unrelated Ideas:**
   - ○ Example: "Cooking" and "Fitness."
2. **Find Connections:**
   - ○ Combine them into something new, like a cooking class focused on healthy meal prep for fitness enthusiasts.
3. **Test Your Idea:**
   - ○ Share your combination with others or prototype it to see how it works.

Why This Technique Works

Combining ideas fosters innovation by breaking down silos between disciplines or concepts. It allows you to create something greater than the sum of its parts.

Closing Thought

Creativity thrives at the intersection of ideas. Combine, experiment, and watch innovation emerge.

Chapter 47: Think in Opposites to Break Norms

What Does It Mean to Think in Opposites?

Thinking in opposites involves challenging conventional assumptions. Instead of asking how to improve something the usual way, you challenge norms by asking what would happen if you did the opposite. This method encourages unconventional thinking and helps you uncover fresh ideas that break through creative blocks.

For example:

- A traditional restaurant focuses on offering as many menu options as possible. Thinking in opposites might lead to a limited-menu concept, like a chef's tasting menu or a single-dish restaurant, which could create a unique experience and attract attention.

Why Thinking in Opposites is Effective

1. **Challenges Assumptions:**
    o   It forces you to question why things are done a certain way and whether the opposite could work better.
2. **Breaks Habits:**
    o   By reversing your usual approach, you disrupt mental ruts and open the door to creative solutions.
3. **Encourages Bold Ideas:**
    o   Thinking in opposites often leads to unexpected, high-impact innovations.

How to Think in Opposites

1. **Identify the Norm:**
    o   Start with a common assumption or approach related to your problem.
    o   Example: "A bookstore should sell as many titles as possible."
2. **Flip It Around:**
    o   Ask, "What if we did the opposite?"
    o   Example: "What if the bookstore sold only a curated selection of 50 books?"
3. **Explore the Possibilities:**
    o   Think about how this reversal could create value or solve the problem.
4. **Test the Idea:**
    o   Experiment with your opposite-thinking solution to see how it performs in practice.

Examples of Thinking in Opposites

1. **In Business:**
    o   **Scenario:** A clothing brand wants to stand out in a crowded market.
    o   **Opposite Thinking:** Instead of launching a seasonal collection, they release one timeless design and focus on sustainability.

- Outcome: The minimalist approach appeals to eco-conscious customers.

2. **In Education:**
   - **Scenario:** A teacher wants to improve student participation.
   - **Opposite Thinking:** Instead of leading the discussion, they let students design and teach lessons.
   - **Outcome:** Students engage more deeply and develop leadership skills.

3. **In Daily Life:**
   - **Scenario:** You want to relax after a stressful day.
   - **Opposite Thinking:** Instead of unwinding with TV, you try something stimulating, like a creative hobby or learning a new skill.
   - **Outcome:** You feel refreshed and accomplished.

Practical Exercise: Try Thinking in Opposites

1. **Choose a Problem or Goal:**
   - Example: "How can I make my morning routine more productive?"

2. **Identify the Norm:**
   - Example: "I should follow a structured checklist every morning."

3. **Flip the Approach:**
   - Ask, "What if I didn't follow a checklist and started my day spontaneously?"

4. **Brainstorm Solutions:**
   - Consider hybrid approaches, like reserving part of your morning for creative or unstructured activities.

Why This Technique Works

Thinking in opposites disrupts the status quo, encouraging fresh perspectives and bold innovations. By reversing assumptions, you expand your creative range and uncover possibilities others might overlook.

Closing Thought

Innovation often lives in the unexpected. Flip the script, break norms, and discover transformative ideas through opposite thinking.

Chapter 48: Set Constraints to Foster Creativity

How Do Constraints Spark Creativity?

While it might seem counterintuitive, setting boundaries or limitations can actually boost your creativity. Constraints force you to think resourcefully, encouraging you to explore innovative solutions within the given limits.

For example:

- If you're tasked with creating a 30-second video, the time constraint compels you to focus on the most impactful ideas, cutting unnecessary fluff.

Why Constraints Are Powerful

1. **Sharpen Focus:**
   - Constraints eliminate distractions, helping you zero in on what matters most.

2. **Encourage Resourcefulness:**
   - Limitations push you to think outside the box and find unconventional solutions.
3. **Boost Productivity:**
   - Knowing your boundaries prevents overthinking and accelerates decision-making.

How to Use Constraints to Foster Creativity

1. **Set Clear Boundaries:**
   - Define specific limits related to time, budget, materials, or scope.
   - Example: "Create a meal using only five ingredients."
2. **Reframe Constraints as Opportunities:**
   - View limits as challenges that inspire innovation rather than obstacles.
3. **Focus on Core Goals:**
   - Use the constraint to prioritize what's most important.
4. **Experiment and Iterate:**
   - Work within the limits, test your ideas, and refine them as needed.

Examples of Creativity Within Constraints

1. **In Design:**
   - **Scenario:** A graphic designer is asked to create a striking logo using only black and white.
   - **Constraint:** No color.
   - **Outcome:** The designer focuses on bold shapes and negative space, creating a timeless, eye-catching design.
2. **In Writing:**
   - Scenario: A writer enters a contest requiring a 100-word story.
   - **Constraint:** Word count.

- o **Outcome:** They craft a concise, impactful narrative that resonates with readers.

3. **In Business:**
   - o **Scenario:** A startup launches with a small marketing budget.
   - o **Constraint:** Limited funds.
   - o **Outcome:** The team focuses on low-cost strategies like social media and word-of-mouth marketing, which build a loyal community.

Practical Exercise: Create Within Constraints

1. **Choose a Task or Goal:**
   - o Example: "Plan a weekend getaway."
2. **Set Constraints:**
   - o Example: "Plan the trip for under $200 and within 50 miles of home."
3. **Brainstorm Solutions:**
   - o Explore creative ways to meet the goal, such as finding free local attractions or carpooling to reduce costs.

Why This Technique Works

Constraints are a catalyst for innovation. By forcing you to work within limits, they spark resourcefulness and lead to solutions that might not have emerged in a limitless environment.

Closing Thought

Creativity thrives on challenge. Embrace constraints as opportunities to think boldly, work efficiently, and innovate beyond expectations.

Chapter 49: Borrow from Other Fields

We're stuck solving this logistics issue.

What if we borrow ideas from how emergency rooms triage patients?

What Does It Mean to Borrow from Other Fields?

Borrowing from other fields involves taking ideas, strategies, or practices from unrelated industries or disciplines and applying them to your current challenge. It's based on the idea that innovation often happens at the intersection of different perspectives.

For example:

- The concept of an assembly line revolutionized car manufacturing, but it was inspired by techniques used in meatpacking plants.

By looking beyond your own area of expertise, you gain fresh insights and discover unconventional solutions that others might overlook.

Why Borrowing from Other Fields Works

1. **Encourages Cross-Pollination of Ideas:**
   o Different fields often solve similar problems in unique ways. Borrowing their methods leads to creative breakthroughs.

2. **Expands Your Perspective:**
   o It challenges you to think beyond the limits of your industry or situation.

3. **Inspires Novel Solutions:**
   o Applying an unfamiliar idea to your challenge often results in innovation.

How to Borrow Ideas from Other Fields

1. **Study Different Disciplines:**
   o Learn about fields unrelated to your own, such as science, art, engineering, or psychology.
   o Example: If you work in marketing, study storytelling techniques used in filmmaking.

2. **Look for Analogies:**
   o Identify similarities between your problem and challenges faced in other industries.
   o Example: A hospital's triage system could inspire how a tech company prioritizes customer support tickets.

3. **Ask How Others Solve Similar Problems:**
   o Explore how unrelated industries approach challenges like efficiency, customer satisfaction, or innovation.

4. **Test and Adapt the Ideas:**
   o Apply the borrowed idea to your context, making adjustments as needed.

Examples of Borrowing from Other Fields

1. **In Product Design:**
   o **Scenario:** A fashion designer seeks to create a stain-proof fabric.

o **Borrowed Idea:** They study how lotus leaves repel water and develop a material with similar properties.

2. **In Business Strategy:**

   o **Scenario:** A grocery store wants to improve customer flow.

   o **Borrowed Idea:** They adapt the layout of airport terminals to create clear pathways and reduce congestion.

3. **In Personal Life:**

   o **Scenario:** You're struggling to organize your daily tasks.

   o **Borrowed Idea:** You adopt an athlete's training schedule, structuring your day into focused "workout" sessions with breaks.

Practical Exercise: Apply Ideas from Another Field

1. **Define Your Challenge:**

   o Example: "I want to make my online store more user-friendly."

2. **Choose a Field to Explore:**

   o Example: Study hospitality to understand how hotels create welcoming environments.

3. **Find Analogies:**

   o Ask, "What do hotels do to make guests comfortable, and how can I apply that to my website?"

   o Example: Simplify navigation like a concierge simplifies guest services.

4. **Test the Idea:**

   o Implement and refine the borrowed concept in your context.

Why This Technique Works

Borrowing from other fields breaks you out of your routine, exposing you to new ways of thinking. It leverages the creativity of others and applies it in ways they might never have imagined.

Closing Thought

The best ideas aren't always new — they're often borrowed. Look beyond your field, find inspiration in unexpected places, and innovate boldly.

Chapter 50: Play 'What If?' with Scenarios

What Does It Mean to Play 'What If?'

Playing "What If?" is a creativity technique where you ask hypothetical questions to explore new possibilities. It encourages you to imagine alternate realities, scenarios, or outcomes, often leading to fresh ideas and unconventional solutions.

For example:

- "What if cars could drive themselves?" sparked the development of autonomous vehicles.

This approach unlocks your imagination by challenging assumptions and inspiring innovative thinking.

Why Asking 'What If?' Sparks Creativity

1. **Breaks Conventional Thinking:**
   - o It frees you from the constraints of "what is" and allows you to imagine "what could be."
2. **Encourages Curiosity:**
   - o By asking open-ended questions, you uncover possibilities you might not have considered before.
3. **Opens Pathways to Innovation:**
   - o Hypothetical scenarios often lead to ground-breaking ideas.

How to Play 'What If?' Effectively

1. **Start with a Challenge or Goal:**
   - o Define the problem or area where you want to innovate.
   - o Example: "How can we reduce energy consumption in the office?"
2. **Ask Open-Ended 'What If?' Questions:**
   - o Encourage imaginative thinking by posing hypothetical scenarios.
   - o Example: "What if the office only operated during daylight hours?"
3. **Explore the Implications:**
   - o Consider how each scenario could work in practice and what challenges it might address.
4. **Refine and Test Ideas:**
   - o Choose the most promising "What If?" scenarios and experiment with them.

Examples of 'What If?' Thinking in Action

1. **In Technology:**
   - o **Scenario:** A tech company wants to improve smartphone design.
   - o **What If?:** "What if smartphones were wearable instead of handheld?"

- o **Outcome:** This question leads to the development of smartwatches.

2. **In Education:**
   - o **Scenario:** A school wants to increase student engagement.
   - o **What If?:** "What if students designed their own curriculum?"
   - o **Outcome:** The school creates a program where students choose project-based learning paths.

3. **In Personal Growth:**
   - o **Scenario:** You're stuck in a career rut.
   - o **What If?:** "What if I started a side hustle in my passion area?"
   - o **Outcome:** You explore freelancing opportunities, eventually transitioning to a fulfilling new career.

Practical Exercise: Try 'What If?' Thinking

1. **Choose a Challenge or Opportunity:**
   - o Example: "How can I make my weekends more relaxing?"

2. **Ask 'What If?' Questions:**
   - o Examples: "What if I planned no activities at all? What if I dedicated Saturdays to hobbies and Sundays to rest?"

3. **Explore the Scenarios:**
   - o Consider how each option might impact your weekend experience.

4. **Take Action:**
   - o Experiment with one scenario and refine it based on your results.

Why This Technique Works

'What If?' thinking opens the door to new possibilities by encouraging curiosity and exploration. It's a playful yet powerful way to unlock ideas that challenge the status quo.

Closing Thought

The world changes when we ask, "What if?" Let your imagination roam, and you'll find ideas that push the boundaries of what's possible.

Part VI: Techniques for Mental Clarity

Mental clarity is the foundation of good decision-making, creativity, and focus. In this section, you'll explore tools to declutter your thoughts, prioritize effectively, and stay present in the moment. By mastering these methods, you'll learn to approach challenges with a clear mind and make thoughtful, deliberate decisions.

Chapter 51: Practice Mental Hygiene: Eliminate Mental Clutter

I keep jumping between tasks and forgetting what I started.
Try writing everything down first—it clears the mental clutter.

What is Mental Hygiene?

Mental hygiene is the practice of regularly clearing your mind of unnecessary thoughts, worries, and distractions. Just as you clean your physical space, maintaining a "clean" mental space helps you think more clearly and reduces stress.

Mental clutter often comes from unfinished tasks, unresolved emotions, and an overwhelming amount of information. Without regular mental hygiene, this clutter can cloud your judgment and reduce your productivity.

Why Mental Hygiene is Essential

1. **Improves Focus:**
   - A clear mind allows you to concentrate on what matters most.
2. **Reduces Stress:**
   - Letting go of unnecessary worries frees up

mental energy.

3. **Enhances Decision-Making:**
   o With fewer distractions, you can think critically and act decisively.

How to Eliminate Mental Clutter

1. **Create a Thought Dump:**
   o Write down everything on your mind, no matter how small or trivial. This helps offload mental "junk" and organize your priorities.

2. **Resolve Open Loops:**
   o Identify unfinished tasks or decisions weighing on your mind. Take action or schedule a time to address them.

3. **Let Go of What You Can't Control:**
   o Focus on what's within your power to change and release worries about the rest.

4. **Declutter Your Environment:**
   o Your physical space often mirrors your mental state. Tidying up can create a sense of calm and order.

5. **Limit Mental Input:**
   o Reduce unnecessary information by unsubscribing from irrelevant emails, turning off notifications, and avoiding excessive media consumption.

Examples of Mental Hygiene in Action

1. **In Work:**
   o **Scenario:** You feel overwhelmed by a long to-do list.
   o **Action:** Write down all tasks, prioritize them, and delegate what you can.

2. **In Personal Life:**
   o **Scenario:** You keep replaying a recent argument in your mind.
   o **Action:** Reflect on the issue, resolve what you can, and then let it go.
3. **In Daily Habits:**
   o **Scenario:** Your phone constantly distracts you with notifications.
   o **Action:** Turn off unnecessary alerts and set specific times to check your phone.

Practical Exercise: Clean Your Mental Space

1. **Spend 10 Minutes Writing a Thought Dump:**
   o List everything on your mind—tasks, worries, ideas, or random thoughts.
2. **Categorize Your Thoughts:**
   o Group them into "actionable," "non-urgent," and "let go."
3. **Take Action:**
   o Address one actionable item immediately and schedule others. Release the rest.

Why This Technique Works

Practicing mental hygiene creates space for clearer thinking and greater focus. It's a simple habit that makes room for your best ideas and most thoughtful decisions.

Closing Thought

A cluttered mind can't function at its best. Clear the mental "junk" regularly to free your thoughts and regain clarity.

Chapter 52: Write It Out: Organize Thoughts on Paper

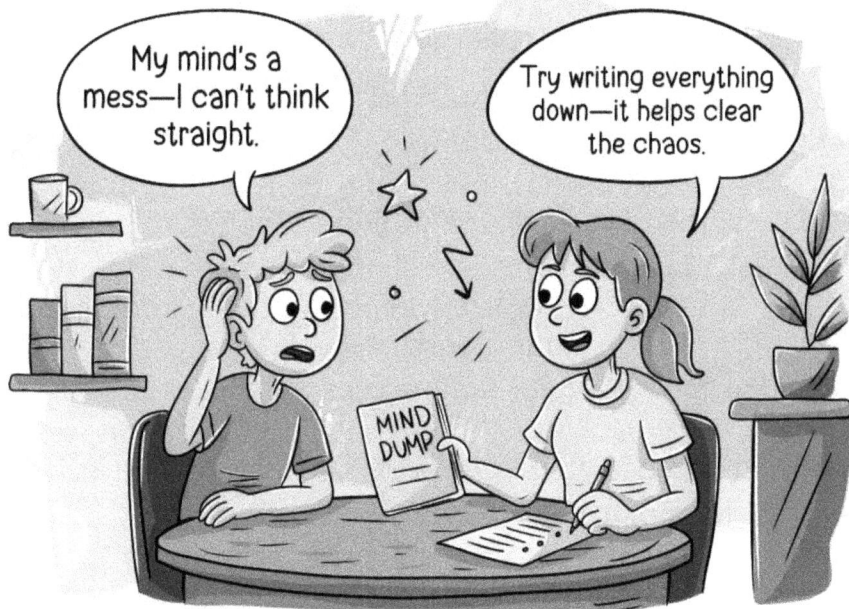

Why Writing Clarifies Thinking

Writing is one of the simplest yet most effective ways to organize your thoughts. When you put your ideas, worries, or plans on paper, you free up mental space and gain clarity about what matters. Writing helps you sort through confusion, prioritize tasks, and process emotions.

For example:

- Writing out a plan for a big project can help you break it into manageable steps, while journaling about a tough day can bring emotional relief.

Benefits of Writing It Out

1. **Organizes Your Thoughts:**
    - Writing turns abstract ideas into concrete words, making them easier to understand.

2. **Improves Memory:**
   - o Putting thoughts on paper helps you retain information better than keeping it in your head.
3. **Relieves Mental Overload:**
   - o Offloading thoughts onto paper reduces anxiety and clears your mind for focused thinking.

How to Use Writing for Mental Clarity

1. **Start a Daily Brain Dump:**
   - o Spend a few minutes each morning or evening writing down everything on your mind.
2. **Make Lists:**
   - o Organize tasks or ideas into categories, such as "to-do," "questions," or "goals."
3. **Use Journaling for Reflection:**
   - o Write about your feelings, challenges, or successes to process emotions and gain insights.
4. **Write to Solve Problems:**
   - o Outline a problem and brainstorm possible solutions in writing.
5. **Create Visuals:**
   - o Use bullet points, diagrams, or mind maps to structure your thoughts more clearly.

Examples of Writing It Out in Action

1. **In Work:**
   - o **Scenario:** You're overwhelmed by a complex project.
   - o **Action:** Write down the project's goals, break it into smaller tasks, and create a timeline.
2. **In Personal Life:**
   - o **Scenario:** You're feeling stuck in a decision.
   - o **Action:** Write out the pros and cons of each option to clarify your choice.
3. **In Emotional Health:**
   - o **Scenario:** You're feeling anxious about the future.

o **Action:** Journal about your worries to explore what's causing them and what steps you can take.

Practical Exercise: Start Writing for Clarity

1. **Take Five Minutes:**
   o Write down everything on your mind without worrying about grammar or structure.

2. **Organize Your Thoughts:**
   o Highlight the most important items and group related ideas together.

3. **Choose One Item to Act On:**
   o Take immediate action on a task or reflect further on an insight you gained.

Why This Technique Works

Writing simplifies your thoughts and gives you a clearer picture of what matters. It's an easy way to process emotions, plan effectively, and regain focus.

Closing Thought

Don't let your thoughts swirl around in your mind. Write them down, organize them, and find the clarity you need to move forward.

Chapter 53: Mind Mapping for Visual Clarity

I don't even know where to start with this topic.

"Let's make a mind map—it'll help connect everything.

What is Mind Mapping?

Mind mapping is a visual technique for organizing information, ideas, or thoughts. It starts with a central concept, with related ideas branching out like the limbs of a tree. This method allows you to see connections between ideas, brainstorm effectively, and structure your thoughts clearly.

For example:

- If you're planning a vacation, you could create a mind map with "Vacation" at the center, branching into categories like "Destinations," "Activities," "Budget," and "Packing List." Each branch can have its own sub-branches, breaking down details like specific places or items.

Why Mind Mapping is Effective

1. **Visualizes Complexity:**
   - By laying out ideas visually, mind mapping makes it easier to see relationships and organize thoughts.
2. **Encourages Creativity:**
   - The open-ended structure allows for free-flowing ideas and brainstorming.
3. **Improves Memory:**
   - The combination of words, colors, and shapes helps you retain information better than linear lists.
4. **Simplifies Planning:**
   - Mind maps provide a clear overview of a project, goal, or problem, making it easier to manage.

How to Create a Mind Map

1. **Start with a Central Idea:**
   - Write the main topic or goal in the center of a blank page. Use a circle, box, or another shape to highlight it.
   - Example: "Start a Small Business."
2. **Add Branches:**
   - Draw lines radiating from the center and label them with related categories or subtopics.
   - Example: Branches might include "Marketing," "Budget," "Products," and "Logistics."
3. **Develop Sub-Branches:**
   - Add smaller lines branching from the main categories, detailing specific ideas or tasks.
   - Example: Under "Marketing," sub-branches might include "Social Media," "Website," and "Networking."
4. **Use Colors, Images, and Keywords:**
   - Highlight key points with colors or symbols to make the map visually engaging and easier to remember.

5. **Review and Refine:**
   - Rearrange branches, add new ideas, or simplify as needed to clarify your thoughts.

Examples of Mind Mapping in Action

1. **In Personal Goals:**
   - **Scenario:** You want to improve your health.
   - **Mind Map:**
     - Central Idea: "Health."
     - Branches: "Exercise," "Nutrition," "Sleep," and "Stress Management."
     - Sub-branches: "Strength Training" under "Exercise," "Meal Prep" under "Nutrition," and so on.

2. **In Problem-Solving:**
   - **Scenario:** You're trying to fix a recurring issue at work.
   - **Mind Map:**
     - Central Idea: "Problem."
     - Branches: "Causes," "Possible Solutions," "Resources Needed," and "Next Steps."

3. **In Learning:**
   - **Scenario:** You're studying for an exam.
   - **Mind Map:**
     - Central Idea: "History Exam."
     - Branches: "Key Dates," "Important Figures," "Themes," and "Essay Topics."

Practical Exercise: Create Your Own Mind Map

1. **Pick a Topic or Goal:**
   - Example: "Organize a Family Event."
2. **Write the Central Idea:**
   - Place "Family Event" in the center of the page.
3. **Add Main Branches:**
   - Example: "Venue," "Guests," "Food," and "Activities."

4. **Develop Sub-Branches:**
   o Under "Food," add options like "Catering," "Potluck," or "DIY."

5. **Use Colors and Symbols:**
   o Highlight deadlines in red or draw a clock next to time-sensitive tasks.

Why This Technique Works

Mind mapping transforms scattered thoughts into an organized, visual format. It encourages creativity, simplifies planning, and provides clarity at a glance.

Closing Thought

When your thoughts feel tangled, map them out. A well-crafted mind map turns chaos into clarity, helping you see the big picture and the details all at once.

Chapter 54: Practice Single-Tasking: Focus on One Thing at a Time

What is Single-Tasking?

Single-tasking means focusing on one task at a time, giving it your full attention until it's complete. In contrast to multitasking, which divides your attention and reduces efficiency, single-tasking helps you work more effectively and with greater quality.

For example:

- Instead of checking emails while writing a report, you focus solely on the report, finishing it faster and with fewer errors.

Why Single-Tasking is Essential

1. **Boosts Productivity:**
   - Concentrating on one task allows you to complete it faster and with better results.
2. **Improves Quality:**
   - Fewer distractions mean fewer mistakes and higher-quality work.
3. **Reduces Stress:**
   - Single-tasking feels less overwhelming than juggling multiple priorities.
4. **Builds Mindfulness:**
   - It keeps you present in the moment, helping you enjoy and engage with what you're doing.

How to Practice Single-Tasking

1. **Prioritize Your Tasks:**
   - Choose the most important task to work on first.
   - Example: Start with the report due tomorrow, not your email inbox.
2. **Eliminate Distractions:**
   - Turn off notifications, close unnecessary tabs, and create a focused workspace.
3. **Set a Time Block:**
   - Commit to working on one task for a set period, such as 25 minutes using the Pomodoro Technique.
4. **Finish Before Switching:**
   - Complete or make significant progress on your current task before moving to the next one.
5. **Take Breaks:**
   - Pause between tasks to recharge your focus and energy.

Examples of Single-Tasking in Action

1. **In Work:**
   - o **Scenario:** Writing a proposal while managing team emails.
   - o **Action:** Schedule time to write the proposal without interruptions, then dedicate time to emails later.

2. **In Personal Life:**
   - o **Scenario:** Cooking dinner while checking your phone.
   - o **Action:** Put the phone away and focus on cooking, enjoying the process and improving the meal.

3. **In Learning:**
   - o **Scenario:** Studying for a test while texting friends.
   - o **Action:** Turn off your phone and focus solely on studying for a set time.

Practical Exercise: Try Single-Tasking

1. **Pick One Task:**
   - o Example: "Write a weekly report."

2. **Eliminate Distractions:**
   - o Silence your phone, close unrelated browser tabs, and let others know you need focused time.

3. **Work in Focused Blocks:**
   - o Spend 25–30 minutes on the task, then take a short break.

4. **Evaluate Results:**
   - o Notice how much more you accomplish and how your stress levels improve.

Why This Technique Works

Single-tasking channels your energy into what matters most. By reducing distractions and improving focus, it helps you work more efficiently and enjoy the process.

Closing Thought

In a world that glorifies multitasking, single-tasking is your superpower. Focus on one thing at a time and watch your productivity and peace of mind soar.

Chapter 55: Declutter Information Overload

I've got tabs, emails, and messages open—I can't focus.

Start by cutting the noise. What's actually important right now?

What is Information Overload?

Information overload happens when you're bombarded with more information than you can process. From emails to news updates, social media, and endless articles, it's easy to feel overwhelmed and distracted. This overload can cloud your thinking, hinder decision-making, and leave you feeling mentally drained.

Decluttering information prioritizes what's relevant and eliminates unnecessary noise so you can focus on what truly matters.

Why Decluttering Information Matters

1. **Improves Focus:**
    o With less irrelevant information competing for attention, you can concentrate better.
2. **Reduces Stress:**

o A cleaner mental environment feels more manageable and less overwhelming.

3. Enhances Decision-Making:

o By focusing on quality over quantity, you gain clearer insights and make better choices.

How to Declutter Information Overload

1. Limit Your Inputs:

o Identify the sources of information in your life and cut back on non-essential ones.

o Example: Unsubscribe from newsletters you never read or follow fewer social media accounts.

2. Set Boundaries for Consumption:

o Designate specific times for checking email, news, or social media.

o Example: Limit news reading to 20 minutes a day.

3. Use Filters:

o Prioritize information by relevance and importance.

o Example: Use tools like email filters to separate urgent messages from routine ones.

4. Focus on One Topic at a Time:

o Instead of multitasking between multiple sources, dive deeply into one subject before moving to the next.

5. Take Digital Breaks:

o Step away from screens periodically to recharge your mind.

6. Practice the 80/20 Rule:

o Focus on the 20% of information that delivers 80% of the value.

o Example: Read summaries instead of full articles for non-critical topics.

Examples of Managing Information Overload

1. **In Work:**
   - ○ **Scenario:** Your inbox is flooded with unread emails.
   - ○ **Action:** Use folders or tags to sort emails by priority, respond to urgent ones first, and archive irrelevant messages.

2. **In Personal Life:**
   - ○ **Scenario:** You spend hours scrolling through social media without gaining much value.
   - ○ **Action:** Unfollow accounts that don't add meaning or joy, and set a daily time limit for scrolling.

3. **In Learning:**
   - ○ **Scenario:** You're overwhelmed by conflicting advice on a topic.
   - ○ **Action:** Identify a few trusted sources and stick to them, instead of trying to absorb everything.

Practical Exercise: Declutter Your Information Inputs

1. **Audit Your Inputs:**
   - ○ List all the ways you consume information — news, social media, emails, podcasts, etc.

2. **Identify Unnecessary Sources:**
   - ○ Ask: "Which of these truly add value to my life or work?"

3. **Reduce and Streamline:**
   - ○ Unsubscribe, unfollow, or delete apps that don't serve a clear purpose.

4. **Set Boundaries:**
   - ○ Establish rules, like "no emails after 7 PM" or "news only in the morning."

Why This Technique Works

Decluttering information overload creates mental space for what's important. It reduces distractions and allows you to focus on meaningful tasks and decisions.

Closing Thought

You don't need to know everything — just the right things. Declutter your mind by decluttering your inputs, and let clarity lead the way.

Chapter 56: Use White Space: Schedule Thinking Time

What is White Space?

White space refers to the deliberate gaps or pauses you create in your schedule to think, reflect, or recharge. In a packed day, it's easy to rush from task to task without pausing to process or plan. White space gives your brain room to breathe, fostering clarity, creativity, and better decision-making.

For example:

- Setting aside 30 minutes of quiet time in the morning can help you prioritize your day and approach tasks with a clear mind.

Why White Space is Powerful

1. **Encourages Reflection:**
   - It provides time to think critically, solve problems, and gain new insights.

2. **Boosts Creativity:**
   - o Downtime allows your mind to wander, often leading to innovative ideas.
3. **Reduces Burnout:**
   - o Scheduling breaks prevents mental exhaustion and improves focus.

How to Incorporate White Space into Your Day

1. **Block Time on Your Calendar:**
   - o Schedule thinking time as you would any other task. Treat it as non-negotiable.
2. **Start Small:**
   - o Begin with 10–15 minutes of white space each day and gradually increase as needed.
3. **Eliminate Distractions:**
   - o Use this time for quiet reflection, not for catching up on emails or social media.
4. **Use Prompts:**
   - o If you're unsure how to use white space, ask questions like, "What's my top priority today?" or "How can I solve this challenge creatively?"
5. **Combine with Restorative Activities:**
   - o Take a walk, meditate, or simply sit in silence to clear your mind.

Examples of Using White Space

1. **In Work:**
   - o **Scenario:** Your calendar is packed with back-to-back meetings.
   - o **Action:** Block 15 minutes between meetings to reflect, take notes, and reset.
2. **In Personal Life:**
   - o **Scenario:** You feel overwhelmed by daily chores.
   - o **Action:** Schedule quiet time each evening to plan and relax.

3. **In Creative Projects:**
   - Scenario: You're stuck on a writing project.
   - Action: Take a 20-minute walk to let your mind wander and generate fresh ideas.

Practical Exercise: Add White Space to Your Day

1. **Pick a Time:**
   - Choose a block of time when you can step away from tasks—e.g., the first 10 minutes after lunch.
2. **Set Boundaries:**
   - Turn off notifications and let others know you're unavailable during this time.
3. **Reflect or Recharge:**
   - Use the time to think strategically, journal, or simply rest.
4. **Evaluate the Benefits:**
   - Notice how white space improves your focus, clarity, and creativity.

Why This Technique Works

White space gives your brain a chance to reset. It allows you to process information, reflect on priorities, and recharge for what's next.

Closing Thought

Productivity isn't about doing more; it's about doing what matters. Create space to think, and you'll find clarity and purpose in your work and life.

Chapter 57: Decline to Decide: Avoid Decision Fatigue

What is Decision Fatigue?

Decision fatigue occurs when the mental energy required to make repeated decisions leaves you feeling exhausted and less capable of making good choices. Every decision, no matter how small, drains your cognitive resources. Over time, this can lead to poor judgment, procrastination, or defaulting to the easiest option.

For example:

- After a long day of decision-making, you might skip cooking dinner in favor of ordering unhealthy fast food simply because it feels easier.

The key to combating decision fatigue is learning to reduce unnecessary decisions and streamline your choices.

Why Avoiding Decision Fatigue Matters

1. **Preserves Mental Energy:**
   o Fewer decisions mean more focus for the choices that truly matter.
2. **Improves Decision Quality:**
   o By reserving energy for important decisions, you make better, more thoughtful choices.
3. **Reduces Stress:**
   o Simplifying your choices creates a sense of clarity and ease.

How to Avoid Decision Fatigue

1. **Automate Routine Choices:**
   o Simplify daily decisions by creating routines or habits.
   o Example: Plan your meals for the week or wear a "uniform" of go-to outfits.
2. **Set Priorities:**
   o Focus on making high-impact decisions first and defer less important ones.
3. **Limit Options:**
   o Too many choices can be overwhelming. Narrow your options to a manageable number.
   o Example: Instead of browsing an entire streaming library, pick one genre or create a shortlist.
4. **Batch Similar Decisions:**
   o Group similar tasks together to minimize decision-making throughout the day.
   o Example: Reply to emails in one session rather than sporadically.
5. **Delegate or Decline Decisions:**
   o Empower others to make certain choices or say "no" to decisions that aren't your responsibility.

6. Schedule Decision-Free Time:

- o Reserve parts of your day for creativity, relaxation, or reflection, free from decision-making.

Examples of Avoiding Decision Fatigue

1. In Work:

- o **Scenario:** You're constantly interrupted by co-workers asking for input.
- o **Action:** Create clear guidelines or delegate decision-making authority for routine questions.

2. In Personal Life:

- o **Scenario:** You struggle to decide what to eat for dinner every night.
- o **Action:** Plan meals in advance or rotate a set menu of favorite dishes.

3. In Shopping:

- o **Scenario:** You spend hours choosing between products.
- o **Action:** Research and set criteria beforehand to limit your options, such as price range or brand preference.

Practical Exercise: Simplify Your Decisions

1. Identify Recurring Decisions:

- o Write down daily or weekly decisions that drain your mental energy.

2. Create a Plan:

- o Automate, batch, or limit options for these decisions.
- o Example: "I'll check emails twice a day, at 10 AM and 3 PM, instead of constantly."

3. Evaluate the Impact:

- o Notice how much mental space and energy you free up by simplifying choices.

Why This Technique Works

Declining to decide on trivial matters conserves mental energy for what's truly important. It reduces stress, boosts productivity, and helps you approach big decisions with clarity and focus.

Closing Thought

Not every choice deserves your energy. Simplify your life by eliminating, automating, or delegating low-stakes decisions, and watch your mental clarity soar.

Chapter 58: Set Clear Goals for Mental Direction

Speech bubble (left): I want to grow my side business, but I don't know where to start.

Speech bubble (right): Set a clear target—like gaining 5 new clients this month—and plan backward from there.

Why Clear Goals Are Essential for Mental Clarity

Clear goals act as a mental compass, guiding your thoughts and actions toward a specific outcome. Without defined objectives, it's easy to feel scattered or overwhelmed by competing priorities. Setting clear goals not only focuses your energy but also provides a sense of purpose and direction.

For example:

- Instead of a vague goal like "Get in shape," a clear goal would be "Run three times a week and lose 10 pounds in three months." This specificity gives you a clear target and actionable steps.

Benefits of Clear Goals

1. **Improves Focus:**
    - Goals help you prioritize what's important and avoid distractions.

2. **Boosts Motivation:**
   - o Having a clear objective gives you something to work toward, increasing your drive.
3. **Simplifies Decision-Making:**
   - o With a defined goal, it's easier to determine which actions align with your priorities.

How to Set Clear Goals

1. **Use the SMART Framework:**
   - o **Specific:** Clearly define what you want to achieve.
   - o **Measurable:** Include criteria to track your progress.
   - o **Achievable:** Set a goal that's realistic and within your control.
   - o **Relevant:** Align the goal with your broader objectives.
   - o **Time-Bound:** Set a deadline to create urgency.
2. **Break Goals into Steps:**
   - o Divide larger goals into smaller, actionable tasks.
   - o Example: To "write a book," break it into tasks like "outline chapters" and "write 500 words daily."
3. **Write Down Your Goals:**
   - o Putting goals in writing solidifies your commitment and makes them easier to track.
4. **Review Regularly:**
   - o Check your progress and adjust your goals as needed.

Examples of Setting Clear Goals

1. **In Career:**
   - o **Vague Goal:** "Be successful at work."
   - o **Clear Goal:** "Get a promotion within the next year by completing two key projects and improving my leadership skills."

2. **In Fitness:**
   - **Vague Goal:** "Get healthier."
   - **Clear Goal:** "Run a 5K in under 30 minutes by training four times a week for eight weeks."

3. **In Finances:**
   - **Vague Goal:** "Save more money."
   - **Clear Goal:** "Save $5,000 in six months by cutting unnecessary expenses and taking on freelance work."

Practical Exercise: Set Your Clear Goals

1. **Choose an Area to Focus On:**
   - Example: "Career," "Health," or "Relationships."

2. **Write a SMART Goal:**
   - Example: "Apply to three jobs each week to secure a new role within six months."

3. **List Actionable Steps:**
   - Break the goal into smaller tasks, such as "Update resume," "Research job openings," and "Practice interviews."

4. **Track Progress:**
   - Use a planner, app, or journal to monitor your progress and milestones.

Why This Technique Works

Clear goals cut through mental clutter by giving you a specific direction to follow. They help you focus, stay motivated, and measure progress, leading to greater clarity and success.

Closing Thought

Goals are roadmaps. Set clear, actionable goals, and watch your mental focus and productivity soar.

Chapter 59: Use a Daily Reflection Routine

Each day blurs into the next—I can't tell what I'm improving.

Try ending each day with a short reflection. It helps me see

What is a Daily Reflection Routine?

A daily reflection routine is the practice of setting aside time to review your day — what went well, what didn't, and what you learned. This intentional pause helps you process experiences, identify areas for improvement, and set clear intentions for the next day.

For example:

- At the end of each day, you might ask yourself: "What am I proud of today? What could I do better tomorrow?" Writing down your reflections allows you to track progress and maintain focus on your goals.

Why Daily Reflection is Essential

1. **Promotes Self-Awareness:**
   - Reflecting on your thoughts, actions, and emotions helps you better understand yourself.

2. **Improves Decision-Making:**
   o By identifying patterns in your behavior, you can make more thoughtful choices in the future.
3. **Boosts Productivity:**
   o Reviewing your progress keeps you aligned with your goals and highlights areas for improvement.
4. **Reduces Stress:**
   o Reflection provides a sense of closure, helping you let go of the day's challenges.

How to Start a Daily Reflection Routine

1. **Choose a Time and Space:**
   o Set aside 10–15 minutes at the same time each day, such as before bed, in a quiet, comfortable space.
2. **Use a Journal or Digital Tool:**
   o Write your reflections in a notebook or use an app to keep your thoughts organized and accessible.
3. **Ask Key Questions:**
   o Use prompts to guide your reflection:
     ▪ What went well today?
     ▪ What didn't go as planned?
     ▪ What did I learn?
     ▪ What are my priorities for tomorrow?
4. **Celebrate Successes:**
   o Acknowledge what you accomplished, no matter how small. This builds motivation and positivity.
5. **Set Intentions for Tomorrow:**
   o Reflect on what you can improve and outline a few actionable steps for the next day.

Examples of Daily Reflection in Action

1. **In Work:**
   o **Scenario:** A project manager reflects on a hectic day.

- Routine:
    - What went well? "We completed the presentation on time."
    - What can improve? "I need to communicate more clearly during team meetings."
    - Tomorrow's intention: "Prepare a checklist for my next meeting to stay organized."

2. **In Personal Life:**
   - **Scenario:** A parent reflects on their interactions with their children.
   - **Routine:**
       - What went well? "I spent quality time reading with my kids."
       - What didn't go as planned? "I lost my patience during dinner."
       - Tomorrow's intention: "Stay calm and practice active listening."

3. **In Fitness:**
   - **Scenario:** Someone is working on a new fitness routine.
   - **Routine:**
       - What went well? "I completed my workout and stayed hydrated."
       - What can improve? "I need to eat healthier snacks."
       - Tomorrow's intention: "Prep a healthy snack pack."

Practical Exercise: Begin Your Daily Reflection Routine

1. **Choose a Time:**
   - Commit to reflecting at a consistent time each day, like before bed.

2. **Use Reflection Prompts:**
   - Write down your answers to three questions:
       - What am I grateful for today?

- What challenged me today?
- What is my top focus for tomorrow?

3. **Track Your Progress:**
   - Review your reflections weekly to notice patterns and celebrate improvements.

Why This Technique Works

Daily reflection helps you pause and reset. It keeps you connected to your goals, builds self-awareness, and ensures each day becomes a stepping stone toward personal growth.

Closing Thought

Reflection turns experiences into lessons. Take time daily to look back, learn, and step forward with clarity and purpose.

Chapter 60: Practice Mindfulness to Stay Present

What is Mindfulness?

Mindfulness is the practice of paying full attention to the present moment without judgment. It means being aware of your thoughts, feelings, and surroundings as they are, rather than dwelling on the past or worrying about the future.

For example:

- While eating a meal, mindfulness involves savoring each bite, noticing the flavors and textures, and focusing on the act of eating instead of scrolling through your phone.

Why Mindfulness is Powerful

1. **Reduces Stress:**
   - Mindfulness calms the mind by shifting focus away from worries and distractions.

2. **Enhances Focus:**
   o By staying present, you improve your ability to concentrate on tasks.
3. **Improves Emotional Regulation:**
   o Awareness of your emotions helps you respond thoughtfully rather than react impulsively.
4. **Boosts Well-Being:**
   o Mindfulness fosters a sense of gratitude, contentment, and peace.

How to Practice Mindfulness

1. **Start with Breathing:**
   o Take a few minutes to focus on your breath. Inhale deeply, hold briefly, and exhale slowly, paying attention to the sensations.
2. **Use Mindful Activities:**
   o Engage fully in everyday tasks, like washing dishes or walking, by focusing on the sensory details.
3. **Practice a Body Scan:**
   o Close your eyes and mentally scan your body from head to toe, noticing any tension or sensations.
4. **Bring Awareness to Thoughts:**
   o Observe your thoughts without judgment. Let them come and go, like clouds passing in the sky.
5. **Set a Daily Reminder:**
   o Schedule mindfulness breaks throughout your day to check in with yourself.

Examples of Mindfulness in Action

1. **In Work:**
   o **Scenario:** You feel overwhelmed by a long to-do list.
   o **Action:** Take a 5-minute breathing break to calm your mind before tackling one task at a time.

2. **In Relationships:**
   - ○ **Scenario:** You're distracted while spending time with loved ones.
   - ○ **Action:** Put away your phone and give your full attention to the conversation.
3. **In Stressful Moments:**
   - ○ **Scenario:** You feel anxious before a presentation.
   - ○ **Action:** Focus on your breath, grounding yourself in the present moment to reduce nervousness.

Practical Exercise: Try a Mindfulness Routine

1. **Morning Mindfulness:**
   - ○ Spend 5 minutes after waking up focusing on your breath or practicing gratitude.
2. **Mindful Breaks:**
   - ○ Pause during the day to observe your surroundings and check in with how you feel.
3. **Evening Reflection:**
   - ○ Before bed, spend 5 minutes journaling about what you noticed or appreciated that day.

Why This Technique Works

Mindfulness anchors you in the present, reducing the mental clutter caused by past regrets or future worries. It's a simple practice with profound benefits for your mind, body, and emotions.

Closing Thought

The present moment is where life happens. Practice mindfulness to experience it fully and live with greater clarity and peace.

Part VII: Advanced Critical Thinking Techniques

Critical thinking is the cornerstone of sound decision-making and problem-solving. It involves questioning assumptions, analysing probabilities, and thinking deeply about how ideas interact and evolve. This section dives into techniques that help you sharpen your analytical skills, anticipate consequences, and approach challenges with a structured, thoughtful mindset.

Chapter 61: Bayesian Thinking: Update Beliefs with New Evidence

I was sure the campaign would work, but early feedback isn't great.

Then let's adjust expectations and revise the plan.

Initial Prediction: 80% success

Revised: 50% success

What is Bayesian Thinking?

Bayesian thinking is a method of updating your beliefs or assumptions based on new evidence. Instead of sticking rigidly to your initial ideas, you adjust your confidence in those beliefs as you encounter new information.

For example:

- Imagine you believe there's a 70% chance of rain today based on the forecast. If you later see clear skies and bright sunshine, you might revise that belief to a 20% chance of rain.

This approach is named after Bayes' theorem, a mathematical formula used to calculate probabilities, but its practical application doesn't require complex math — just a willingness to adapt your thinking.

Why Bayesian Thinking is Powerful

1. **Reduces Cognitive Bias:**
   - o It prevents you from clinging to outdated assumptions by encouraging evidence-based updates.
2. **Improves Decision-Making:**
   - o By regularly integrating new information, you stay aligned with reality.
3. **Encourages Flexibility:**
   - o It helps you remain open to change and adjust your strategies when circumstances shift.

How to Apply Bayesian Thinking

1. **Start with a Baseline Belief (Your Prior):**
   - o Estimate the likelihood of something based on existing knowledge.
   - o Example: "There's a 50% chance this project will succeed based on similar past efforts."
2. **Gather New Evidence:**
   - o Look for relevant data, observations, or feedback that could affect your belief.
   - o Example: Early feedback from team members indicates potential roadblocks.
3. **Update Your Belief:**
   - o Adjust the probability of your belief based on the new evidence.
   - o Example: "Given the roadblocks, I now think there's a 30% chance of success unless we address the issues."
4. **Repeat as More Evidence Arrives:**
   - o Continuously refine your belief as new information becomes available.

Examples of Bayesian Thinking in Action

1. **In Personal Decisions:**
   - o **Scenario:** You're deciding whether to buy a house.
   - o **Belief:** "This neighborhood is ideal for me."
   - o **New Evidence:** A friend mentions the area has frequent traffic issues.
   - o **Updated Belief:** You revise your confidence in the neighborhood and research further before committing.

2. **In Business:**
   - o **Scenario:** A company believes a new product will sell well.
   - o **New Evidence:** Early customer feedback highlights confusion about the product's features.
   - o **Updated Belief:** The company lowers its sales expectations and adjusts its marketing strategy.

3. **In Health:**
   - o **Scenario:** You think a new diet will work for you.
   - o **New Evidence:** After two weeks, you notice no weight loss and low energy levels.
   - o **Updated Belief:** You re-evaluate the diet and explore alternatives.

Practical Exercise: Try Bayesian Thinking

1. **Pick a Current Belief:**
   - o Example: "I think I'll enjoy this new hobby."
2. **List Your Initial Confidence Level:**
   - o Example: "I'm 70% confident I'll enjoy it."
3. **Gather Evidence:**
   - o Try the hobby or talk to others who've done it.
4. **Revise Your Confidence:**
   - o Adjust your belief based on what you learn.

5. Repeat:

  o   Continue updating as you gather more data.

Why This Technique Works

Bayesian thinking keeps your beliefs grounded in reality by encouraging regular updates based on evidence. It helps you avoid stubbornness, adapt to change, and make smarter decisions.

Closing Thought

The world isn't static, and neither should your beliefs be. Stay open to new information, update your thinking, and align yourself with the truth.

Chapter 62: Game Theory Basics: Think Strategically About Others

What is Game Theory?

Game theory is the study of how people make decisions when their choices depend on the actions of others. It's like a mental chess game where you consider not only your own strategy but also how others might respond to it.

For example:

- If you're negotiating a salary, game theory involves predicting how your employer will react to your counteroffer and adjusting your approach accordingly.

Game theory helps you anticipate outcomes, make strategic moves, and find win-win solutions when working with or competing against others.

Why Game Theory is Valuable

1. **Encourages Strategic Thinking:**
   - o It teaches you to plan your actions while considering others' perspectives.
2. **Improves Negotiation Skills:**
   - o Anticipating the other party's moves helps you craft better strategies.
3. **Fosters Cooperation:**
   - o Game theory can reveal opportunities for mutual benefit, even in competitive situations.

How to Apply Game Theory

1. **Define the Players:**
   - o Identify everyone involved in the situation and their potential goals.
   - o Example: In a business negotiation, the players are you and the other party.
2. **Understand the Incentives:**
   - o Consider what each player wants to gain or avoid.
   - o Example: You want a higher salary; the employer wants to minimize costs.
3. **Predict Possible Moves:**
   - o Think through the actions each player might take and how those actions affect everyone else.
4. **Consider Payoffs:**
   - o Evaluate the outcomes of different strategies for all players.
   - o Example: Will pushing too hard for a raise risk the relationship or job offer?
5. **Choose Your Strategy:**
   - o Select the approach that balances your goals with the likely responses of others.

Examples of Game Theory in Action

1. **In Business:**
   - o **Scenario:** Two competing stores are deciding whether to lower prices.
   - o **Strategy:** Each store considers how the other might react and the potential impact on profits.
2. **In Relationships:**
   - o **Scenario:** A couple is deciding how to spend their weekend.
   - o **Strategy:** Each person shares their preferences, looking for activities that make both happy.
3. **In Everyday Decisions:**
   - o **Scenario:** You're deciding which line to join at a grocery store.
   - o **Strategy:** You predict how quickly the line will move based on the number of people and the cashier's speed.

Practical Exercise: Use Game Theory in a Decision

1. **Pick a Situation Involving Others:**
   - o Example: "Should I ask for a promotion at work?"
2. **Identify the Players and Goals:**
   - o You: Secure a raise.
   - o Employer: Retain talent while managing costs.
3. **Predict Their Moves:**
   - o How might your manager react to your request?
4. **Plan Your Strategy:**
   - o Prepare evidence of your value to the company to strengthen your case.

Why This Technique Works

Game theory gives you a framework for analyzing decisions involving others. It helps you think ahead, and choose strategies that increase your chances of success.

Closing Thought

Life is full of strategic interactions. Think like a game theorist to make smarter moves, build stronger relationships, and achieve your goals.

Chapter 63: Think in Probabilities, Not Certainties

This campaign will definitely work!

Let's say it's 60% likely—we should plan for the other 40% too.

SUCCESS
NEUTRAL
FAIL

What Does It Mean to Think in Probabilities?

Thinking in probabilities means acknowledging uncertainty and evaluating the likelihood of different outcomes instead of treating events as black-and-white certainties. Life is rarely 100% predictable, and viewing decisions in terms of probabilities allows you to prepare for a range of scenarios rather than relying on absolute predictions.

For example:

- Instead of thinking, "This investment will definitely succeed," you might estimate, "There's a 70% chance of success based on market trends, but a 30% chance it won't perform as expected."

This mindset shifts you from rigid thinking to flexible, data-driven decision-making.

Why Thinking in Probabilities is Valuable

1. **Reduces Overconfidence:**
   - Acknowledging uncertainty helps you avoid assuming you're always right.
2. **Encourages Better Planning:**
   - By preparing for multiple outcomes, you minimize risks and increase adaptability.
3. **Improves Decision-Making:**
   - Assessing probabilities ensures your decisions are based on evidence and logic, not wishful thinking.

How to Think in Probabilities

1. **Estimate Likelihoods:**
   - Assign probabilities to different outcomes based on available information.
   - Example: "There's a 60% chance this marketing campaign will increase sales, based on past data."
2. **Consider Multiple Scenarios:**
   - Identify the best-case, worst-case, and most likely outcomes.
   - Example: Launching a new product could result in high profits, moderate success, or a loss.
3. **Weigh Risks vs. Rewards:**
   - Calculate whether the potential benefits outweigh the risks, given the probabilities.
4. **Update Your Estimates:**
   - As new evidence emerges, revise your probabilities.
   - Example: If early results show strong customer interest, you might increase your confidence in success.
5. **Avoid Absolutes:**
   - Replace phrases like "This will happen" with "This is likely" or "This has a 30% chance."

Examples of Thinking in Probabilities

1. **In Career Decisions:**
   - o **Scenario:** You're considering switching jobs.
   - o **Probabilities:**
     - ▪ 50% chance the new role is a better fit.
     - ▪ 30% chance it's similar to your current role.
     - ▪ 20% chance it's less satisfying.
   - o **Action:** You weigh the risks and prepare for the less favorable outcomes while pursuing the opportunity.

2. **In Health:**
   - o **Scenario:** You're deciding whether to follow a new diet plan.
   - o **Probabilities:**
     - ▪ 70% chance it helps you lose weight.
     - ▪ 20% chance it's ineffective.
     - ▪ 10% chance it causes side effects.
   - o **Action:** You research further to reduce the uncertainty and plan alternatives if it doesn't work.

3. **In Investing:**
   - o **Scenario:** You're evaluating a stock.
   - o **Probabilities:**
     - ▪ 40% chance it grows significantly.
     - ▪ 50% chance of steady, moderate growth.
     - ▪ 10% chance of loss.
   - o **Action:** You diversify your investments to mitigate the 10% risk.

Practical Exercise: Start Thinking in Probabilities

1. **Pick a Decision:**
   - o Example: "Should I take a weekend trip?"
2. **Identify Possible Outcomes:**
   - o Outcome 1: You have a great time and return refreshed.

o   Outcome 2: You overspend and feel stressed about finances.

3. **Assign Probabilities:**

    o   Great time: 70%.

    o   Financial stress: 30%.

4. **Plan Accordingly:**

    o   If the trip is worth the risk, set a budget to reduce the 30% downside.

Why This Technique Works

Thinking in probabilities replaces emotional or biased decision-making with logical, evidence-based approaches. It prepares you for uncertainty and helps you make informed, confident choices.

Closing Thought

Nothing in life is guaranteed. By thinking in probabilities, you'll approach decisions with clarity, flexibility, and a stronger sense of control.

Chapter 64: Second-Order Thinking: Anticipate the Ripple Effects

What is Second-Order Thinking?

Second-order thinking is the practice of looking beyond immediate consequences to anticipate the ripple effects of your actions. While first-order thinking focuses on the direct result of a decision, second-order thinking considers how that result will trigger additional outcomes, both positive and negative.

For example:

- First-order thinking: "Eating fast food is convenient."
- Second-order thinking: "Eating fast food regularly might save time today, but it could harm my health and increase medical expenses later."

This technique is crucial for making thoughtful, long-term decisions.

Why Second-Order Thinking is Essential

1. **Reveals Hidden Consequences:**
   - It helps you anticipate outcomes that might not be immediately obvious.
2. **Prepares You for Complex Systems:**
   - In interconnected situations, one action often triggers multiple reactions.
3. **Improves Long-Term Planning:**
   - Considering future effects ensures your decisions align with your bigger goals.

How to Practice Second-Order Thinking

1. **Identify the Immediate Result:**
   - Start with the most obvious consequence of your decision.
   - Example: "Switching to cheaper materials will reduce costs."
2. **Ask, 'What Happens Next?'**
   - Consider the next layer of consequences.
   - Example: "Cheaper materials might lower product quality, leading to customer dissatisfaction."
3. **Go Beyond the Second Order:**
   - Continue exploring the ripple effects.
   - Example: "If customers leave, sales might drop, and profits could ultimately decline."
4. **Weigh Short-Term vs. Long-Term Effects:**
   - Balance immediate benefits with potential future costs.
5. **Consider Trade-Offs:**
   - Think about what you might lose in pursuit of short-term gains.

Examples of Second-Order Thinking in Action

1. **In Personal Finance:**
   o **Scenario:** You're tempted to use credit for a big purchase.
   o **First Order:** You get the item immediately.
   o **Second Order:** You accumulate debt and pay interest over time.
   o **Action:** You decide to save and buy the item later, avoiding the ripple effect of debt.

2. **In Leadership:**
   o **Scenario:** A manager considers cutting staff to save money.
   o **First Order:** Costs decrease.
   o **Second Order:** Remaining staff becomes overworked, leading to lower morale and productivity.
   o **Action:** The manager explores alternative cost-saving measures instead.

3. **In Health:**
   o **Scenario:** You skip sleep to finish a project.
   o **First Order:** You meet the deadline.
   o **Second Order:** Fatigue lowers your performance the next day, leading to more mistakes.
   o **Action:** You plan better to avoid sacrificing sleep.

Practical Exercise: Practice Second-Order Thinking

1. **Pick a Decision:**
   o Example: "Should I take on a new project at work?"

2. **Identify the First-Order Effect:**
   o "I'll earn recognition and develop new skills."

3. **Consider the Ripple Effects:**
   o "I might become overcommitted, leading to stress and lower-quality work."

4. Plan Accordingly:

- o Accept the project but set boundaries to manage your workload effectively.

Why This Technique Works

Second-order thinking helps you avoid unintended consequences by thinking beyond the obvious. It ensures your decisions create positive, sustainable outcomes.

Closing Thought

Every choice creates ripples. Think beyond the immediate result to make decisions that serve you well in the long run.

Chapter 65: Counterfactual Thinking: Imagine the 'What-Ifs'

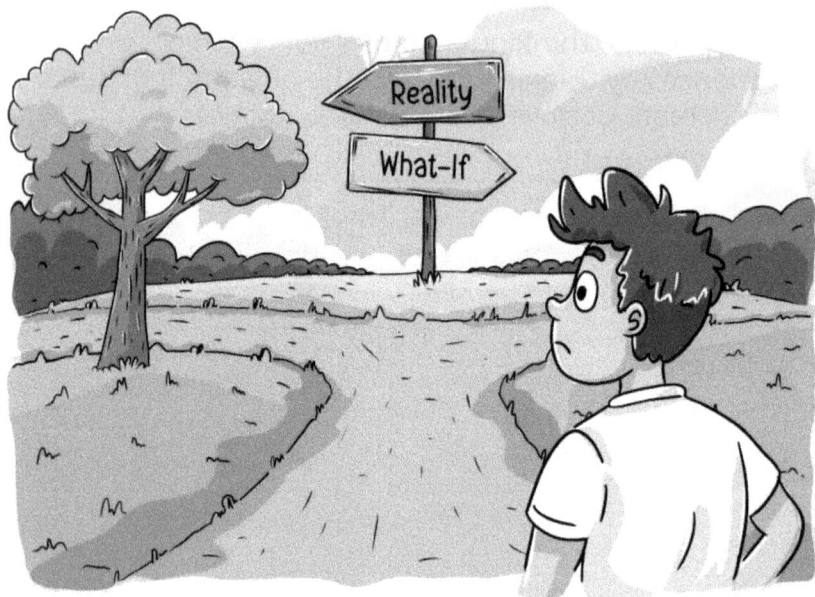

What is Counterfactual Thinking?

Counterfactual thinking is the process of imagining alternate outcomes to events that have already occurred. It involves asking "what if" questions to explore how different choices or circumstances might have led to different results.

For example:

- "What if I had studied a different major in college?"
- "What if I had taken that job offer in another city?"

While counterfactual thinking doesn't change the past, it sharpens your understanding of cause and effect and helps you make better decisions in the future.

Why Counterfactual Thinking is Valuable

1. **Identifies Key Turning Points:**
   - o It helps you understand which decisions or factors had the biggest impact on outcomes.
2. **Enhances Learning:**
   - o By reflecting on alternate scenarios, you gain insights into what worked, what didn't, and why.
3. **Encourages Better Planning:**
   - o Counterfactuals reveal hidden risks or opportunities, enabling you to prepare more effectively for future situations.
4. **Builds Gratitude:**
   - o Reflecting on how things could have gone worse can increase appreciation for what went well.

How to Practice Counterfactual Thinking

1. **Focus on a Specific Event:**
   - o Choose a situation where the outcome was significant or unexpected.
   - o Example: A missed opportunity, a major decision, or a surprising success.
2. **Ask Two Types of Questions:**
   - o **Upward Counterfactuals:** Imagine how the outcome could have been better.
     - ▪ Example: "What if I had started my project earlier?"
   - o **Downward Counterfactuals:** Imagine how the outcome could have been worse.
     - ▪ Example: "What if I hadn't caught that mistake in time?"
3. **Identify the Key Factors:**
   - o Reflect on the decisions, actions, or external factors that shaped the outcome.
4. **Extract Lessons:**
   - o Use the insights from your counterfactuals to refine your approach in the future.

Examples of Counterfactual Thinking in Action

1. **In Personal Growth:**
   - ○ **Scenario:** You didn't get a job you applied for.
   - ○ **Upward Counterfactual:** "What if I had prepared better for the interview?"
     - ▪ **Lesson:** Invest more time in interview practice for future applications.
   - ○ **Downward Counterfactual:** "What if I hadn't applied at all and missed the experience?"
     - ▪ **Lesson:** Appreciate that you gained valuable practice for next time.

2. **In Relationships:**
   - ○ **Scenario:** You had a falling out with a friend.
   - ○ **Upward Counterfactual:** "What if I had communicated more openly about my feelings?"
     - ▪ **Lesson:** Prioritize honest communication in future interactions.
   - ○ **Downward Counterfactual:** "What if I hadn't apologized afterward and lost the friendship entirely?"
     - ▪ **Lesson:** Recognize the value of reconciliation efforts.

3. **In Work:**
   - ○ **Scenario:** A project succeeded despite tight deadlines.
   - ○ **Upward Counterfactual:** "What if we had planned the timeline more carefully?"
     - ▪ **Lesson:** Allow more lead time for future projects.
   - ○ **Downward Counterfactual:** "What if the team hadn't collaborated so effectively?"
     - ▪ **Lesson:** Reinforce the importance of teamwork and communication.

Practical Exercise: Try Counterfactual Thinking

1. **Choose an Event to Reflect On:**
   - Example: "I didn't achieve my fitness goal this month."
2. **Ask Upward and Downward Questions:**
   - Upward: "What if I had stuck to my meal plan more consistently?"
   - Downward: "What if I hadn't exercised at all?"
3. **Identify Lessons:**
   - Extract actionable insights, such as revising your goals or finding more sustainable habits.
4. **Apply the Lessons:**
   - Use what you've learned to improve your future decisions and actions.

Why This Technique Works

Counterfactual thinking provides clarity by exploring alternative paths, making it easier to identify what led to success or failure. It's a powerful tool for reflection, learning, and future planning.

Closing Thought

The past is unchangeable, but it's full of lessons. Ask "what if" to uncover insights, refine your approach, and create better outcomes moving forward.

Chapter 66: The Feynman Technique: Explain to Learn

What is the Feynman Technique?

Named after physicist Richard Feynman, this technique involves breaking down complex ideas and explaining them in simple terms to ensure true understanding. If you can explain something clearly, you've mastered it. If not, it highlights gaps in your knowledge that need further attention.

For example:

- To understand a complicated financial concept like compound interest, you might try explaining it to a friend as if they were new to the topic. Simplifying it for someone else clarifies it for yourself.

Why the Feynman Technique is Powerful

1. **Reveals Knowledge Gaps:**
   - It quickly shows you which parts of a concept you don't fully grasp.

2. **Deepens Understanding:**
   o Explaining something forces you to process it at a deeper level.
3. **Builds Communication Skills:**
   o Translating complex ideas into simple language improves your ability to share knowledge.

How to Use the Feynman Technique

1. **Choose a Topic You Want to Learn:**
   o Pick something you want to understand better.
   o Example: "How does the immune system work?"
2. **Explain It to a Beginner:**
   o Write down or verbalize the explanation as if teaching someone with no prior knowledge.
3. **Identify Gaps in Your Explanation:**
   o Notice where you struggle to explain clearly or where you use jargon instead of simple terms.
4. **Go Back to the Source:**
   o Study those weak areas until you can explain them effectively.
5. **Simplify Further:**
   o Refine your explanation until it's concise, clear, and easy to understand.

Examples of the Feynman Technique in Action

1. **In Studying:**
   o **Scenario:** You're preparing for a biology exam.
   o **Action:** Explain photosynthesis to a friend as if they were new to the topic.
   o **Outcome:** You identify gaps in your understanding and revisit the textbook for clarity.
2. **In Work:**
   o **Scenario:** You need to present a technical concept to a non-expert team.
   o **Action:** Simplify the concept into a step-by-step process, ensuring you fully grasp each part.

- o **Outcome:** Your audience gains a clear understanding, and you deepen your own knowledge.

3. **In Personal Growth:**
   - o **Scenario:** You're trying to understand mindfulness techniques.
   - o **Action:** Explain mindfulness to a friend as if they've never heard of it.
   - o **Outcome:** You refine your practice by identifying key principles and misconceptions.

Practical Exercise: Use the Feynman Technique

1. **Pick a Concept to Learn:**
   - o Example: "How does GPS work?"
2. **Write an Explanation:**
   - o Use simple, clear language to describe the concept as if to a child.
3. **Review for Gaps:**
   - o Identify areas where your explanation feels incomplete or unclear.
4. **Refine and Simplify:**
   - o Research and revise until the explanation feels intuitive and concise.

Why This Technique Works

The Feynman Technique pushes you to engage deeply with a topic, ensuring you truly understand it rather than memorizing surface details. It's a method that combines learning with teaching.

Closing Thought

To master a topic, teach it. Simplify, clarify, and refine your understanding until it becomes second nature.

Chapter 67: Ask, 'What Am I Missing?'

Why Ask, 'What Am I Missing?'

Humans tend to focus on what's immediately visible or obvious, often overlooking hidden factors that influence outcomes. Asking, "What am I missing?" prompts them to examine assumptions, identify gaps in information, and consider alternative viewpoints. This question sharpens their thinking, reduces errors, and encourages a broader understanding of complex situations.

For example:

- Before launching a new business, asking "What am I missing?" might lead you to research competitors, customer needs, or market trends you hadn't initially considered.

Why This Question is Powerful

1. **Exposes Blind Spots:**
   - o It reveals overlooked risks, opportunities, or details that could influence outcomes.
2. **Encourages Humility:**
   - o Acknowledging that you might not have the full picture keeps your ego in check and opens your mind to learning.
3. **Leads to Better Decisions:**
   - o By uncovering hidden factors, you can make more informed and strategic choices.
4. **Strengthens Collaboration:**
   - o Asking for input from others often uncovers what you might have missed on your own.

How to Use 'What Am I Missing?' Effectively

1. **Question Your Assumptions:**
   - o Challenge what you believe to be true about the situation.
   - o Example: "Am I assuming this project will succeed just because it worked in the past?"
2. **Seek Alternative Perspectives:**
   - o Ask others—especially those with different viewpoints—what they see that you don't.
3. **Consider What's Not Visible:**
   - o Think about hidden factors, such as underlying motivations, indirect consequences, or missing data.
4. **Look for Contradictions:**
   - o Ask, "Does anything about this situation not add up?"
5. **Reassess Your Plan:**
   - o Use what you uncover to adjust your approach, fill gaps, or mitigate risks.

Examples of Asking 'What Am I Missing?' in Action

1. **In Business:**
   - **Scenario:** A company plans to expand into a new market.
   - **Question:** "What are we missing about local regulations, customer preferences, or competitors?"
   - **Outcome:** The company discovers cultural differences that require adjustments to its marketing strategy.

2. **In Personal Life:**
   - **Scenario:** You're deciding whether to move to a new city for a job.
   - **Question:** "What am I missing about the cost of living, social opportunities, or long-term career growth?"
   - **Outcome:** You research further and realize the high cost of living would outweigh the salary increase.

3. **In Problem-Solving:**
   - **Scenario:** A team is troubleshooting a recurring issue in their workflow.
   - **Question:** "What are we missing about the root cause of this problem?"
   - **Outcome:** They discover a lack of training is causing repeated mistakes, not faulty equipment as initially assumed.

Practical Exercise: Apply This Question

1. **Choose a Current Challenge:**
   - Example: "Should I invest in a new skill or course?"

2. **List What You Know:**
   - Write down everything you're certain about regarding the decision.

3. **Ask, 'What Am I Missing?':**
   - ○ Look for gaps, such as hidden costs, time commitments, or better alternatives.
4. **Consult Others:**
   - ○ Seek input from a mentor, colleague, or friend to gain additional perspectives.
5. **Adjust Your Plan:**
   - ○ Use the insights to refine your decision or strategy.

Why This Technique Works

Asking "What am I missing?" challenges your blind spots, broadens your thinking, and reduces overconfidence. It ensures you approach decisions with greater awareness and preparedness.

Closing Thought

No one has all the answers. Keep asking, keep digging, and uncover the hidden factors that could make or break your decisions.

Chapter 68: Test Your Assumptions Before Acting

Why Test Your Assumptions?

Assumptions are beliefs we accept as true without proof, and they often shape our decisions. While some assumptions are harmless, others can lead to costly mistakes if they're incorrect. Testing your assumptions before acting ensures your decisions are based on reality, not guesswork.

For example:

- If you assume your target audience prefers a certain style of content, you might invest heavily in creating it — only to find it doesn't resonate. Testing that assumption beforehand could save time and resources.

Benefits of Testing Assumptions

1. **Reduces Risk:**
   o Validating assumptions prevents you from acting on faulty beliefs.

2. **Improves Outcomes:**
   o Decisions based on tested assumptions are more likely to succeed.
3. **Encourages Critical Thinking:**
   o Testing forces you to analyze whether your beliefs hold up under scrutiny.
4. **Saves Time and Resources:**
   o It helps you avoid pursuing strategies that aren't grounded in reality.

How to Test Your Assumptions

1. **Identify Your Assumptions:**
   o Write down the beliefs or expectations underlying your decisions.
   o Example: "Customers prefer digital products over physical ones."
2. **Ask, 'How Do I Know This is True?'**
   o Examine whether you have evidence to support the assumption.
3. **Run Small Tests:**
   o Experiment on a small scale to gather data.
   o Example: Launch a survey or pilot a digital product with a test audience.
4. **Seek Feedback:**
   o Ask others, especially those affected by the decision, for their input.
5. **Adjust Based on Results:**
   o Use what you learn to refine your strategy or replace faulty assumptions.

Examples of Testing Assumptions

1. **In Business:**
   o **Scenario:** A team assumes a new feature will attract more users.
   o **Test:** They launch the feature to a small group and track engagement metrics.

- o **Outcome:** The data shows low interest, prompting them to revise the feature before a full rollout.

2. **In Personal Goals:**
   - o **Scenario:** You assume you'll enjoy a new hobby.
   - o **Test:** You try it out through a one-day workshop before committing to expensive gear.
   - o **Outcome:** You discover it's not a good fit and explore other options.

3. **In Relationships:**
   - o **Scenario:** You assume your partner would prefer a certain type of gift.
   - o **Test:** You casually ask about their preferences before making the purchase.
   - o **Outcome:** You find they'd prefer an experience over a physical gift, avoiding a disappointing choice.

Practical Exercise: Test Your Assumptions

1. **Choose a Decision or Goal:**
   - o Example: "I think this career move will be rewarding."

2. **Identify the Assumptions:**
   - o Example: "The new role will have better growth opportunities."

3. **Design a Test:**
   - o Research the company's promotion rates, talk to current employees, or request a job shadow.

4. **Evaluate the Results:**
   - o Use the data to confirm or challenge your assumption.

Why This Technique Works

Testing assumptions replaces guesswork with evidence. It helps you avoid acting on faulty beliefs and ensures your decisions are based on solid foundations.

Closing Thought

Don't let untested assumptions steer your decisions. Test them, validate them, and move forward with confidence.

Chapter 69: Use Small Experiments to Test Ideas

Why Test Ideas with Small Experiments?

Ideas often seem great in theory but fail when put into practice. Small experiments allow you to test your ideas on a manageable scale, gathering valuable insights without committing too many resources upfront. This approach reduces risk, encourages learning, and increases the chances of success by refining your idea based on real-world results.

For example:

- Before launching a full-scale marketing campaign, you could test your ad with a small target audience to gauge its effectiveness and refine it based on feedback.

Benefits of Small Experiments

1. **Minimizes Risk:**
   - Testing on a small scale prevents costly mistakes if the idea doesn't work as planned.
2. **Encourages Iteration:**
   - Experiments reveal strengths and weaknesses, allowing you to improve your idea incrementally.
3. **Builds Confidence:**
   - Positive results from small tests validate your idea, giving you the assurance to move forward.
4. **Saves Resources:**
   - You invest only what's necessary to test the concept, preserving time, money, and effort.

How to Use Small Experiments to Test Ideas

1. **Define Your Hypothesis:**
   - Clearly state what you want to test and what outcome you expect.
   - Example: "If I promote my product on social media, I'll gain 50 new followers in a week."
2. **Design a Simple Experiment:**
   - Create a low-cost, low-risk way to test your idea.
   - Example: Post one ad on your social media page and track engagement.
3. **Run the Test:**
   - Implement your experiment and gather data.
4. **Analyze the Results:**
   - Compare the outcome to your expectations. Did your idea perform as hoped?
5. **Refine and Retest:**
   - Use the insights to improve your idea, then test again to see if the changes lead to better results.

Examples of Small Experiments in Action

1. **In Business:**
   - **Scenario:** A restaurant wants to introduce a new dish to the menu.
   - **Experiment:** They offer it as a weekly special to gauge customer interest.
   - **Outcome:** If it's popular, they add it to the permanent menu; if not, they tweak the recipe or scrap it.

2. **In Personal Life:**
   - **Scenario:** You're considering a new workout routine.
   - **Experiment:** Try the routine for one week to see if it fits your schedule and goals.
   - **Outcome:** You discover what works and what doesn't, allowing you to adjust accordingly.

3. **In Learning:**
   - **Scenario:** You're unsure if an online course will help your career.
   - **Experiment:** Take a free trial or complete one module before committing to the full program.
   - **Outcome:** The test reveals whether the course aligns with your learning style and needs.

Practical Exercise: Test Your Own Idea

1. **Choose an Idea You Want to Test:**
   - Example: "Start a side hustle selling handmade crafts."

2. **Define Your Hypothesis:**
   - Example: "If I sell my crafts at a local market, I'll make at least $200 in a weekend."

3. **Design a Small Test:**
   - Set up a booth at one market and track your sales and customer feedback.

4. Evaluate the Results:

   o   Did you hit your goal? What feedback did you receive?

5. Refine and Scale:

   o   Use what you learned to improve your pricing, display, or product selection before scaling up.

Why This Technique Works

Small experiments provide real-world feedback, turning abstract ideas into actionable plans. By testing on a small scale, you gain insights that help you avoid costly missteps and refine your approach for success.

Closing Thought

Big ideas start with small tests. Experiment, learn, and refine until your idea is ready to shine on a larger stage.

Chapter 70: Always Ask for Feedback

Why Feedback is Essential

Feedback is one of the most powerful tools for growth. It provides fresh perspectives, uncovers blind spots, and helps you refine your ideas, skills, or decisions. Whether you're working on a project, pursuing a personal goal, or navigating relationships, asking for feedback ensures you stay aligned with reality and continuously improve.

For example:

- If you're creating a presentation, feedback from colleagues can highlight unclear sections, allowing you to make adjustments before the final delivery.

Benefits of Asking for Feedback

1. **Reveals Blind Spots:**
    - Others can identify issues or opportunities you might have overlooked.

2. **Encourages Growth:**
   - o Constructive criticism helps you improve your skills and strategies.
3. **Builds Stronger Relationships:**
   - o Inviting feedback shows openness and humility, fostering trust and collaboration.
4. **Improves Decision-Making:**
   - o Feedback provides diverse viewpoints, leading to more informed choices.

How to Ask for Feedback Effectively

1. **Be Specific:**
   - o Ask targeted questions to get actionable insights.
   - o Example: "What do you think about the structure of my proposal?"
2. **Choose the Right People:**
   - o Seek feedback from individuals with relevant expertise or perspectives.
   - o Example: For career advice, ask a mentor or trusted colleague.
3. **Listen Without Defensiveness:**
   - o Approach feedback with an open mind, focusing on improvement rather than taking criticism personally.
4. **Clarify if Needed:**
   - o Ask follow-up questions to ensure you fully understand the feedback.
   - o Example: "Can you give an example of where my explanation felt unclear?"
5. **Act on the Feedback:**
   - o Use the insights to make specific changes or adjustments.

Examples of Asking for Feedback in Action

1. **In Work:**
   o **Scenario:** You're drafting an important report.
   o **Feedback Request:** "Does this address the client's key concerns clearly?"
   o **Outcome:** A colleague points out areas needing clarification, helping you polish the report.
2. **In Personal Growth:**
   o **Scenario:** You're working on improving your communication skills.
   o **Feedback Request:** "Do you feel I listen actively during conversations?"
   o **Outcome:** Friends share that you sometimes interrupt, giving you a specific behavior to work on.
3. **In Creative Projects:**
   o **Scenario:** You're designing a website.
   o **Feedback Request:** "Is the navigation intuitive, or does anything feel confusing?"
   o **Outcome:** Test users suggest reorganizing the menu for easier access to key features.

Practical Exercise: Ask for Feedback

1. **Pick an Area You Want to Improve:**
   o Example: "My presentation skills."
2. **Identify Who to Ask:**
   o Choose people who can provide honest, relevant feedback, like colleagues or friends.
3. **Ask Specific Questions:**
   o Example: "What's one thing I did well in this presentation, and what's one thing I could improve?"
4. **Reflect and Take Action:**
   o Use the feedback to make targeted changes, then seek additional feedback to measure progress.

Why This Technique Works

Feedback accelerates improvement by highlighting strengths to build on and weaknesses to address. It helps you make more informed decisions and creates opportunities for growth.

Closing Thought

Growth thrives on honest feedback. Embrace it as a gift, act on it with intention, and watch yourself improve in ways you never imagined.

Part VIII: Techniques for Identifying Hidden Influences

We're constantly influenced in ways we may not even notice — whether it's the language someone uses, the way information is framed, or subtle social pressures.

This section equips you with tools to uncover those invisible forces. By learning to identify manipulative tactics, trace motivations, and evaluate credibility, you'll sharpen your ability to think critically and make decisions based on reality.

Chapter 71: Spot Manipulative Language

What is Manipulative Language?

Manipulative language is designed to influence your thoughts or actions without you realizing it. It often appeals to emotions, oversimplifies complex issues, or frames information in a way that pushes you toward a specific conclusion.

For example:

- Instead of saying, "We need to cut costs," someone might say, "If we don't cut costs, the company will fail, and everyone will lose their jobs." The latter statement uses fear to manipulate your response.

Why Recognizing Manipulative Language is Important

1. **Protects Your Autonomy:**
   - o Identifying manipulation helps you think for yourself rather than being swayed by others' agendas.
2. **Encourages Logical Thinking:**
   - o It enables you to focus on facts and logic instead of emotional appeals or deceptive tactics.
3. **Improves Communication Skills:**
   - o Recognizing manipulative tactics helps you communicate more clearly and ethically.

Common Manipulative Language Tactics

1. **Loaded Words:**
   - o Using emotionally charged terms to sway your opinion.
   - o Example: Calling a policy "freedom-crushing" instead of "restrictive."
2. **False Dichotomies:**
   - o Presenting only two extreme options as if no middle ground exists.
   - o Example: "You're either with us or against us."
3. **Generalizations:**
   - o Using words like "always," "never," or "everyone" to oversimplify issues.
   - o Example: "You always ignore my ideas."
4. **Appeals to Fear or Pity:**
   - o Manipulating emotions instead of presenting rational arguments.
   - o Example: "If we don't act now, everything will be lost."
5. **Name-Calling or Labels:**
   - o Using derogatory terms to dismiss ideas or people without addressing the issue.
   - o Example: "Only a fool would believe that."

How to Spot and Respond to Manipulative Language

1. **Pay Attention to Emotional Appeals:**
   - Ask yourself: "Is this argument making me feel scared, guilty, or angry instead of offering facts?"
2. **Look for Absolutes:**
   - Be wary of words like "always" or "never" that oversimplify reality.
3. **Identify Missing Details:**
   - Manipulative language often leaves out context or alternative perspectives.
4. **Ask for Clarification:**
   - Challenge vague or emotional statements with questions like, "Can you explain that in more detail?"
5. **Focus on Facts:**
   - Separate emotional language from the actual information being presented.

Examples of Spotting Manipulative Language

1. **In Advertising:**
   - **Scenario:** A commercial says, "If you truly care about your family, you'll buy our product."
   - **Manipulation:** It uses guilt to influence your decision rather than providing evidence of the product's value.
2. **In Debates:**
   - **Scenario:** A speaker says, "Only someone ignorant would disagree with this policy."
   - **Manipulation:** It dismisses opposing views through name-calling instead of addressing their merits.
3. **In Personal Conversations:**
   - **Scenario:** A friend says, "You never listen to me."
   - **Manipulation:** The word "never" exaggerates the issue, turning a single instance into a sweeping accusation.

Practical Exercise: Identify Manipulative Language

1. **Pick a News Article or Ad:**
   - Look for emotionally charged words, oversimplifications, or appeals to fear or guilt.
2. **Highlight the Tactics:**
   - Mark instances of loaded language, false dichotomies, or generalizations.
3. **Rewrite the Statement Logically:**
   - Example: Rewrite "This plan will destroy the economy!" as "This plan may have economic downsides, such as increased costs."

Why This Technique Works

Recognizing manipulative language empowers you to think critically and independently. It helps you focus on the truth, avoid emotional traps, and respond thoughtfully.

Closing Thought

Words are powerful tools — but they can also be weapons. Learn to spot manipulative language so you can navigate the world with clarity and confidence.

Chapter 72: Identify Emotional Triggers in Arguments

Speech bubble (left): That ad made me nervous—but it didn't explain anything.

Speech bubble (right): That's a fear trigger. Let's look at the facts before reacting.

What are Emotional Triggers?

Emotional triggers in arguments are words, phrases, or tactics designed to provoke a strong emotional response — often at the expense of rational thinking. These triggers can make you feel scared, angry, guilty, or hopeful, influencing your decisions without presenting clear facts.

For example:

- A politician might say, "Our way of life is under attack!" to incite fear and urgency, even without specific evidence.

Why Identifying Emotional Triggers is Important

1. **Helps You Stay Rational:**
   o Recognizing triggers allows you to focus on facts rather than being swayed by emotions.

2. **Reduces Manipulation:**
   - o It protects you from being influenced by arguments that exploit your feelings.
3. **Encourages Informed Decisions:**
   - o By filtering out emotional noise, you can evaluate arguments more objectively.

Common Emotional Triggers in Arguments

1. **Fear:**
   - o Example: "If we don't act now, disaster will strike!"
2. **Anger:**
   - o Example: "Those people are ruining everything we've worked for."
3. **Guilt:**
   - o Example: "If you don't support this cause, you're part of the problem."
4. **Hope:**
   - o Example: "This plan will finally fix everything and lead us to success."
5. **Shame:**
   - o Example: "How could anyone with common sense think that way?"

How to Identify and Respond to Emotional Triggers

1. **Notice Your Emotional Reaction:**
   - o Ask yourself: "Is this argument making me feel angry, scared, or guilty? Why?"
2. **Separate Emotions from Facts:**
   - o Focus on the actual information being presented, not how it makes you feel.
3. **Ask for Evidence:**
   - o Challenge emotionally charged statements with questions like, "What evidence supports this claim?"

4. **Stay Calm:**
   o Emotional triggers often rely on creating urgency or tension. Take a moment to reflect before responding.

Examples of Identifying Emotional Triggers

1. **In Media:**
   o **Scenario:** A headline reads, "The shocking truth about what's happening in your neighborhood!"
   o **Trigger:** The word "shocking" is designed to provoke fear or curiosity without providing details.
   o **Response:** Investigate the facts behind the headline before reacting.

2. **In Debates:**
   o **Scenario:** A speaker says, "If you care about your family, you'll support this policy."
   o **Trigger:** Guilt is used to push agreement without explaining the policy's actual impact.
   o **Response:** Focus on understanding the policy's details instead of reacting emotionally.

3. **In Personal Interactions:**
   o **Scenario:** Someone says, "You're just like everyone else who doesn't understand."
   o **Trigger:** Shame is used to dismiss your perspective.
   o **Response:** Redirect the conversation to focus on the actual argument.

Practical Exercise: Spot Emotional Triggers

1. **Analyze a Speech or Ad:**
   o Identify words or phrases designed to provoke emotions.

2. **Rewrite the Argument:**
   o Remove the emotional language and focus on the facts.

3. Reflect on Your Reactions:

   o Consider how emotional triggers affected your initial response.

Why This Technique Works

Emotional triggers are powerful but often distort reality. Recognizing them helps you stay grounded, think critically, and make decisions based on evidence rather than manipulation.

Closing Thought

Your emotions are valid, but they shouldn't control your decisions. Spot emotional triggers, stay rational, and take charge of your thinking.

Chapter 73: Follow the Money: Trace Motivations

This proposal really pushes that new software.

Let's check if the team pitching it has a stake in the company.

What Does It Mean to 'Follow the Money'?

"Follow the money" is a phrase often used to uncover hidden motivations behind decisions, actions, or claims. By tracing who benefits financially, you can reveal potential biases, conflicts of interest, or ulterior motives that might influence someone's behavior or arguments.

For example:

- A company heavily promoting a particular health supplement might have financial incentives to exaggerate its benefits while downplaying side effects.

This principle is vital for critical thinking because financial interests can shape narratives, policies, and even public opinion.

Why Tracing Motivations Matters

1. **Reveals Conflicts of Interest:**
   - Understanding who benefits financially helps you evaluate whether information is trustworthy or biased.
2. **Increases Scepticism:**
   - It encourages you to question claims that may be more about profit than truth.
3. **Helps You Make Informed Decisions:**
   - Knowing the financial motivations behind actions allows you to weigh information critically.

How to Follow the Money

1. **Identify the Stakeholders:**
   - Determine who is involved in the situation, claim, or decision.
   - Example: In a pharmaceutical ad, stakeholders might include the company, doctors, and patients.
2. **Ask Who Benefits Financially:**
   - Consider who stands to gain or lose money based on the outcome.
   - Example: If a study praises a new drug, check whether the study was funded by the drug's manufacturer.
3. **Investigate Funding Sources:**
   - Look into the origins of funding for campaigns, research, or advertisements.
   - Example: A charity promoting a product might be sponsored by the company that makes it.
4. **Examine Patterns:**
   - Trace the flow of money to identify whether similar actions or decisions have benefited the same parties.

5. **Look Beyond the Surface:**
   - ○ Hidden financial ties, such as lobbying efforts or undisclosed partnerships, may influence outcomes.

Examples of Following the Money

1. **In Media:**
   - ○ **Scenario:** A news outlet repeatedly promotes a particular industry.
   - ○ **Action:** Investigate whether the outlet receives advertising revenue or funding from that industry.
   - ○ **Outcome:** You discover potential bias in their coverage and seek alternative sources.

2. **In Healthcare:**
   - ○ **Scenario:** A doctor recommends a specific medical device.
   - ○ **Action:** Research whether the doctor has financial ties to the device manufacturer.
   - ○ **Outcome:** You find that they're a paid consultant, prompting you to get a second opinion.

3. **In Politics:**
   - ○ **Scenario:** A politician supports legislation that benefits a specific corporation.
   - ○ **Action:** Check campaign donation records to see if the corporation contributed to their campaign.
   - ○ **Outcome:** You identify a possible conflict of interest and scrutinize their arguments more carefully.

Practical Exercise: Trace Financial Motivations

1. **Choose a Claim or Action:**
   - ○ Example: "This sunscreen is the best on the market."

2. **Identify Stakeholders:**
   - ○ Who benefits financially from you buying this sunscreen?

3. Investigate Funding or Promotions:

- o Is the research supporting the claim funded by the sunscreen company?

4. Assess the Credibility:

- o Consider whether financial ties might bias the claim, and seek independent reviews.

Why This Technique Works

Money often drives decisions and narratives. By tracing financial motivations, you uncover biases and conflicts of interest that might otherwise go unnoticed, helping you make more informed judgments.

Closing Thought

When in doubt, follow the money. Understanding who stands to gain reveals the true motivations behind decisions and claims.

Chapter 74: Question the Source: Evaluate Credibility

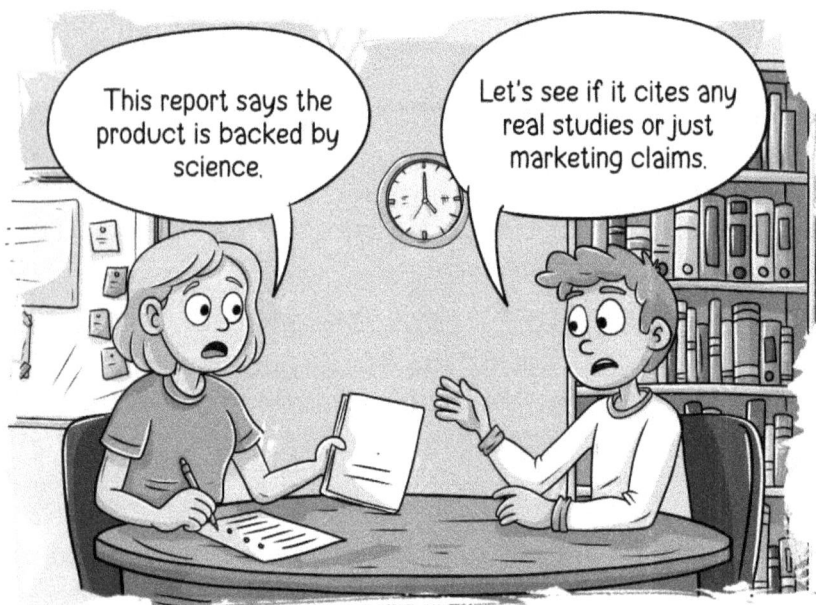

Why Questioning the Source is Crucial

Not all information is created equal. Questioning the source helps you determine whether the information you're receiving is reliable, accurate, and free from bias. In an age of information overload, where opinions often masquerade as facts, this skill is critical for separating trustworthy sources from misleading ones.

For example:

- A social media post claiming a ground-breaking health cure might not be credible if it comes from an unverified account with no supporting evidence.

What Makes a Source Credible?

1. **Expertise:**
   - The source should have relevant knowledge or experience in the topic.

2. **Evidence:**
   - Credible sources back their claims with data, research, or verifiable facts.
3. **Impartiality:**
   - Reliable sources present information objectively, without clear bias or hidden agendas.
4. **Reputation:**
   - Established, respected organizations or individuals are more likely to provide credible information.

How to Evaluate the Credibility of a Source

1. **Check the Author or Organization:**
   - Research the qualifications and background of the individual or group providing the information.
2. **Look for Supporting Evidence:**
   - Credible sources cite data, studies, or expert opinions to back their claims.
3. **Analyze the Tone:**
   - Be cautious of overly emotional or sensational language, which may indicate bias.
4. **Verify the Date:**
   - Ensure the information is current and relevant to the topic at hand.
5. **Cross-Check with Other Sources:**
   - Compare the information with reputable sources to ensure consistency.

Examples of Questioning the Source

1. **In News:**
   - **Scenario:** A headline claims a miraculous cure for a disease.
   - **Action:** Check whether the article cites peer-reviewed studies or credible health organizations.

- Outcome: You discover the claim is based on preliminary research, not established science.

2. **In Social Media:**
   - **Scenario:** A viral post says a celebrity endorsed a controversial product.
   - **Action:** Verify the claim through official channels or the celebrity's verified account.
   - **Outcome:** You find the endorsement is fake, preventing you from spreading misinformation.

3. **In Conversations:**
   - **Scenario:** A coworker shares a statistic that seems off.
   - **Action:** Politely ask where they found the information and verify it yourself.
   - **Outcome:** You identify the statistic as outdated or inaccurate.

Practical Exercise: Evaluate a Source

1. **Pick a Recent Claim:**
   - Example: "This diet guarantees weight loss in two weeks."

2. **Investigate the Source:**
   - Who is making the claim? Are they an expert in nutrition?

3. **Check for Evidence:**
   - Does the claim cite scientific research or rely on testimonials?

4. **Cross-Check:**
   - Compare the claim with information from trusted health organizations.

Why This Technique Works

Questioning the source prevents you from accepting misinformation at face value. By evaluating credibility, you ensure that your beliefs and decisions are grounded in fact.

Closing Thought

The source of information matters as much as the information itself. Question, verify, and rely on credible voices to guide your thinking.

Chapter 75: Detect Spin in Media Narratives

What is Spin in Media Narratives?

Spin refers to the deliberate framing of information to influence public perception. Media outlets often use selective facts, emotionally charged language, or biased framing to present a story in a way that aligns with their agenda or target audience. Detecting spin helps you recognize when information is being presented in a way that prioritizes persuasion over accuracy.

For example:

- A news report might describe a tax policy as "an attack on hardworking families" rather than simply explaining its details, which appeals to emotion rather than providing a neutral analysis.

Why Detecting Spin is Important

1. **Promotes Critical Thinking:**
   - Recognizing spin encourages you to analyze information objectively instead of accepting it at face value.

2. **Reduces Bias:**
   - Understanding how narratives are framed helps you form balanced opinions.

3. **Improves Decision-Making:**
   - Avoiding spun narratives ensures your decisions are based on facts, not manipulated perceptions.

How to Detect Spin in Media Narratives

1. **Analyze Word Choice:**
   - Look for emotionally charged or exaggerated language designed to provoke a reaction.
   - Example: "Devastating cuts" versus "necessary budget adjustments."

2. **Check for Selective Facts:**
   - Determine whether the story includes all relevant details or omits key information to support a specific angle.

3. **Identify the Source's Agenda:**
   - Consider the outlet's target audience, political leanings, or funding sources that might influence their narrative.

4. **Compare Coverage:**
   - Cross-check the same story across multiple media outlets to identify differences in framing and tone.

5. **Watch for False Balance:**
   - Be cautious of attempts to present two sides as equally valid when one side lacks credible evidence.

Common Signs of Spin in Media

1. **Loaded Headlines:**
   - Example: "Scandalous Leak Exposes Government Corruption!" The headline might sensationalize minor details to attract clicks.

2. **Cherry-Picked Data:**
   - Example: Highlighting only the benefits of a policy without mentioning potential drawbacks.

3. **Out-of-Context Quotes:**
   - Example: Using a snippet of a speech to misrepresent the speaker's full message.

4. **Exaggeration or Oversimplification:**
   - Example: Claiming a complex issue has a simple solution, such as "This one law will fix the economy!"

5. **Emotional Appeals:**
   - Example: Including stories or images designed to elicit strong emotions rather than convey facts.

Examples of Detecting Spin in Action

1. **In Political News:**
   - **Scenario:** A news outlet describes a new law as "a dangerous overreach."
   - **Detection:** Analyze whether the report explains the actual content of the law or focuses only on criticism from one side.

2. **In Health Reporting:**
   - **Scenario:** An article claims, "This new diet is revolutionizing weight loss!"
   - **Detection:** Check whether the story cites peer-reviewed studies or relies on testimonials and hype.

3. **In Business Coverage:**
   - **Scenario:** A financial site declares, "Stock market crash imminent!"

- o **Detection:** Look for supporting data and compare the report with other financial analyses.

Practical Exercise: Detect Spin in Media

1. **Choose a News Story:**
   - o Pick an article on a controversial topic from a media outlet.
2. **Highlight Emotional Language:**
   - o Identify words or phrases that seem designed to provoke fear, anger, or excitement.
3. **Look for Missing Context:**
   - o Ask yourself, "What information might be missing or deliberately left out?"
4. **Compare Sources:**
   - o Read the same story from another outlet to see how the framing differs.

Why This Technique Works

Detecting spin sharpens your ability to separate facts from opinion and evaluate the integrity of media narratives. It keeps you informed without being swayed by manipulative framing.

Closing Thought

Don't let spin cloud your judgment. Seek the full picture, think critically, and approach every narrative with a discerning eye.

Chapter 76: Read Between the Lines of Ambiguity

What Does It Mean to Read Between the Lines?

Reading between the lines involves interpreting the underlying meaning or intentions behind vague or ambiguous language. People often use ambiguity to obscure details, evade accountability, or manipulate perception. Learning to decode these hidden messages helps you uncover the truth and make better decisions.

For example:

- A company's press release stating, "We are committed to exploring options for improvement," might sound promising but lacks concrete details about actions or timelines.

Why Understanding Ambiguity is Valuable

1. **Reveals Hidden Agendas:**
   - Ambiguous language often masks true intentions or unfavorable details.
2. **Encourages Critical Analysis:**
   - It forces you to question what isn't being said, rather than focusing only on what is.
3. **Prevents Misinterpretation:**
   - Clarifying vague statements ensures you don't make decisions based on incomplete information.

Common Types of Ambiguity

1. **Vague Promises:**
   - Example: "We're working to make things better." (What does "better" mean, and when will it happen?)
2. **Evasive Answers:**
   - Example: Politicians avoiding direct responses to specific questions.
3. **Overly Broad Statements:**
   - Example: "This product is suitable for everyone." (Is it really, or are exceptions being ignored?)
4. **Unclear Accountability:**
   - Example: "Mistakes were made." (By whom? When? How will they be addressed?)

How to Read Between the Lines

1. **Look for Missing Details:**
   - Ask, "What specifics are missing that would clarify this statement?"
2. **Consider the Context:**
   - Analyze whether the ambiguity serves a purpose, such as avoiding criticism or buying time.

3. **Ask Follow-Up Questions:**
   - o Press for specifics to fill in the gaps. Example: "What actions are being taken to improve the situation?"
4. **Watch for Patterns:**
   - o Repeated use of vague language may indicate a lack of transparency or accountability.
5. **Seek Independent Verification:**
   - o Look for evidence or alternative sources to clarify the ambiguous statement.

Examples of Reading Between the Lines

1. **In Corporate Communication:**
   - o **Scenario:** A company announces, "We're streamlining operations to better serve customers."
   - o **Hidden Meaning:** This might imply layoffs or budget cuts without explicitly stating them.
2. **In Politics:**
   - o **Scenario:** A candidate says, "We're working on solutions to reduce unemployment."
   - o **Hidden Meaning:** The lack of specifics suggests they don't have a concrete plan yet.
3. **In Personal Relationships:**
   - o **Scenario:** A friend says, "I'll try to be there."
   - o **Hidden Meaning:** They may not intend to show up but want to avoid directly declining.

Practical Exercise: Practice Decoding Ambiguity

1. **Choose an Ambiguous Statement:**
   - o Example: "We're committed to improving customer satisfaction."
2. **Identify Missing Information:**
   - o What actions, timelines, or metrics are missing from this statement?

3. **Ask Clarifying Questions:**
   - Example: "What specific steps are you taking to improve satisfaction?"
4. **Cross-Check for Evidence:**
   - Look for supporting actions or data to verify the claim.

Why This Technique Works

Ambiguity often hides key information or intentions. By reading between the lines, you uncover what's being left unsaid, ensuring you base your decisions on clear and accurate information.

Closing Thought

Don't take vague statements at face value. Dig deeper, ask questions, and uncover the truth hidden in ambiguity.

Chapter 77: Look for the Hidden Agenda

What is a Hidden Agenda?

A hidden agenda is an underlying motive or goal that isn't openly stated. People, companies, and organizations often hide their true intentions to persuade, manipulate, or achieve their objectives without attracting scrutiny. By learning to spot hidden agendas, you can uncover the real reasons behind actions, claims, or decisions.

For example:

- A company might market a product as eco-friendly to appeal to environmentally conscious consumers, even if the product's environmental benefits are negligible.

Why Identifying Hidden Agendas is Crucial

1. **Reveals True Motivations:**
   - o Spotting hidden agendas helps you understand what someone or an organization really wants to achieve.

2. **Prevents Manipulation:**
   - o Knowing the real intent behind a message reduces the chances of being misled.

3. **Encourages Better Decision-Making:**
   - o Understanding the hidden motives allows you to assess situations more accurately and act accordingly.

How to Spot a Hidden Agenda

1. **Analyze the Message's Purpose:**
   - o Ask yourself, "What is this person or organization trying to achieve?"
   - o Example: Is a politician advocating for a policy because it benefits the public—or because it helps their campaign donors?

2. **Look for Discrepancies:**
   - o Notice if actions don't match stated goals.
   - o Example: A company claiming to support local businesses might still outsource jobs overseas.

3. **Investigate Who Benefits:**
   - o Follow the outcomes of the action or decision to determine who gains the most.
   - o Example: A charity promoting a specific product might be funded by the product's manufacturer.

4. **Check for Consistency:**
   - o Look for patterns in past behavior to determine if the stated motives align with actions over time.

5. **Ask Questions:**
   - o Seek clarification about vague or contradictory statements to reveal hidden motives.

Examples of Hidden Agendas in Action

1. **In Marketing:**
   - o **Scenario:** A food brand promotes a product as "all-natural."
   - o **Hidden Agenda:** The branding might distract consumers from the fact that the product is still high in sugar or calories.
2. **In Politics:**
   - o **Scenario:** A bill is marketed as "improving public safety."
   - o **Hidden Agenda:** Upon closer inspection, it might primarily benefit private contractors or special interest groups.
3. **In Social Situations:**
   - o **Scenario:** A friend encourages you to attend a party with them.
   - o **Hidden Agenda:** They may want you there to make themselves more comfortable or to help them network.

Practical Exercise: Uncover Hidden Agendas

1. **Choose a Recent Decision or Statement:**
   - o Example: "This new tax will strengthen the economy."
2. **Ask Who Benefits:**
   - o Identify individuals or groups who stand to gain financially, politically, or socially.
3. **Look for Discrepancies:**
   - o Does the stated reason align with the likely outcomes?
4. **Research Background Information:**
   - o Investigate funding sources, partnerships, or past actions that might reveal deeper motives.

Why This Technique Works

Hidden agendas often distort truth and mislead decision-making. By uncovering the real motives behind actions or claims, you empower yourself to act based on facts and logic rather than appearances.

Closing Thought

Always look beyond the surface. The true story often lies in the hidden motives, not the stated goals.

Chapter 78: Understand Framing Effects

"Same Facts, Different Frames."

What are Framing Effects?

Framing effects occur when the way information is presented influences how you interpret it. The same facts can evoke different reactions depending on how they're worded or emphasized. Understanding framing helps you spot attempts to shape your perceptions and make more objective decisions.

For example:

- A health study might report that a drug has a "95% survival rate," which sounds reassuring. However, framing the same fact as a "5% mortality rate" feels more alarming, even though the numbers are identical.

Why Framing Effects Matter

1. **Shapes Perceptions:**
   - The way information is framed can alter how you feel about a situation, even if the facts remain the same.
2. **Influences Decisions:**
   - Framing can push you toward certain choices without you realizing it.
3. **Encourages Critical Thinking:**
   - Recognizing framing effects helps you focus on the facts rather than the presentation.

Common Examples of Framing Effects

1. **Positive vs. Negative Framing:**
   - Example: A product labeled "80% lean" sounds healthier than one labeled "20% fat," even though they're the same.
2. **Gain vs. Loss Framing:**
   - Example: "You'll save $100 by switching plans" versus "You'll lose $100 if you don't switch plans."
3. **Highlighting Benefits or Drawbacks:**
   - Example: A company emphasizes a car's fuel efficiency while downplaying its high repair costs.
4. **Selective Statistics:**
   - Example: Highlighting the "4 out of 5 doctors recommend" statistic while ignoring the sample size or methodology.

How to Recognize and Counter Framing Effects

1. **Reframe the Information:**
   - Restate the facts in a neutral way to see how they sound without the spin.
   - Example: Instead of "95% survival rate," think of it as "5% mortality rate."
2. **Ask for Context:**
   - Investigate whether the frame emphasizes one aspect of the situation while ignoring others.

3. **Compare Alternatives:**
   - Evaluate how different framings of the same information influence your perception.
4. **Focus on the Facts:**
   - Strip away the emotional language or emphasis and concentrate on the underlying data.

Examples of Understanding Framing Effects in Action

1. **In Advertising:**
   - **Scenario:** A toothpaste ad says, "Clinically proven to fight cavities!"
   - **Detection:** Research whether the claim is based on a significant improvement or just minimal results.
2. **In Health Decisions:**
   - **Scenario:** A doctor says, "This surgery has a 90% success rate."
   - **Detection:** Ask about the 10% risk of complications to get a complete picture.
3. **In Personal Finance:**
   - **Scenario:** A credit card promises "1% cash back on every purchase."
   - **Detection:** Consider whether the benefits outweigh potential interest fees or annual charges.

Practical Exercise: Reframe the Message

1. **Pick a Statement:**
   - Example: "This plan will save you $500 per year!"
2. **Restate It Differently:**
   - Example: "Not choosing this plan will cost you $500 per year."
3. **Analyze the Impact:**
   - Consider whether the framing changes how you feel about the decision.

Why This Technique Works

Framing effects can distort your judgment by playing on emotions and cognitive biases. Recognizing these tactics ensures you focus on facts, not just the way they're presented.

Closing Thought

Words matter, but context matters more. Learn to see through the frame and focus on what's inside the picture.

Chapter 79: Notice What's Left Out

What Does It Mean to Notice What's Left Out?

When someone presents an argument or narrative, what they omit can be just as important as what they include. Missing information — whether intentional or accidental — can skew your understanding, leading you to make decisions based on an incomplete picture. By training yourself to notice what's left out, you uncover hidden gaps, ask better questions, and form a more balanced perspective.

For example:

- A product review might highlight its strengths but conveniently leave out its known flaws, giving you a distorted view.

Why Noticing What's Left Out Matters

1. **Fills in the Gaps:**
   - Missing information often hides key details that are critical to understanding the full context.
2. **Prevents Misleading Conclusions:**
   - Omissions can create bias, pushing you toward a particular interpretation or decision.
3. **Encourages Deeper Investigation:**
   - Recognizing gaps motivates you to ask questions and seek additional sources.

Common Types of Missing Information

1. **Selective Reporting:**
   - Highlighting favorable data while ignoring unfavorable results.
   - Example: A study on a drug's effectiveness might exclude data about its side effects.
2. **Lack of Context:**
   - Presenting facts without the background that makes them meaningful.
   - Example: "Crime rates have doubled" without mentioning they're still historically low.
3. **Overgeneralization:**
   - Making broad claims without addressing exceptions or limitations.
   - Example: "This method works for everyone" without considering individual differences.
4. **Unspoken Assumptions:**
   - Failing to mention underlying beliefs or conditions that influence the argument.
   - Example: A plan to reduce taxes assumes government spending won't increase.

How to Spot What's Missing

1. **Ask What's Not Being Said:**
   - Look beyond the surface of the information presented and question what might have been omitted.

2. **Compare Multiple Sources:**
   - Cross-reference information to identify gaps or contradictions between different accounts.

3. **Look for Vague or Sweeping Claims:**
   - Be wary of statements that lack specifics or supporting details.

4. **Identify the Stakes:**
   - Consider who benefits from leaving out certain details and why they might do so.

5. **Request Clarification:**
   - Directly ask for more information to fill in the blanks.

Examples of Noticing What's Left Out

1. **In Marketing:**
   - **Scenario:** A car ad boasts excellent fuel efficiency.
   - **Omission:** It doesn't mention the car's high repair costs or lack of safety features.
   - **Action:** Research reviews and specifications to uncover the missing details.

2. **In News:**
   - **Scenario:** An article reports that a new policy "has widespread support."
   - **Omission:** It doesn't specify how "widespread" was measured or who was surveyed.
   - **Action:** Investigate polling data or consult alternative reports for context.

3. **In Social Interactions:**
   - o **Scenario:** A friend recounts an argument but only shares their side of the story.
   - o **Omission:** Key details about what the other person said or did.
   - o **Action:** Encourage them to share the full context or speak to the other person involved.

Practical Exercise: Find the Missing Pieces

1. **Pick a Recent Claim:**
   - o Example: "This diet plan guarantees results in two weeks!"
2. **Identify Potential Omissions:**
   - o Are there details about the diet's long-term effects or health risks?
3. **Seek Additional Information:**
   - o Look for independent reviews or studies to fill in the gaps.
4. **Ask Clarifying Questions:**
   - o Example: "What specific results are guaranteed, and for whom does this plan work best?"

Why This Technique Works

Noticing what's left out prevents you from being misled by partial information. It ensures you see the whole picture, allowing you to make more informed and balanced decisions.

Closing Thought

Don't just focus on what's said, pay attention to what isn't. The truth often lies in the gaps.

Chapter 80: Track the Influence of Social Pressure

What is Social Pressure?

Social pressure is the influence others exert on your decisions, beliefs, or behavior. It often comes from a desire to fit in, avoid conflict, or gain approval. While it's a natural human experience, unchecked social pressure can push you to conform to ideas or actions that don't align with your values or reasoning.

For example:

- A group of friends might pressure you into agreeing with their opinion on a controversial issue, even if you have doubts or disagree.

Why Recognizing Social Pressure is Important

1. **Encourages Independent Thinking:**
   o Identifying social pressure helps you resist conformity and think for yourself.

2. **Reduces Manipulation:**
   o Awareness of group influence makes you less susceptible to peer pressure or mob mentality.
3. **Strengthens Integrity:**
   o Standing firm against social pressure builds confidence in your values and beliefs.

Common Signs of Social Pressure

1. **Groupthink:**
   o A group prioritizes consensus over critical evaluation, discouraging dissent.
2. **Fear of Rejection:**
   o You agree with others to avoid conflict or exclusion, even if you disagree internally.
3. **Bandwagon Effect:**
   o You adopt an idea or behavior because it's popular, not because it's logical or right.
4. **Appeals to Authority:**
   o You feel compelled to agree because the pressure comes from a respected figure.

How to Track and Resist Social Pressure

1. **Pause Before Agreeing:**
   o Ask yourself whether you genuinely agree or are just conforming to fit in.
2. **Seek Diverse Opinions:**
   o Expose yourself to differing perspectives to counter the influence of group bias.
3. **Clarify Your Values:**
   o Reflect on your core beliefs to strengthen your ability to stand firm under pressure.
4. **Ask Questions:**
   o Challenge the group's assumptions or reasoning by raising thoughtful, open-ended questions.
5. **Practice Assertiveness:**
   o Learn to voice your opinions respectfully, even when they differ from the majority.

Examples of Social Pressure in Action

1. **In Group Decisions:**
   - o **Scenario:** Your team supports a risky project you think is flawed.
   - o **Pressure:** Fear of being labeled a "naysayer" makes you hesitant to speak up.
   - o **Action:** Raise concerns by focusing on the project's potential risks and alternatives.

2. **In Social Media Trends:**
   - o **Scenario:** Everyone in your network shares an unverified news story.
   - o **Pressure:** You feel compelled to share it too, even though you haven't fact-checked it.
   - o **Action:** Research the story before deciding whether to share it.

3. **In Friend Groups:**
   - o **Scenario:** Your friends pressure you to agree with a controversial political stance.
   - o **Pressure:** You worry disagreeing will cause tension.
   - o **Action:** Politely express your differing opinion and explain your reasoning.

Practical Exercise: Track Social Pressure

1. **Reflect on a Recent Group Decision:**
   - o Did you agree because you believed in the idea or to avoid conflict?

2. **Identify the Source of Pressure:**
   - o Was it peer approval, fear of rejection, or a desire to fit in?

3. **Practice Independent Thinking:**
   - o Next time, pause and ask yourself, "What do I truly think about this?"

Why This Technique Works

Social pressure can cloud your judgment and stifle critical thinking. By recognizing and resisting it, you empower yourself to act with integrity and clarity.

Closing Thought

Don't let the crowd dictate your choices. Stay true to your values, think independently, and let logic guide your decisions.

Part IX: Mastering Interpersonal Clarity

Clear thinking is not only an individual skill — it's also essential for building strong, meaningful connections with others. This section equips you with practical techniques to improve communication, resolve conflicts, and foster understanding in any relationship. By mastering these skills, you'll connect with others more authentically and collaboratively.

Chapter 81: Practice Active Listening

What is Active Listening?

Active listening is the practice of fully focusing on what someone is saying, without distractions or judgment. It goes beyond simply hearing words — it's about understanding the message, acknowledging the speaker, and responding thoughtfully.

For example:

- Instead of thinking about your response while someone talks, active listening means giving your full attention, nodding to show understanding, and asking clarifying questions if needed.

Why Active Listening is Crucial

1. **Builds Trust:**
    o   When people feel heard, they're more likely to open up and collaborate with you.

2. **Reduces Misunderstandings:**
   - o Fully understanding someone's message prevents unnecessary confusion or conflict.
3. **Fosters Empathy:**
   - o Active listening helps you see things from the speaker's perspective.
4. **Strengthens Relationships:**
   - o It shows you value and respect the other person, deepening your connection.

How to Practice Active Listening

1. **Eliminate Distractions:**
   - o Put away your phone, close unnecessary tabs, and focus entirely on the speaker.
2. **Show You're Engaged:**
   - o Use nonverbal cues like nodding, eye contact, and an open posture to signal you're paying attention.
3. **Don't Interrupt:**
   - o Let the speaker finish their thought before jumping in with questions or comments.
4. **Paraphrase and Reflect:**
   - o Repeat key points in your own words to confirm understanding.
   - o Example: "So what you're saying is that the timeline feels too rushed?"
5. **Ask Clarifying Questions:**
   - o Encourage the speaker to elaborate by asking open-ended questions like, "Can you explain more about what you mean?"

Examples of Active Listening in Action

1. **In Work:**
   - o **Scenario:** A coworker shares frustrations about a project.

- o **Action:** Instead of offering solutions immediately, you listen fully, paraphrase their concerns, and ask, "What do you think could help improve the situation?"

2. **In Relationships:**
   - o **Scenario:** A partner expresses feeling ignored.
   - o **Action:** You put aside your assumptions, focus on their words, and say, "I hear that you feel I haven't been as present. How can I do better?"

3. **In Friendships:**
   - o **Scenario:** A friend talks about a personal challenge.
   - o **Action:** Instead of steering the conversation to your experiences, you ask questions like, "How has this been affecting you?"

Practical Exercise: Strengthen Your Active Listening

1. **Pick a Conversation to Focus On:**
   - o Choose a daily interaction, such as a meeting or a talk with a friend.

2. **Use Nonverbal Cues:**
   - o Maintain eye contact, nod, and eliminate distractions during the conversation.

3. **Summarize Key Points:**
   - o After the speaker finishes, paraphrase what you heard to ensure you understand their message.

4. **Ask Thoughtful Questions:**
   - o Encourage deeper dialogue with questions like, "What else would you like to share about this?"

Why This Technique Works

Active listening transforms communication from a passive exchange to a meaningful connection. It ensures clarity, builds trust, and deepens your understanding of others' perspectives.

Closing Thought

Listening isn't just hearing — it's understanding. Practice active listening to connect, clarify, and build stronger relationships.

Chapter 82: Ask Open-Ended Questions

What Are Open-Ended Questions?

Open-ended questions are inquiries that encourage detailed responses rather than simple "yes" or "no" answers. They invite exploration, discussion, and deeper understanding, making them a powerful tool for uncovering thoughts, feelings, or ideas.

For example:

- Instead of asking, "Did you like the event?" you might ask, "What was your favorite part of the event?"

Why Open-Ended Questions Are Powerful

1. **Encourage Thoughtful Responses:**
    - They prompt people to share more, providing richer insights and perspectives.

2. **Build Better Connections:**
   - o Open-ended questions show genuine interest, fostering trust and openness.
3. **Promote Problem-Solving:**
   - o They encourage others to think critically and consider multiple angles.
4. **Uncover Hidden Details:**
   - o These questions reveal nuances that might otherwise go unnoticed.

How to Ask Effective Open-Ended Questions

1. **Start with 'What,' 'How,' or 'Why':**
   - o Example: "What led you to this decision?" or "How did you feel about the outcome?"
2. **Avoid Leading Questions:**
   - o Example: Replace "Don't you think this is the best solution?" with "What do you think about this solution?"
3. **Encourage Exploration:**
   - o Example: "What challenges do you see in this plan?" instead of "Are there any challenges?"
4. **Follow Up Thoughtfully:**
   - o Ask additional questions to explore their response further, such as, "Can you elaborate on that?"
5. **Be Patient:**
   - o Give the other person time to think and respond fully.

Examples of Open-Ended Questions in Action

1. **In Work:**
   - o **Scenario:** You're seeking feedback on a project.
   - o **Question:** "What do you think worked well, and what could we improve?"
   - o **Outcome:** You gain detailed insights rather than a simple thumbs-up or thumbs-down.

2. **In Relationships:**
   - o **Scenario:** A partner seems upset.
   - o **Question:** "How are you feeling right now, and what's been on your mind?"
   - o **Outcome:** They feel invited to share their emotions in depth.
3. **In Teaching or Mentoring:**
   - o **Scenario:** A student struggles with a concept.
   - o **Question:** "What part of this feels most confusing, and how do you think we could approach it differently?"
   - o **Outcome:** The student identifies their stumbling blocks, helping you tailor your guidance.

Practical Exercise: Practice Open-Ended Questions

1. **Choose a Conversation:**
   - o Select an interaction where you want to learn more about someone's thoughts or feelings.
2. **Plan Three Questions:**
   - o Write down three open-ended questions that begin with "What," "How," or "Why."
3. **Listen Fully:**
   - o Ask the questions and give the other person space to respond without interrupting.
4. **Reflect on the Outcome:**
   - o Notice how the open-ended questions deepened the conversation or revealed new insights.

Why This Technique Works

Open-ended questions invite others to share their thoughts more fully, fostering understanding and trust. They transform conversations into opportunities for discovery and connection.

Closing Thought

The right question opens doors. Use open-ended questions to explore ideas, connect with others, and unlock deeper insights.

Chapter 83: Clarify What You Heard

What Does It Mean to Clarify What You Heard?

Clarifying what you heard involves restating or paraphrasing someone's message to confirm your understanding. It ensures that both parties are on the same page, reducing the risk of misunderstandings or assumptions.

For example:

- If someone says, "I'm worried about our deadline," you might clarify by asking, "Are you saying the timeline feels too short, or is there another concern?"

Why Clarifying is Essential

1. **Prevents Misunderstandings:**
   - Misinterpretations can lead to unnecessary confusion, mistakes, or conflict. Clarifying resolves ambiguity before it becomes an issue.

2. **Builds Trust:**
   - o It shows the speaker that you care about understanding their message accurately.
3. **Encourages Open Communication:**
   - o Clarifying invites others to elaborate, fostering deeper and more productive conversations.
4. **Improves Decision-Making:**
   - o Clear communication ensures that everyone has the same information, leading to better decisions and outcomes.

How to Clarify Effectively

1. **Paraphrase the Key Points:**
   - o Restate the main ideas in your own words to confirm understanding.
   - o Example: "So, if I understand correctly, you're suggesting we prioritize the new feature over fixing bugs?"
2. **Ask Specific Questions:**
   - o Use clarifying questions to explore ambiguous statements.
   - o Example: "When you say 'soon,' do you mean within the next week or the next few days?"
3. **Check for Agreement:**
   - o After paraphrasing, ask, "Did I get that right?" or "Is there anything I missed?"
4. **Watch for Nonverbal Cues:**
   - o Pay attention to tone, facial expressions, or body language that might signal whether the speaker feels understood.
5. **Avoid Assumptions:**
   - o If something seems unclear, don't guess—ask for clarification.

Examples of Clarifying in Action

1. **In Work Settings:**
   - **Scenario:** Your manager says, "Let's make this project top priority."
   - **Clarification:** "Does that mean we should pause all other tasks until this is complete?"
   - **Outcome:** Your manager specifies that the team should still address urgent issues as they arise.

2. **In Personal Relationships:**
   - **Scenario:** A partner says, "I feel like we're not spending enough time together."
   - **Clarification:** "Do you mean you'd like to schedule more date nights, or is it something else?"
   - **Outcome:** Your partner explains that they'd like to spend more quality time during the weekends.

3. **In Education:**
   - **Scenario:** A teacher says, "Focus on the key themes for the exam."
   - **Clarification:** "Can you clarify which themes are most important to review?"
   - **Outcome:** The teacher provides a list of specific topics to prioritize.

Practical Exercise: Practice Clarifying What You Heard

1. **Choose a Recent Conversation:**
   - Think of an interaction where you weren't entirely sure about what the other person meant.

2. **Paraphrase the Key Message:**
   - Write down how you could have restated their message to confirm understanding.

3. **Ask Clarifying Questions:**
   - Imagine follow-up questions you could have asked to gather more details.

4. Apply in Future Conversations:

- During your next interaction, practice paraphrasing and asking questions to ensure clarity.

Why This Technique Works

Clarifying prevents small misunderstandings from turning into bigger issues. It fosters trust, ensures mutual understanding, and paves the way for more effective communication.

Closing Thought

Clarity isn't just about what's said — it's about what's understood. Take the time to confirm, clarify, and communicate effectively.

Chapter 84: Use Empathy to Understand Others' Views

What is Empathy in Communication?

Empathy is the ability to put yourself in someone else's shoes — to see the world from their perspective and understand their feelings, even if you don't share their experiences. It's a cornerstone of effective communication and a powerful tool for resolving conflicts and building stronger relationships.

For example:

- If a co-worker is frustrated about changes in a project, empathy helps you see how the changes might impact their workload or priorities.

Why Empathy Matters

1. **Fosters Connection:**
   - Empathy builds trust and rapport, making others feel valued and understood.

2. **Reduces Conflict:**
   - Understanding someone's perspective makes it easier to address disagreements constructively.

3. **Improves Collaboration:**
   - Empathy encourages cooperation by helping you align with others' needs and goals.

4. **Encourages Open Dialogue:**
   - When people feel heard, they're more likely to share openly and work toward solutions.

How to Use Empathy Effectively

1. **Listen Without Judgment:**
   - Focus on understanding the other person's feelings and experiences without immediately forming opinions.

2. **Acknowledge Their Perspective:**
   - Let them know you see where they're coming from.
   - Example: "I can see why that situation feels overwhelming for you."

3. **Ask Questions to Explore Their Viewpoint:**
   - Use open-ended questions to learn more about their perspective.
   - Example: "Can you tell me more about what's been challenging for you?"

4. **Mirror Emotions:**
   - Reflect their emotions to show you understand.
   - Example: "It sounds like you're feeling frustrated because of the tight deadlines."

5. **Validate Their Feelings:**
   - Even if you don't agree with their actions, acknowledge that their feelings are valid.
   - Example: "I understand why you'd feel upset in that situation."

Examples of Using Empathy in Action

1. **In Work Settings:**
   - o **Scenario:** A teammate is upset about a new process.
   - o **Empathy in Action:** "I can see how this change might feel like extra work for you. Let's figure out how to make it easier."
   - o **Outcome:** The teammate feels supported and works with you to find solutions.

2. **In Relationships:**
   - o **Scenario:** Your partner is stressed about a family issue.
   - o **Empathy in Action:** "That sounds really tough. I'm here if you want to talk about it more."
   - o **Outcome:** Your partner feels comforted and opens up about their concerns.

3. **In Friendships:**
   - o **Scenario:** A friend cancels plans last minute, citing exhaustion.
   - o **Empathy in Action:** "I understand—sometimes you just need to recharge. Let's reschedule when you're feeling better."
   - o **Outcome:** Your friend feels supported rather than judged.

Practical Exercise: Practice Empathy

1. **Reflect on a Recent Interaction:**
   - o Think of a conversation where you could have shown more empathy.

2. **Identify Their Perspective:**
   - o What might the other person have been feeling or experiencing?

3. **Write a Response:**
   - o Draft an empathetic statement you could have used to acknowledge their feelings.

4. Apply in Future Conversations:

- During your next interaction, consciously practice empathy by listening and validating the other person's perspective.

Why This Technique Works

Empathy bridges the gap between differing views, fostering understanding and collaboration. It transforms communication from surface-level exchanges into meaningful connections.

Closing Thought

Empathy isn't just about hearing — it's about understanding. Use it to connect, support, and communicate with clarity and compassion.

Chapter 85: Reframe Conflict into Problem-Solving

What Does It Mean to Reframe Conflict into Problem-Solving?

Conflict often feels like a battle. Reframing conflict into problem-solving changes the dynamic. Instead of focusing on who's right or wrong, you shift your energy toward resolving the issue collaboratively. It's not about defeating the other person; it's about finding a solution that works for everyone involved.

For example:

- Instead of arguing about who caused a mistake at work, you could focus on how to prevent similar errors in the future.

Why Reframing Conflict is Effective

1. **Reduces Tension:**
    o   Shifting the focus to solutions defuses emotions and promotes calm, constructive discussions.
2. **Fosters Collaboration:**
    o   Problem-solving encourages teamwork rather than opposition, improving relationships.
3. **Leads to Better Outcomes:**
    o   A focus on solutions often uncovers creative, mutually beneficial answers.
4. **Builds Long-Term Trust:**
    o   Handling conflict constructively shows respect and strengthens communication.

How to Reframe Conflict into Problem-Solving

1. **Pause and Shift Your Mindset:**
    o   Remind yourself that the goal is resolution, not "winning."
2. **Focus on the Problem, Not the Person:**
    o   Avoid personal attacks and frame the issue as a shared challenge.
    o   Example: Replace "You're always late" with "How can we make sure we're both on time for meetings?"
3. **Use Collaborative Language:**
    o   Say "we" instead of "you" or "I" to emphasize teamwork.
    o   Example: "How can we work together to solve this?"
4. **Acknowledge Emotions:**
    o   Validate the other person's feelings to show understanding.
    o   Example: "I see that this situation has been frustrating for you."

5. **Brainstorm Solutions Together:**
   - o Invite the other person to contribute ideas for resolving the conflict.
   - o Example: "What do you think would help us move forward?"
6. **Agree on Action Steps:**
   - o End the conversation with a clear plan for addressing the issue.

Examples of Reframing Conflict in Action

1. **In Work Settings:**
   - o **Scenario:** Two team members disagree on how to approach a project.
   - o **Reframe:** "We both want the project to succeed. Let's list the pros and cons of each approach and decide together."
   - o **Outcome:** The team finds a compromise that combines the best aspects of both ideas.
2. **In Relationships:**
   - o **Scenario:** A partner is upset about feeling ignored.
   - o **Reframe:** "I understand you feel like I haven't been present. Let's talk about what would help you feel more connected."
   - o **Outcome:** The conversation shifts from blame to actionable solutions, like scheduling regular quality time.
3. **In Friendships:**
   - o **Scenario:** A friend feels hurt about a missed event.
   - o **Reframe:** "I can see how missing the event upset you. Let's talk about how I can make it up to you."
   - o **Outcome:** The focus moves from the past mistake to repairing the relationship.

Practical Exercise: Practice Reframing Conflict

1. **Reflect on a Recent Conflict:**
   - o Identify a situation where you and someone else were at odds.
2. **Reframe the Issue:**
   - o Write down how you could have turned the argument into a collaborative discussion.
3. **Plan Collaborative Questions:**
   - o Example: "What's most important to you in this situation?" or "How can we work together to resolve this?"
4. **Apply in Future Conflicts:**
   - o When disagreements arise, consciously shift to problem-solving language and mindset.

Why This Technique Works

Reframing conflict into problem-solving redirects negative energy into constructive action. It helps you work through disagreements collaboratively, strengthening relationships and achieving better outcomes.

Closing Thought

Conflict doesn't have to be a fight. Reframe it as a shared challenge, and watch problems turn into opportunities for growth and connection.

Chapter 86: Communicate in Simple, Clear Language

Why Does Clear Communication Matter?

Clear communication ensures that your message is understood the way you intend. Overcomplicated language, jargon, or vague statements can confuse others and create misunderstandings. Speaking and writing simply and clearly makes your ideas accessible, strengthens relationships, and fosters trust.

For example:

- Instead of saying, "We need to synergize our paradigms for optimized solutions," clear communication would be: "Let's work together to find the best solution."

Benefits of Simple, Clear Language

1. **Improves Understanding:**
   - Clear language reduces ambiguity and ensures your audience grasps your message.
2. **Saves Time:**
   - Simplicity prevents long explanations, keeping conversations focused and efficient.
3. **Builds Credibility:**
   - People trust speakers who communicate clearly and avoid unnecessary complexity.
4. **Encourages Collaboration:**
   - When everyone understands the message, they're more likely to engage and contribute.

How to Communicate Clearly

1. **Know Your Audience:**
   - Tailor your language to the listener's level of knowledge or expertise.
   - Example: Use plain language for non-experts and specific terminology only when necessary.
2. **Organize Your Thoughts:**
   - Structure your ideas logically, starting with the main point and supporting it with details.
3. **Use Short, Simple Sentences:**
   - Avoid overly complex sentences that bury your main point.
4. **Avoid Jargon and Buzzwords:**
   - Replace technical terms or trendy phrases with straightforward language.
   - Example: Instead of "leverage cross-platform solutions," say "use tools that work on different devices."
5. **Be Specific:**
   - Use precise examples or details to make your point clear.

o   Example: Replace "soon" with "by next Friday."

6. **Ask for Feedback:**
   o   Confirm that your message was understood by asking, "Does that make sense?" or "Do you have any questions?"

Examples of Clear Communication in Action

1. **In Work Settings:**
   o   **Scenario:** Explaining a project update to your team.
   o   **Clear Communication:** "We've completed 80% of the tasks. The remaining work includes testing and final revisions, which should take two more weeks."

2. **In Relationships:**
   o   **Scenario:** Asking for help with household chores.
   o   **Clear Communication:** "Can you please take care of the dishes today?" instead of vaguely saying, "I need help around the house."

3. **In Problem-Solving:**
   o   **Scenario:** Giving feedback to a colleague.
   o   **Clear Communication:** "Your presentation was strong, but adding a summary slide would make the key points even clearer."

Practical Exercise: Simplify Your Communication

1. **Choose a Message:**
   o   Think of something you recently explained, like an email or conversation.

2. **Rewrite It Simply:**
   o   Remove jargon, simplify sentences, and organize it logically.

3. **Share and Get Feedback:**
   o   Present the simplified version and ask if it's clear. Adjust if needed.

Why This Technique Works

Clear communication eliminates confusion and ensures everyone is on the same page. It builds trust, saves time, and strengthens connections by making your message easy to understand.

Closing Thought

Simplicity is the ultimate sophistication. Speak clearly, listen carefully, and watch your relationships and results thrive.

Chapter 87: Know When to Say Nothing

Why Knowing When to Say Nothing is Powerful

In conversations, silence can be as impactful as words. Knowing when to stay quiet allows you to observe, listen, and respond thoughtfully. It also prevents you from saying things in the heat of the moment that you might regret later. Silence isn't about avoiding communication — it's about choosing your words wisely and creating space for deeper understanding.

For example:

- If someone criticizes your work, pausing to reflect before responding can prevent a defensive reaction and allow you to address their points more constructively.

Benefits of Saying Nothing

1. **Encourages Reflection:**
   - Silence gives you time to process information and form a thoughtful response.
2. **Defuses Conflict:**
   - In heated situations, staying quiet can prevent escalation and help calm emotions.
3. **Invites Others to Share:**
   - Silence creates space for others to express themselves, leading to richer conversations.
4. **Demonstrates Self-Control:**
   - Resisting the urge to speak impulsively shows emotional intelligence and maturity.
5. **Enhances Listening Skills:**
   - Staying quiet helps you focus on what others are saying instead of planning your next response.

When to Say Nothing

1. **When You're Angry or Upset:**
   - Emotional reactions often lead to regrettable words. Silence allows you to cool down and respond thoughtfully.
2. **When You Don't Have Enough Information:**
   - If you're unsure about a topic, it's better to listen and learn than to speculate.
3. **When Someone Needs to Vent:**
   - Sometimes, people just need to be heard. Staying silent lets them express their feelings fully.
4. **When Silence Creates Impact:**
   - Pausing before responding can emphasize your words when you do speak.
5. **When It's Not Your Turn:**
   - Interrupting others disrupts the flow of conversation. Waiting shows respect and attentiveness.

How to Master the Art of Silence

1. **Count to Three Before Responding:**
   - A short pause ensures your response is thoughtful and measured.
2. **Observe Body Language:**
   - Use silence to pick up on nonverbal cues that might reveal deeper meanings.
3. **Resist the Urge to Fill Gaps:**
   - Silence in conversations can feel awkward, but allowing it can lead to more meaningful exchanges.
4. **Reflect Instead of Reacting:**
   - Ask yourself, "Will my words add value to this conversation?" before speaking.
5. **Practice Active Listening:**
   - Focus on understanding the speaker's message fully instead of planning your next comment.

Examples of Saying Nothing in Action

1. **In Work Settings:**
   - **Scenario:** A colleague critiques your idea during a meeting.
   - **Silence in Action:** You pause, listen to their concerns, and respond constructively instead of reacting defensively.
2. **In Relationships:**
   - **Scenario:** Your partner vents about a tough day.
   - **Silence in Action:** You stay quiet, nodding and listening attentively, allowing them to feel heard.
3. **In Conflicts:**
   - **Scenario:** A heated argument begins to escalate.
   - **Silence in Action:** You stop speaking, take a breath, and suggest returning to the discussion later when emotions have cooled.

Practical Exercise: Practice Silence in Conversations

1. **Choose a Conversation to Observe:**
   - Pick an interaction where you'll focus on staying silent and listening more than usual.

2. **Pause Before Speaking:**
   - Count to three after someone finishes speaking to ensure you're responding thoughtfully.

3. **Resist Interrupting:**
   - Let the other person finish their thoughts, even if there are pauses.

4. **Reflect Afterward:**
   - Consider how silence influenced the conversation's tone and outcome.

Why This Technique Works

Silence is a powerful communication tool. It allows you to process emotions, observe nuances, and respond thoughtfully. By speaking less and listening more, you create space for clarity and connection.

Closing Thought

Words have power, but so does silence. Know when to speak and when to hold back — it's a skill that strengthens every relationship.

Chapter 88: Mirror for Understanding

What is Mirroring in Communication?

Mirroring involves repeating or rephrasing someone's words or emotions to show you understand their message. It's about reflecting their thoughts back to them to confirm that you've interpreted their message correctly.

For example:

- If a colleague says, "I'm frustrated because the deadline feels unrealistic," you might mirror by saying, "It sounds like the timeline is causing you stress."

Why Mirroring is Valuable

1. **Ensures Clarity:**
    - o Mirroring confirms that you've understood the speaker's message accurately.

2. **Builds Trust:**
   - o It shows the other person that you're truly listening and care about their perspective.

3. **Defuses Tension:**
   - o Reflecting emotions can help de-escalate conflicts by acknowledging feelings.

4. **Encourages Deeper Sharing:**
   - o When people feel understood, they're more likely to open up.

How to Mirror Effectively

1. **Listen Fully:**
   - o Pay attention to both the speaker's words and emotions.

2. **Paraphrase Their Message:**
   - o Rephrase what they said in your own words.
   - o Example: "So you're saying the meeting schedule is making it hard to stay productive?"

3. **Acknowledge Emotions:**
   - o Reflect the speaker's feelings to show empathy.
   - o Example: "It sounds like you're feeling overwhelmed by everything on your plate."

4. **Ask for Confirmation:**
   - o Check if your reflection is accurate.
   - o Example: "Did I get that right?"

5. **Avoid Mimicking:**
   - o Don't repeat their words verbatim—use your own language to convey understanding.

Examples of Mirroring in Action

1. **In Work Settings:**
   - o **Scenario:** A team member says, "I'm concerned we won't have enough time to finish this."
   - o **Mirroring:** "You're worried the timeline might be too tight to get everything done. Is that right?"
   - o **Outcome:** They feel heard and can work with you to address their concerns.

2. **In Relationships:**
   - **Scenario:** A partner says, "I feel like we're not spending enough time together."
   - **Mirroring:** "It sounds like you'd like us to prioritize more time for each other. What would that look like for you?"
   - **Outcome:** They feel understood, opening the door for a constructive discussion.

3. **In Friendships:**
   - **Scenario:** A friend says, "I'm nervous about this big presentation."
   - **Mirroring:** "It sounds like you're feeling anxious about how it will go. What's making you the most nervous?"
   - **Outcome:** Your friend feels supported and shares more about their concerns.

Practical Exercise: Practice Mirroring

1. **Choose a Conversation to Focus On:**
   - During your next interaction, consciously practice mirroring the other person's message.

2. **Reflect Back:**
   - Use phrases like, "It sounds like you're saying..." or "I hear that you feel..."

3. **Ask for Feedback:**
   - Check if your reflection matches their intended meaning.

4. **Refine Your Technique:**
   - Adjust your mirroring approach based on their response.

Why This Technique Works

Mirroring fosters understanding, builds trust, and ensures clarity in communication. It strengthens connections by showing that you're truly listening and valuing what the other person has to say.

Closing Thought

Communication isn't just about speaking — it's about understanding. Mirror to reflect, connect, and build stronger relationships.

Chapter 89: Summarize for Mutual Clarity

What Does It Mean to Summarize for Clarity?

Summarizing involves condensing the key points of a conversation into a concise statement to confirm mutual understanding. It ensures that everyone is on the same page and eliminates the risk of miscommunication. A good summary highlights the most important ideas, agreements, or action steps without introducing new information.

For example:

- At the end of a meeting, you might say, "So, to recap, we've agreed to complete the report by Friday, divide the tasks equally, and reconvene next Monday."

Why Summarizing is Crucial

1. **Prevents Misunderstandings:**
   - Summarizing ensures that all parties have the same understanding of the discussion.

2. **Saves Time:**
   - o By distilling key points, you avoid unnecessary repetition or confusion later.

3. **Encourages Focus:**
   - o It helps prioritize the most important aspects of the conversation.

4. **Improves Accountability:**
   - o A clear summary outlines expectations and action items, making follow-ups easier.

How to Summarize Effectively

1. **Listen Actively Throughout the Conversation:**
   - o Pay attention to the main ideas, agreements, or concerns as they're discussed.

2. **Highlight Key Points:**
   - o Focus on the most important information or decisions rather than restating everything.
   - o Example: "Here's what we've discussed so far: we'll adjust the timeline and allocate more resources to the project."

3. **Use Clear and Concise Language:**
   - o Keep your summary brief and to the point.

4. **Confirm Agreement:**
   - o End with a question like, "Does that sound right to you?" to ensure everyone agrees with your summary.

5. **Include Next Steps:**
   - o If relevant, outline any action items or deadlines.

Examples of Summarizing in Action

1. **In Work Settings:**
   - o **Scenario:** A project meeting with your team.
   - o **Summary:** "To summarize, John will handle the research, Sarah will draft the report, and I'll review it by Wednesday. We'll meet again Friday to finalize everything. Does that cover everything?"

- o **Outcome:** Everyone leaves the meeting with clear roles and deadlines.

2. **In Relationships:**
   - o **Scenario:** Discussing weekend plans with your partner.
   - o **Summary:** "So, we'll leave at 10 AM, grab lunch on the way, and visit your parents in the afternoon. Sound good?"
   - o **Outcome:** Misunderstandings about timing or plans are avoided.

3. **In Customer Service:**
   - o **Scenario:** A customer explains their issue with a product.
   - o **Summary:** "If I understand correctly, the product isn't functioning as expected, and you'd like a replacement. Is that correct?"
   - o **Outcome:** The customer feels heard, and the resolution process begins smoothly.

Practical Exercise: Practice Summarizing Conversations

1. **Choose a Daily Interaction:**
   - o After a meeting or discussion, take a moment to summarize what was said.

2. **Use a Simple Structure:**
   - o Start with "Here's what I understood..." and outline the key points.

3. **Ask for Confirmation:**
   - o Check if your summary matches the other person's understanding.

4. **Reflect and Adjust:**
   - o Note any feedback and improve your summarizing skills in future conversations.

Why This Technique Works

Summarizing helps clarify discussions, reinforce shared understanding, and prevent errors or misunderstandings. It ensures that everyone involved leaves the conversation with a clear, unified direction.

Closing Thought

Don't assume clarity, create it. Summarize to ensure mutual understanding and a smoother path forward.

Chapter 90: Adapt to Your Audience's Needs

What Does It Mean to Adapt to Your Audience?

Adapting to your audience involves tailoring your communication style, language, and message to suit the needs, preferences, and level of understanding of the people you're speaking to. This ensures that your message resonates and is clearly understood, regardless of who you're addressing.

For example:

- You might explain a technical concept differently to a group of experts than you would to a non-technical audience.

Why Adapting to Your Audience is Vital

1. **Increases Understanding:**
   - People are more likely to grasp your message when it's delivered in a way they relate to.

2. **Builds Rapport:**
   o Tailoring your communication shows respect and consideration for your audience's perspective.

3. **Enhances Persuasion:**
   o When your message aligns with your audience's needs, it becomes more compelling and impactful.

4. **Avoids Miscommunication:**
   o Adapting your language prevents confusion or misinterpretation.

How to Adapt to Your Audience

1. **Understand Your Audience:**
   o Consider their knowledge level, interests, and expectations.
   o Example: Are you speaking to beginners or experts? A formal or casual group?

2. **Match Your Tone and Style:**
   o Use formal language for professional settings and a conversational tone for casual discussions.

3. **Simplify or Expand as Needed:**
   o Avoid technical jargon with non-experts but provide in-depth details for specialized audiences.

4. **Use Relevant Examples:**
   o Tailor your examples to resonate with the audience's experiences or concerns.
   o Example: Use sports analogies for a sports-focused audience, or business examples for a corporate group.

5. **Ask for Feedback:**
   o Check if your message is landing by asking questions like, "Does that make sense?" or "Would you like more detail on that?"

Examples of Adapting to Your Audience

1. **In Work Presentations:**
    - o **Scenario:** Presenting project results to a client.
    - o **Adaptation:** Focus on high-level outcomes and business impacts rather than technical details.
    - o **Outcome:** The client understands the value of your work without being overwhelmed by data.

2. **In Education:**
    - o **Scenario:** Teaching a complex topic to students.
    - o **Adaptation:** Use simple language, diagrams, and real-world examples to make the concept accessible.
    - o **Outcome:** Students grasp the topic more easily and engage in the discussion.

3. **In Social Settings:**
    - o **Scenario:** Explaining your job to a friend with no knowledge of your field.
    - o **Adaptation:** Avoid industry jargon and describe your role in everyday terms.
    - o **Outcome:** Your friend gains a clear understanding of what you do.

Practical Exercise: Tailor Your Message

1. **Choose an Audience:**
    - o Identify a person or group you'll be speaking to soon (e.g. co-workers, friends, or a client).

2. **Analyze Their Needs:**
    - o What do they know about the topic? What details would interest or benefit them?

3. **Plan Your Message:**
    - o Adjust your tone, language, and examples to match their level of understanding.

4. **Seek Feedback:**
    - o After the conversation, ask if your message was clear and useful.

Why This Technique Works

Adapting to your audience ensures your message is relevant, understandable, and impactful. It strengthens your connection with others and makes communication more effective.

Closing Thought

Great communicators don't just speak — they adjust. Tailor your message to meet your audience's needs, and watch your conversations flourish.

Part X: Building a Clear Thinking Lifestyle

Clear thinking is a way of life. The habits and routines you adopt shape how you approach challenges, make decisions, and connect with the world around you. This final part focuses on integrating clarity into your everyday life. These techniques go beyond isolated strategies, helping you build a mindset and lifestyle that support clear, intentional thinking in all areas.

Chapter 91: Develop a Growth Mindset for Continuous Learning

What is a Growth Mindset?

A growth mindset is the belief that abilities, intelligence, and skills can be developed through effort, learning, and persistence. It contrasts with a fixed mindset, which assumes that these traits are static and unchangeable.

For example:

- A person with a growth mindset sees failure as an opportunity to learn and improve, rather than as a permanent setback.

Why a Growth Mindset Matters for Clear Thinking

1. **Encourages Resilience:**
   - A growth mindset helps you see challenges as opportunities rather than roadblocks.

2. **Fosters Adaptability:**
   - By believing you can improve, you're more open to learning new skills and adjusting your strategies.
3. **Reduces Fear of Failure:**
   - Viewing mistakes as a natural part of growth makes it easier to take risks and innovate.
4. **Supports Lifelong Learning:**
   - A growth mindset keeps you curious and motivated to expand your knowledge.

How to Develop a Growth Mindset

1. **Reframe Challenges as Opportunities:**
   - Instead of saying, "I can't do this," try, "I can't do this yet, but I can learn."
2. **Embrace Feedback:**
   - View criticism as valuable input for growth, rather than as a personal attack.
3. **Focus on Effort, Not Outcomes:**
   - Celebrate progress and persistence, even if the result isn't perfect.
   - Example: "I worked hard to improve my presentation skills, and it's paying off."
4. **Learn from Mistakes:**
   - Reflect on failures to identify lessons and use them to improve.
5. **Surround Yourself with Growth-Oriented People:**
   - Spend time with individuals who inspire and challenge you to grow.

Examples of a Growth Mindset in Action

1. **In Work:**
   - **Scenario:** You struggle with a new software program.
   - **Growth Mindset:** "I may not know this yet, but I can take a course or practice until I improve."

- o **Outcome:** You gain confidence and master the tool over time.

2. **In Relationships:**
   - o **Scenario:** You make a mistake that upsets a friend.
   - o **Growth Mindset:** "I can learn from this and communicate better in the future."
   - o **Outcome:** You strengthen the relationship through self-improvement.

3. **In Hobbies:**
   - o **Scenario:** You fail at your first attempt to bake bread.
   - o **Growth Mindset:** "This didn't work, but I can tweak the recipe and try again."
   - o **Outcome:** Each attempt brings you closer to success.

Practical Exercise: Build a Growth Mindset

1. **Identify a Current Challenge:**
   - o Write down a skill or area where you're struggling.

2. **Reframe Your Thoughts:**
   - o Replace fixed mindset thoughts like "I can't do this" with "I'm learning to do this."

3. **Set a Small Goal:**
   - o Choose one action to improve, such as practicing for 10 minutes daily or seeking feedback.

4. **Reflect on Progress:**
   - o After a week, note how your efforts have helped you grow, even if progress feels small.

Why This Technique Works

A growth mindset creates the foundation for continuous improvement and resilience. It empowers you to face challenges with optimism and see every experience as a stepping stone for personal development.

Closing Thought

Your potential is limitless. Adopt a growth mindset, and watch how it transforms the way you think, learn, and grow.

Chapter 92: Stay Curious: Cultivate a Questioning Habit

What Does It Mean to Stay Curious?

Curiosity is the desire to explore, ask questions, and seek out new knowledge. It's a mindset that keeps you engaged with the world and motivates you to challenge assumptions, uncover hidden truths, and expand your understanding.

For example:

- Instead of accepting a headline at face value, curiosity might lead you to ask, "What's the evidence behind this claim?"

Why Curiosity Fuels Clear Thinking

1. **Challenges Assumptions:**
   - Curiosity prompts you to question what you think you know and explore alternative perspectives.

2. **Encourages Lifelong Learning:**
   - A curious mind is always hungry for new information, keeping you informed and adaptable.
3. **Strengthens Problem-Solving:**
   - Asking "why" or "how" leads to deeper understanding and creative solutions.
4. **Fosters Open-Mindedness:**
   - Curiosity helps you approach ideas with a sense of wonder, not judgment.

How to Cultivate a Questioning Habit

1. **Ask Open-Ended Questions:**
   - Replace "Is this true?" with "What evidence supports this?" or "What else could explain this?"
2. **Explore New Topics:**
   - Regularly seek out subjects you know little about to expand your knowledge.
3. **Challenge Common Beliefs:**
   - Question statements or assumptions you've taken for granted.
   - Example: "Why do we do things this way? Is there a better approach?"
4. **Be Comfortable Not Knowing:**
   - Accepting that you don't have all the answers fuels your desire to learn more.
5. **Follow Your Interests:**
   - Pursue hobbies, books, or conversations that spark your curiosity.

Examples of Staying Curious

1. **In Learning:**
   - **Scenario:** You read about a historical event.
   - **Curiosity:** "What were the cultural and political factors that influenced this event?"

- o **Outcome:** You research further, gaining a deeper understanding of history.

2. **In Work:**
   - o **Scenario:** A coworker suggests a new method for solving a problem.
   - o **Curiosity:** "How does this method work, and why is it better?"
   - o **Outcome:** You uncover insights that improve your approach.

3. **In Conversations:**
   - o **Scenario:** A friend mentions an unfamiliar term.
   - o **Curiosity:** "Can you tell me more about what that means?"
   - o **Outcome:** The conversation deepens, and you learn something new.

Practical Exercise: Practice Curiosity Daily

1. **Start a Question Journal:**
   - o Write down three questions each day about things you encounter.

2. **Research One Question:**
   - o Pick one question to explore through books, articles, or conversations.

3. **Reflect on What You Learn:**
   - o Note how curiosity deepens your understanding or challenges your assumptions.

Why This Technique Works

Curiosity keeps your mind active and engaged, driving deeper understanding and better decision-making. It encourages exploration and opens doors to new possibilities.

Closing Thought

Never stop asking, "Why?" Curiosity is the compass that leads to discovery, growth, and a clearer understanding of the world.

Chapter 93: Learn From Diverse Perspectives

Why Learning from Diverse Perspectives is Vital

The world is full of varied experiences, cultures, and viewpoints. Learning from diverse perspectives broadens your understanding, challenges your assumptions, and helps you think more critically.

For example:

- Discussing a current event with people from different cultural or professional backgrounds can reveal nuances you hadn't considered.

How Diverse Perspectives Enhance Clear Thinking

1. **Challenge Cognitive Biases:**
   - Exposure to differing viewpoints helps you recognize and overcome personal biases.

2. **Expand Knowledge:**
   - o Hearing others' experiences provides information and insights you may not encounter otherwise.
3. **Foster Empathy and Understanding:**
   - o Engaging with diverse perspectives helps you see the world through others' eyes, making you more compassionate and open-minded.
4. **Encourage Creativity:**
   - o Diverse ideas often spark innovative solutions by combining different ways of thinking.

How to Learn From Diverse Perspectives

1. **Seek Out Varied Voices:**
   - o Read books, watch documentaries, or follow media from cultures, professions, or ideologies different from your own.
   - o Example: If you're used to reading mainstream news, explore international or independent outlets for alternative takes.
2. **Have Open Conversations:**
   - o Engage in discussions with people who have different backgrounds, beliefs, or experiences.
   - o Example: Join community events, workshops, or online forums that emphasize diversity.
3. **Ask Questions with Curiosity:**
   - o Approach conversations with a genuine desire to understand, not to debate or defend your views.
   - o Example: "How has your experience shaped your perspective on this issue?"
4. **Avoid Echo Chambers:**
   - o Be cautious of environments where everyone shares the same opinions, as they can reinforce biases.
   - o Example: Diversify your social media feed to include people with different viewpoints.

5. **Reflect on What You Learn:**
    - After exploring a new perspective, ask yourself how it challenges or complements your own understanding.

Examples of Learning From Diverse Perspectives

1. **In Work Settings:**
    - **Scenario:** Your team includes members from different countries.
    - **Action:** Ask how cultural differences influence their approach to problem-solving.
    - **Outcome:** You learn new strategies that enhance collaboration and creativity.

2. **In Personal Growth:**
    - **Scenario:** You read a memoir by someone with a vastly different life experience.
    - **Action:** Reflect on how their story reshapes your understanding of resilience or privilege.
    - **Outcome:** You gain a deeper appreciation for the complexities of human experience.

3. **In Education:**
    - **Scenario:** A professor presents opposing theories about a historical event.
    - **Action:** Research both viewpoints to understand the context and biases of each.
    - **Outcome:** Your analysis becomes more nuanced and informed.

Practical Exercise: Broaden Your Perspectives

1. **Explore a New Medium:**
    - Watch a foreign film, read a book from a different culture, or listen to a podcast featuring diverse voices.

2. **Join a Group or Event:**
    - Attend a panel discussion, cultural festival, or community gathering that introduces you to new viewpoints.

3. **Have a Conversation:**
   - Talk with someone whose background or experiences differ from yours. Ask open-ended questions to learn from their perspective.
4. **Reflect and Apply:**
   - After exploring a new perspective, think about how it informs or challenges your current beliefs.

Why This Technique Works

Learning from diverse perspectives expands your understanding and reduces blind spots. It sharpens your thinking by exposing you to new ideas, fostering empathy, and encouraging innovation.

Closing Thought

The world is richer when you see it through multiple lenses. Embrace diversity to think more clearly, act more wisely, and connect more deeply.

Chapter 94: Reflect Daily for Self-Awareness

What is Daily Reflection?

Daily reflection is the practice of setting aside time each day to think about your experiences, decisions, and emotions. It helps you identify patterns, understand your behaviour, and learn from your day. This habit cultivates self-awareness, enabling you to approach life with greater clarity and intention.

For example:

- At the end of the day, reflecting on a tough conversation might help you identify what went well, what didn't, and how to improve future interactions.

Why Reflection Matters for Clear Thinking

1. **Builds Self-Awareness:**
   - Reflection helps you understand your strengths, weaknesses, and biases.

2. **Encourages Growth:**
   - o Reviewing your day reveals lessons that guide personal and professional development.
3. **Reduces Reactivity:**
   - o By examining your emotions and triggers, you become less prone to impulsive reactions.
4. **Clarifies Priorities:**
   - o Reflection helps you focus on what truly matters, aligning your actions with your values.

How to Reflect Effectively

1. **Set a Daily Routine:**
   - o Dedicate 10–15 minutes at the end of each day for reflection.
2. **Ask Key Questions:**
   - o Use prompts to guide your thoughts:
     - ▪ What went well today?
     - ▪ What challenges did I face, and how did I respond?
     - ▪ What could I do differently tomorrow?
3. **Write It Down:**
   - o Journaling your reflections makes your thoughts tangible and easier to analyze.
4. **Be Honest:**
   - o Acknowledge both successes and mistakes without judgment.
5. **Focus on Patterns:**
   - o Look for recurring themes or behaviors that might need attention or adjustment.

Examples of Daily Reflection

1. **In Work:**
   - o **Scenario:** A meeting didn't go as planned.
   - o **Reflection:** "What caused the misunderstanding, and how can I communicate more clearly next time?"

- o **Outcome:** You refine your approach for future discussions.

2. **In Relationships:**
   - o **Scenario:** You had an argument with a friend.
   - o **Reflection:** "What triggered the argument, and how could I handle similar situations better?"
   - o **Outcome:** You identify ways to improve your communication.

3. **In Personal Goals:**
   - o **Scenario:** You skipped your workout.
   - o **Reflection:** "Why did I skip it, and how can I stay motivated tomorrow?"
   - o **Outcome:** You plan a specific time for exercise and stick to it.

Practical Exercise: Start a Daily Reflection Practice

1. **Choose a Reflection Time:**
   - o Pick a consistent time each day, such as before bed or after work.

2. **Use Prompts:**
   - o Write or think about questions like, "What did I learn today?" or "What am I grateful for?"

3. **Record Insights:**
   - o Keep a journal or voice notes to track your thoughts over time.

4. **Review Weekly:**
   - o At the end of the week, look back on your reflections to identify growth or recurring challenges.

Why This Technique Works

Daily reflection transforms your experiences into learning opportunities. It enhances self-awareness, sharpens your decision-making, and aligns your actions with your goals and values.

Closing Thought

A clearer mind starts with self-awareness. Reflect daily to grow, learn, and live with purpose.

Chapter 95: Practice Gratitude for Balanced Thinking

What is Gratitude in the Context of Thinking?

Gratitude is the practice of focusing on what's good in your life and being thankful for it. It's not just a feel-good exercise — it's a way to create mental balance. By acknowledging the positive, you prevent negativity or stress from dominating your thoughts, leading to clearer, more rational decision-making.

For example:

- Gratitude for a supportive team at work can shift your mindset from frustration about challenges to appreciation for collaboration.

How Gratitude Enhances Clear Thinking

1. **Balances Negativity:**
   - Gratitude counteracts the brain's natural tendency to focus on problems, creating a more balanced perspective.

2. **Reduces Stress:**
   - o Focusing on what you're thankful for helps lower anxiety and increases emotional resilience.
3. **Improves Decision-Making:**
   - o A positive mindset reduces impulsivity and helps you weigh options more rationally.
4. **Fosters Creativity and Problem-Solving:**
   - o Gratitude shifts your focus from obstacles to opportunities, encouraging creative thinking.

How to Practice Gratitude for Clear Thinking

1. **Start a Gratitude Journal:**
   - o Write down three things you're grateful for each day, no matter how small.
   - o Example: "The sunshine during my morning walk," or "A friend's kind text."
2. **Reflect During Tough Moments:**
   - o When facing a challenge, pause to identify something positive in the situation.
   - o Example: "This problem is hard, but I'm grateful for the skills I'm developing to solve it."
3. **Express Gratitude to Others:**
   - o Tell someone why you appreciate them, either in person or with a note.
   - o Example: "I'm so thankful for how you supported me during that project."
4. **Pause to Appreciate Daily Moments:**
   - o Notice and savor small joys, like a good meal, a beautiful view, or a kind gesture.
5. **Practice Before Problem-Solving:**
   - o Before tackling a stressful decision, list a few things you're grateful for to create a calm, positive mindset.

Examples of Gratitude in Action

1. **In Work Settings:**
   - o **Scenario:** You're frustrated with a tight deadline.
   - o **Gratitude Practice:** Reflect on how your team's support makes the workload manageable.
   - o **Outcome:** You feel more positive and motivated to collaborate effectively.

2. **In Relationships:**
   - o **Scenario:** A disagreement with a loved one leaves you upset.
   - o **Gratitude Practice:** Focus on the aspects of the relationship you value, like their kindness or shared memories.
   - o **Outcome:** This perspective helps you approach the conflict with understanding.

3. **In Personal Challenges:**
   - o **Scenario:** You're recovering from an injury.
   - o **Gratitude Practice:** Appreciate the progress you've made and the support from others.
   - o **Outcome:** Gratitude boosts your emotional resilience during recovery.

Practical Exercise: Build a Gratitude Habit

1. **Set a Daily Gratitude Time:**
   - o Each morning or evening, write or think about three things you're grateful for.

2. **Focus on Specifics:**
   - o Instead of vague entries like "family," write "the laugh I shared with my sister today."

3. **Express Thanks Weekly:**
   - o Share your gratitude with someone who made a positive impact on your week.

4. **Reflect Monthly:**
   - o Review your gratitude journal to notice recurring themes or patterns of positivity.

Why This Technique Works

Gratitude rewires your brain to focus on the positive, creating a balanced mental state that supports clarity and emotional stability. It transforms your mindset from scarcity to abundance, making it easier to think clearly and act wisely.

Closing Thought

Practice gratitude daily to bring balance, clarity, and positivity to your thoughts and decisions.

Chapter 96: Stay Physically Healthy for Mental Sharpness

Why Physical Health is Tied to Mental Sharpness

Your body and mind are deeply connected. Physical health directly impacts your brain's ability to process information, make decisions, and stay focused. Neglecting your physical well-being can cloud your thinking, while maintaining healthy habits sharpens your mental clarity and resilience.

For example:

- Regular exercise improves blood flow to the brain, boosting memory, concentration, and problem-solving skills.

How Physical Health Enhances Clear Thinking

1. **Boosts Cognitive Function:**
   - Physical activity improves memory, focus, and mental agility.

2. **Reduces Stress:**
   - o Healthy habits like exercise and sleep help regulate cortisol levels, keeping your mind calm and focused.
3. **Increases Energy Levels:**
   - o A well-balanced diet and regular exercise prevent mental fatigue and keep you alert.
4. **Supports Emotional Stability:**
   - o Physical health reduces mood swings, helping you approach problems with a balanced mindset.

Key Habits for Physical and Mental Health

1. **Exercise Regularly:**
   - o Aim for at least 30 minutes of physical activity most days of the week.
   - o Example: Walk, jog, do yoga, or try strength training.
2. **Eat Brain-Boosting Foods:**
   - o Incorporate fruits, vegetables, whole grains, and healthy fats into your meals.
   - o Example: Foods rich in omega-3s, like salmon or walnuts, support brain health.
3. **Stay Hydrated:**
   - o Drink enough water to keep your brain functioning optimally.
   - o Example: Even mild dehydration can impair focus and memory.
4. **Prioritize Sleep:**
   - o Aim for 7–9 hours of quality sleep per night to support memory and decision-making.
   - o Example: Create a calming bedtime routine to improve sleep quality.
5. **Take Breaks:**
   - o Periodic breaks during work improve focus and prevent mental burnout.

- o Example: Use the 25/5 Pomodoro technique: 25 minutes of focused work, 5 minutes of rest.

Examples of Physical Health Supporting Mental Sharpness

1. **In Work:**
   - o **Scenario:** You have a big presentation tomorrow.
   - o **Healthy Habit:** A good night's sleep sharpens your memory and ensures peak performance.
   - o **Outcome:** You deliver a confident and clear presentation.
2. **In Stressful Situations:**
   - o **Scenario:** A looming deadline creates anxiety.
   - o **Healthy Habit:** A quick workout reduces stress and helps you refocus.
   - o **Outcome:** You tackle the task with renewed energy and calmness.
3. **In Decision-Making:**
   - o **Scenario:** You're feeling sluggish while weighing a tough choice.
   - o **Healthy Habit:** Drinking water and taking a walk refresh your brain.
   - o **Outcome:** You return to the decision with better clarity and focus.

Practical Exercise: Build Healthy Habits for Clarity

1. **Set a Fitness Goal:**
   - o Start small, like taking a 10-minute walk daily, and build from there.
2. **Track Your Diet:**
   - o Write down what you eat for a week and identify ways to add more brain-boosting foods.
3. **Create a Sleep Routine:**
   - o Go to bed and wake up at consistent times to improve sleep quality.

4. Schedule Breaks:

      o   Set timers to remind yourself to stretch, hydrate, or move throughout the day.

Why This Technique Works

Your brain relies on a healthy body to function at its best. By prioritizing physical well-being, you ensure that your mind stays sharp, focused, and ready to tackle any challenge.

Closing Thought

A healthy body fuels a clear mind. Take care of yourself physically, and your mental clarity will thank you.

Chapter 97: Embrace Failures as Learning Opportunities

What Does It Mean to Embrace Failures?

Failure is often seen as something to avoid, but it's one of the most powerful teachers you'll ever encounter. Embracing failure means recognizing it as an inevitable part of growth and a valuable opportunity to learn, adapt, and improve. It shifts your mindset from fearing mistakes to using them as stepping stones toward success.

For example:

- If a business idea doesn't work out, instead of giving up, you can analyze why it failed, adjust your approach, and try again with a better strategy.

Why Embracing Failure Matters

1. **Promotes Resilience:**
    - Learning from setbacks helps you bounce back stronger and more determined.

2. **Encourages Innovation:**
   - ○ Many breakthroughs come from trial and error. Failure sparks new ideas and approaches.
3. **Improves Decision-Making:**
   - ○ Reflecting on failures reveals what went wrong, helping you make better choices in the future.
4. **Builds Confidence:**
   - ○ Facing and overcoming failure reinforces your belief in your ability to grow and succeed.

How to Turn Failures into Learning Opportunities

1. **Acknowledge the Failure:**
   - ○ Accept responsibility without self-blame or denial.
   - ○ Example: "I missed this deadline because I underestimated the time required."
2. **Analyze What Went Wrong:**
   - ○ Break down the situation to identify specific causes.
   - ○ Example: "Did I lack resources, misunderstand the task, or face unexpected obstacles?"
3. **Extract Lessons:**
   - ○ Ask yourself what the failure taught you about your skills, approach, or environment.
   - ○ Example: "Next time, I'll set smaller milestones to track progress more effectively."
4. **Adjust Your Strategy:**
   - ○ Use what you've learned to improve future efforts.
   - ○ Example: "I'll plan for extra time in case of delays."
5. **Move Forward:**
   - ○ Let go of regret and focus on applying your new insights.

Examples of Embracing Failures

1. **In Work:**
   - o **Scenario:** A product launch fails to meet sales targets.
   - o **Action:** Analyze customer feedback to understand why, and use the insights to improve your next launch.
   - o **Outcome:** The revised product performs significantly better.

2. **In Relationships:**
   - o **Scenario:** A disagreement escalates into an argument.
   - o **Action:** Reflect on how you communicated and identify ways to express yourself more calmly next time.
   - o **Outcome:** Future discussions become more constructive and respectful.

3. **In Personal Goals:**
   - o **Scenario:** You fail to stick to a fitness plan.
   - o **Action:** Adjust your routine to include more manageable goals and accountability.
   - o **Outcome:** You develop a sustainable habit over time.

Practical Exercise: Learn from a Recent Failure

1. **Identify a Failure:**
   - o Choose a recent setback, big or small.

2. **Analyze the Situation:**
   - o Write down what happened, why it happened, and how it made you feel.

3. **Extract Lessons:**
   - o Ask, "What can I learn from this? How can I improve next time?"

4. **Set a New Goal:**
   - o Apply what you've learned to a current or future challenge.

5. Reflect on Your Progress:

- o Over time, revisit this failure to see how it contributed to your growth.

Why This Technique Works

Viewing failure as a learning opportunity transforms it from a source of fear into a tool for growth. It empowers you to take risks, innovate, and adapt with confidence.

Closing Thought

Failure is the beginning of learning. Embrace it, grow from it, and let it guide you to success.

Chapter 98: Take Breaks to Recharge Thinking

Shy Taking Breaks is Essential

Your brain needs rest to function at its best. Taking breaks improves focus, reduces mental fatigue, and boosts creativity. Whether you're solving a problem, learning a new skill, or making decisions, stepping away for a moment can actually enhance your performance.

For example:

- Taking a 10-minute walk during a busy workday can help you return with renewed energy and fresh ideas.

Benefits of Taking Breaks for Mental Clarity

1. **Reduces Cognitive Overload:**
   - Breaks prevent your brain from becoming overwhelmed by constant work or information.

2. **Improves Focus:**
   - Short rests help you sustain concentration and avoid burnout.
3. **Boosts Creativity:**
   - Many creative insights emerge when you step away from the problem.
4. **Enhances Decision-Making:**
   - Breaks create distance from the issue, allowing you to view it more objectively.

How to Take Effective Breaks

1. **Use the Pomodoro Technique:**
   - Work for 25 minutes, then take a 5-minute break. After four cycles, take a longer 15–30 minute break.
2. **Move Your Body:**
   - Physical activity, like stretching or walking, increases blood flow to the brain.
3. **Disconnect From Screens:**
   - Step away from digital devices to rest your eyes and reduce mental fatigue.
4. **Practice Mindfulness or Relaxation:**
   - Take deep breaths, meditate, or listen to calming music to recharge.
5. **Do Something Enjoyable:**
   - Use your break for activities that refresh you, like chatting with a friend or reading a book.

Examples of Breaks Enhancing Productivity

1. **In Work:**
   - **Scenario:** You're stuck on a tough problem.
   - **Action:** Take a short walk outside.
   - **Outcome:** A new solution pops into your mind while you're away from your desk.

2. **In Study Sessions:**
   - o **Scenario:** You're cramming for an exam and feeling overwhelmed.
   - o **Action:** Take a 15-minute break to stretch and hydrate.
   - o **Outcome:** You return more focused and retain information better.

3. **In Creative Work:**
   - o **Scenario:** You're designing a project and hit a mental block.
   - o **Action:** Step away to doodle or listen to music.
   - o **Outcome:** Fresh ideas come to you when you return.

Practical Exercise: Schedule Breaks Into Your Day

1. **Plan Break Intervals:**
   - o Set timers for work and break sessions.

2. **Experiment with Break Activities:**
   - o Try different approaches—physical movement, mindfulness, or creative hobbies—to see what refreshes you most.

3. **Reflect on the Impact:**
   - o Notice how breaks improve your focus, energy, and creativity.

Why This Technique Works

Breaks give your brain the rest it needs to function at its peak. They enhance clarity, creativity, and problem-solving, ensuring you perform better and feel more energized.

Closing Thought

Rest is a tool. Take breaks to refresh your mind and return stronger, sharper, and ready to tackle the next challenge.

Chapter 99: Seek Out Complexity and Simplify It

Why Seek Out Complexity?

The world is full of intricate systems, conflicting ideas, and dense information. While complexity might seem overwhelming, seeking it out helps you develop a deeper understanding of challenging concepts. The key is to simplify complexity—breaking it down into digestible pieces without losing its essence. This process strengthens your analytical skills, enhances decision-making, and empowers you to explain ideas clearly to others.

For example:

- Simplifying a complex business strategy into actionable steps helps your team understand and implement it effectively.

Benefits of Simplifying Complexity

1. **Builds Mastery:**
   - Understanding complex topics strengthens your knowledge and confidence.
2. **Improves Communication:**
   - Simplifying allows you to share insights with others in an accessible way.
3. **Enhances Decision-Making:**
   - Breaking down complexity helps you identify the most important factors in a situation.
4. **Encourages Critical Thinking:**
   - Analyzing and simplifying complexity sharpens your ability to evaluate information.

How to Simplify Complexity

1. **Start with the Big Picture:**
   - Understand the overarching concept or goal before diving into details.
   - Example: If you're learning about climate change, begin with the basics—like the greenhouse effect—before exploring specific policies.
2. **Break It Into Parts:**
   - Divide the topic into smaller, manageable components.
   - Example: For a business project, separate it into planning, execution, and evaluation phases.
3. **Identify Core Ideas:**
   - Focus on the most important elements that drive the topic or problem.
   - Example: Instead of memorizing every law in economics, understand key principles like supply and demand.
4. **Use Analogies and Visuals:**
   - Relate complex concepts to familiar ideas or create diagrams to simplify relationships.

- Example: Compare a computer's CPU to a brain to explain its function.

5. **Explain It to Others:**
   - Teaching forces you to clarify your understanding and spot gaps in your knowledge.

Examples of Simplifying Complexity

1. **In Education:**
   - **Scenario:** You're learning about quantum mechanics.
   - **Simplification:** Use analogies, like comparing quantum superposition to a spinning coin, to grasp the concept.
   - **Outcome:** The analogy makes an abstract idea more tangible and easier to explain.

2. **In Work:**
   - **Scenario:** A project has multiple overlapping deadlines and dependencies.
   - **Simplification:** Create a timeline that highlights key milestones and who's responsible for each.
   - **Outcome:** Your team understands the workflow, improving efficiency and collaboration.

3. **In Everyday Life:**
   - **Scenario:** You're reading a dense news article about economic trends.
   - **Simplification:** Summarize the main takeaway, like "Inflation is rising because demand is outpacing supply."
   - **Outcome:** You gain clarity without getting lost in jargon.

Practical Exercise: Simplify Something Complex

1. **Choose a Complex Topic:**
   - Pick a challenging concept from work, school, or daily life.

2. **Break It Down:**
   o Divide the topic into three to five key points or parts.
3. **Create a Summary:**
   o Write a one-paragraph explanation that captures the essence of the topic.
4. **Share It With Someone:**
   o Explain your summary to a friend or colleague and ask if it makes sense.

Why This Technique Works

Simplifying complexity sharpens your thinking and clarifies your understanding. It reduces overwhelm, helps you focus on what matters, and equips you to communicate effectively.

Closing Thought

Complexity is something you need to embrace and master. Seek it out, simplify it, and turn it into a tool for clarity and understanding.

Chapter 100: Live Intentionally: Align Choices with Values

What Does It Mean to Live Intentionally?

Living intentionally means making deliberate choices that align with your values and long-term goals. It's about focusing on what matters most and letting those priorities guide your actions, instead of being swayed by distractions or societal expectations.

For example:

- If personal growth is a core value, you might choose to invest time in learning new skills rather than mindlessly scrolling through social media.

Why Intentional Living Supports Clear Thinking

1. **Provides Direction:**
   o Aligning actions with values eliminates indecision and keeps you focused on meaningful goals.

2. **Reduces Overwhelm:**
   - Living intentionally helps you prioritize, so you can let go of unnecessary tasks or commitments.
3. **Fosters Resilience:**
   - A strong connection to your values gives you the clarity and strength to navigate challenges.
4. **Promotes Fulfillment:**
   - Intentional living ensures your efforts contribute to a life that feels meaningful and satisfying.

How to Live Intentionally

1. **Identify Your Core Values:**
   - Reflect on what matters most to you—family, honesty, growth, creativity, etc.
2. **Set Clear Goals:**
   - Define what success looks like in each area of your life.
   - Example: "Spend one hour each day connecting with family."
3. **Evaluate Your Choices:**
   - Regularly ask, "Does this align with my values?"
   - Example: If health is a priority, consider whether a late-night binge of TV supports your goals.
4. **Eliminate Distractions:**
   - Let go of habits, commitments, or relationships that don't serve your values.
5. **Reflect and Adjust:**
   - Revisit your values and goals regularly to ensure they remain aligned with your actions.

Examples of Intentional Living

1. **In Work:**
   - **Scenario:** You're offered a promotion that requires more hours but conflicts with your family priorities.

- o **Action:** Evaluate whether the promotion aligns with your values and make a decision accordingly.
- o **Outcome:** You either negotiate a balance or decline the offer, staying true to what matters most.

2. **In Relationships:**
   - o **Scenario:** You feel drained by a friendship that doesn't align with your values of positivity and growth.
   - o **Action:** Choose to spend less time with that person and more time with those who uplift you.
   - o **Outcome:** Your relationships feel more fulfilling and aligned with your values.

3. **In Daily Habits:**
   - o **Scenario:** You value creativity but spend evenings on social media.
   - o **Action:** Dedicate that time to painting, writing, or another creative activity.
   - o **Outcome:** You feel more productive and connected to your passions.

Practical Exercise: Start Living Intentionally

1. **Define Your Values:**
   - o List three to five values that are most important to you.

2. **Assess Your Current Life:**
   - o Reflect on how well your daily choices align with these values.

3. **Set One Intentional Goal:**
   - o Choose one area where you can better align your actions with your values.
   - o Example: "Limit screen time to prioritize family dinners."

4. **Track Progress:**
   - o Monitor how intentional changes improve your clarity, focus, and satisfaction.

Why This Technique Works

Intentional living creates alignment between your thoughts, actions, and values. It clears away distractions and ensures your efforts contribute to a meaningful and fulfilling life.

Closing Thought

Life is too precious to live on autopilot. Choose your path with purpose, align your actions with your values, and watch your life transform into one of clarity and intention.

Conclusion: A Clearer Path Forward

Congratulations on reaching the end of *Clear Thinking Made Simple: An AI's Guide to 100 Techniques for Seeing the World Clearly Without Blind Spots*. By now, you've explored a toolbox of techniques designed to sharpen your thinking, clarify your decisions, and empower you to navigate life with confidence and purpose.

Whether you're questioning assumptions, overcoming biases, solving problems, or connecting with others, every chapter in this book equips you to see the world more clearly and act with greater intention.

Why Clear Thinking Matters

The world is complex and full of noise. It's easy to get overwhelmed by information, fall into mental traps, or be swayed by emotions and biases. Clear thinking cuts through this clutter, allowing you to focus on what truly matters. It's the foundation for better decisions, stronger relationships, and a more fulfilling life.

When you think clearly, you don't just react to the world — you shape it. You approach challenges with curiosity, solve problems with creativity, and align your actions with your values. Clear thinking turns complexity into clarity and confusion into purpose.

Your Next Steps

1. **Practice Daily:**

   Clear thinking isn't learned overnight. Integrate these techniques into your routines, starting with just one or two that resonate most with you. Over time, they'll become second nature.

2. **Stay Curious:**

   The journey to clarity never ends. Keep asking questions, seeking diverse perspectives, and challenging your assumptions.

3. **Reflect and Adjust:**

   Regularly revisit the techniques in this book to see how they apply to new challenges in your life. Self-awareness is the key to growth.

4. **Share the Tools:**

   Clear thinking is contagious. By applying these techniques, you'll inspire others to think more clearly too. Share what you've learned with friends, family, and colleagues—it could transform their lives as much as yours.

A Life Built on Clarity

Imagine a life where your mind is free from mental clutter. Decisions feel lighter, your relationships grow deeper, and your goals align with your values. That's the life clear thinking can help you build. It's not about perfection—it's about progress. Every small step you take toward clarity adds up to a life of meaning, purpose, and impact.

You have everything you need to begin. The world is waiting for your clarity, your ideas, and your actions. Use these tools wisely, stay curious, and keep growing.

Closing Thought

Clear thinking is a superpower. Wield it well, and you'll unlock doors to a brighter, clearer, and more intentional life.

Appendix A: Quick Reference Guide to Clear Thinking

This appendix provides a concise overview of all the techniques covered in this book. Use it as a cheat sheet to refresh your memory or to find the exact tool you need for any situation.

Part I: Foundations of Clear Thinking

The basics you need to sharpen your mind and see the world clearly.

1. **Clean the Window:** Clear your mental filters to avoid distorted perceptions.
2. **Know Your Blind Spots:** Identify the biases and weaknesses in your thinking.
3. **Slow It Down:** Reflective thinking helps you make deliberate, logical decisions.
4. **Think Like a Scientist:** Use the hypothesis method to test ideas and find the truth.
5. **Separate Facts from Feelings:** Keep emotions in check to focus on objective truths.
6. **Distill Complexity:** Simplify complex problems by focusing on the basics.
7. **Zoom Out:** Step back to see the big picture and broader context.
8. **Zoom In:** Focus on crucial details without losing sight of their significance.
9. **Think in Layers:** Peel back assumptions to uncover

deeper truths.

10. **Question Everything:** The Socratic method sharpens your critical thinking.

Part II: Techniques for Logical Thinking

Tools to reason clearly and avoid logical pitfalls.

11. **Spot the Flaw:** Identify and counter logical fallacies in arguments.

12. **Ask the Right Questions:** Good questions lead to better answers and insights.

13. **Use If-Then Thinking for Scenarios:** Anticipate outcomes by mapping logical consequences.

14. **Apply Occam's Razor:** Simplify complex situations by focusing on the simplest explanation.

15. **Connect the Dots:** Recognize patterns to draw insightful conclusions.

16. **Check the Premises:** Ensure your reasoning is built on solid foundations.

17. **Follow the Chain:** Trace causes and effects to understand outcomes clearly.

18. **Think Backward:** Reverse-engineer problems to uncover their solutions.

19. **Use Logic Trees:** Break down problems step-by-step for structured decision-making.

20. **Compare and Contrast for Clearer Choices:** Evaluate options side-by-side for clarity.

Part III: Cognitive Bias-Busting Techniques

Learn to identify and overcome mental shortcuts and distortions.

21. **Fact-Check First:** Verify claims before accepting them as truth.

22. **Spot Confirmation Bias:** Test what you want to believe for accuracy.

23. **Decouple from Anchors:** Avoid being overly influenced by initial impressions.

24. **Think Like a Detective:** Stay objective and avoid

jumping to conclusions.

25. **Challenge the Crowd:** Resist bandwagon thinking by questioning group norms.

26. **Flip the Script:** Consider opposing perspectives to test your beliefs.

27. **Pause Before Reacting:** Manage emotional bias with deliberate thinking.

28. **Think Beyond the Present:** Avoid short-term traps by considering long-term effects.

29. **Don't Fall for Familiar:** Question availability heuristics and assess the evidence.

30. **Step Outside Yourself:** Mitigate egocentric bias by seeing others' perspectives.

Part IV: Practical Decision-Making Techniques

Techniques to make smarter, faster, and more thoughtful decisions.

31. **The 80/20 Rule:** Focus on the few things that produce the biggest impact.

32. **The Eisenhower Matrix:** Prioritize tasks by urgency and importance.

33. **The Premortem:** Plan for failure by anticipating what could go wrong.

34. **Decision Matrix:** Objectively weigh pros and cons for complex decisions.

35. **The 10/10/10 Rule:** Think about decisions' short-, medium-, and long-term impacts.

36. **Scenario Planning:** Prepare for multiple possible futures.

37. **Risk vs. Reward:** Make decisions by balancing potential benefits and risks.

38. **Take Small Steps:** Use iterative decision-making to test ideas gradually.

39. **Start with a Minimum Viable Solution:** Solve problems with simple, quick solutions.

40.Use Weighted Scoring for Big Decisions: Rank choices based on priority criteria.

Part V: Thinking Outside the Box

Break free from conventional thought patterns and unleash creativity.

41. First Principles Thinking: Break problems down to their basic truths.

42.Lateral Thinking: Jump to new perspectives and creative solutions.

43.Brainstorm Without Judgment: Generate ideas freely without overanalyzing.

44. Use Random Input to Spark Ideas: Find inspiration in unrelated concepts.

45.The SCAMPER Method: Improve ideas by modifying and combining them.

46.Combine Ideas to Innovate: Merge concepts to create something new.

47.Think in Opposites to Break Norms: Consider what would happen if you did the opposite.

48.Set Constraints to Foster Creativity: Use limitations to spark innovation.

49.Borrow from Other Fields: Apply ideas from different industries or disciplines.

50.Play 'What If?' with Scenarios: Explore possibilities to generate fresh ideas.

Part VI: Techniques for Mental Clarity

Cultivate habits to organize your thoughts and avoid mental overload.

51. Practice Mental Hygiene: Clear mental clutter for sharper focus.

52. Write It Out: Organize your thoughts by putting them on paper.

53. Mind Mapping for Visual Clarity: Use diagrams to structure and connect ideas.

54. **Practice Single-Tasking:** Focus on one thing at a time for greater productivity.
55. **Declutter Information Overload:** Filter out unnecessary noise to focus on essentials.
56. **Use White Space:** Schedule time for uninterrupted thinking.
57. **Decline to Decide:** Avoid decision fatigue by limiting choices.
58. **Set Clear Goals for Mental Direction:** Define your priorities to guide your actions.
59. **Use a Daily Reflection Routine:** Reflect on the day to improve self-awareness.
60. **Practice Mindfulness to Stay Present:** Stay grounded and focused in the moment.

Part VII: Advanced Critical Thinking Techniques

Deep-dive techniques for sharpening your analytical skills.

61. **Bayesian Thinking:** Update beliefs as new evidence emerges.
62. **Game Theory Basics:** Think strategically by considering others' perspectives.
63. **Think in Probabilities, Not Certainties:** Weigh likelihoods instead of absolutes.
64. **Second-Order Thinking:** Anticipate the ripple effects of decisions.
65. **Counterfactual Thinking:** Imagine "what-if" scenarios to explore alternatives.
66. **The Feynman Technique:** Explain concepts to understand them better.
67. **Ask, 'What Am I Missing?':** Challenge your assumptions to uncover gaps.
68. **Test Your Assumptions Before Acting:** Verify your ideas to avoid costly mistakes.
69. **Use Small Experiments to Test Ideas:** Validate concepts with low-risk trials.
70. **Always Ask for Feedback:** Gain clarity and improve through others' insights.

Part VIII: Techniques for Identifying Hidden Influences

Uncover hidden agendas, biases, and motivations behind information.

71. **Spot Manipulative Language:** Identify when words are used to mislead or influence.

72. **Identify Emotional Triggers in Arguments:** Recognize appeals to emotion over logic.

73. **Follow the Money:** Trace motivations to financial or personal interests.

74. **Question the Source:** Evaluate the credibility of information providers.

75. **Detect Spin in Media Narratives:** Separate facts from biased framing.

76. **Read Between the Lines of Ambiguity:** Uncover hidden meanings in vague statements.

77. **Look for the Hidden Agenda:** Identify the true motives behind actions or claims.

78. **Understand Framing Effects:** Recognize how the presentation of information shapes perception.

79. **Notice What's Left Out:** Identify missing information that distorts the full picture.

80. **Track the Influence of Social Pressure:** Resist groupthink by recognizing its impact.

Part IX: Mastering Interpersonal Clarity

Strengthen relationships with effective communication and understanding.

81. **Practice Active Listening:** Fully engage with others to understand their perspective.

82. **Ask Open-Ended Questions:** Encourage meaningful conversations by inviting detailed responses.

83. **Clarify What You Heard:** Confirm understanding to avoid miscommunication.

84. **Use Empathy to Understand Others' Views:** See the world through others' eyes.

85. **Reframe Conflict into Problem-Solving:** Turn disagreements into collaborative opportunities.

86. **Communicate in Simple, Clear Language:** Make your message easy to understand.

87. **Know When to Say Nothing:** Use silence as a tool for thoughtful communication.

88. **Mirror for Understanding:** Reflect others' thoughts to show you understand them.

89. **Summarize for Mutual Clarity:** Condense conversations to ensure shared understanding.

90. **Adapt to Your Audience's Needs:** Tailor your communication to the listener's perspective.

Part X: Building a Clear Thinking Lifestyle

Integrate clear thinking into every aspect of your life.

91. **Develop a Growth Mindset for Continuous Learning:** Embrace challenges as opportunities for growth.

92. **Stay Curious:** Cultivate a questioning habit to fuel lifelong learning.

93. **Learn From Diverse Perspectives:** Broaden your understanding by seeking varied viewpoints.

94. **Reflect Daily for Self-Awareness:** Use reflection to align actions with your values.

95. **Practice Gratitude for Balanced Thinking:** Focus on the positives to gain perspective.

96. **Stay Physically Healthy for Mental Sharpness:** Support clear thinking with good health habits.

97. **Embrace Failures as Learning Opportunities:** Use setbacks as a springboard for growth.

98. **Take Breaks to Recharge Thinking:** Rest your mind to boost focus and creativity.

99. **Seek Out Complexity and Simplify It:** Break down intricate ideas into manageable insights.

100. **Live Intentionally:** Align your choices with your values for a purposeful life.

Appendix B: Chapter-by-Part Overview

This appendix provides an organized list of all the chapters in the book, grouped by the parts they belong to. Use it as a quick navigation tool to locate specific chapters or revisit entire sections at a glance.

Part I: Foundations of Clear Thinking

- Clean the Window: Clear Your Mental Filters
- Know Your Blind Spots: Identify Cognitive Weaknesses
- Slow It Down: The Power of Reflective Thinking
- Think Like a Scientist: Embrace the Hypothesis Method
- Separate Facts from Feelings
- Distill Complexity: Boil It Down to Basics
- Zoom Out: See the Big Picture
- Zoom In: Focus on the Details That Matter
- Think in Layers: Peel Back Assumptions
- Question Everything: The Socratic Method

Part II: Techniques for Logical Thinking

- Spot the Flaw: Logical Fallacy Detection
- Ask the Right Questions
- Use If-Then Thinking for Scenarios
- Apply Occam's Razor: Simplify the Complex
- Connect the Dots: Pattern Recognition

- Check the Premises: Build on Solid Foundations
- Follow the Chain: Trace Cause to Effect
- Think Backward: Reverse Engineer the Problem
- Use Logic Trees: Break Down Problems Step-by-Step
- Compare and Contrast for Clearer Choices

Part III: Cognitive Bias-Busting Techniques

- Fact-Check First: Verify Before Believing
- Spot Confirmation Bias: Test What You Doubt
- Decouple from Anchors: Avoid First-Impression Traps
- Think Like a Detective: Avoid Jumping to Conclusions
- Challenge the Crowd: Resist Bandwagon Thinking
- Flip the Script: Consider Opposite Perspectives
- Pause Before Reacting: Manage Emotional Bias
- Think Beyond the Present: Avoid Short-Term Traps
- Don't Fall for Familiar: Question Availability Heuristics
- Step Outside Yourself: Mitigate Egocentric Bias

Part IV: Practical Decision-Making Techniques

- The 80/20 Rule: Focus on What Matters Most
- The Eisenhower Matrix: Prioritize Tasks by Importance
- The Premortem: Plan for Failure Before It Happens
- Decision Matrix: Weigh Pros and Cons Objectively
- The 10/10/10 Rule: Think Long-Term
- Scenario Planning: Prepare for All Outcomes
- Risk vs. Reward: Make Calculated Bets
- Take Small Steps: Embrace Iterative Decision-Making
- Start with a Minimum Viable Solution
- Use Weighted Scoring for Big Decisions

Part V: Thinking Outside the Box

- First Principles Thinking: Break It Down to Basics
- Lateral Thinking: Jump to New Perspectives
- Brainstorm Without Judgment
- Use Random Input to Spark Ideas
- The SCAMPER Method: Improve by Modifying
- Combine Ideas to Innovate
- Think in Opposites to Break Norms
- Set Constraints to Foster Creativity
- Borrow from Other Fields
- Play 'What If?' with Scenarios

Part VI: Techniques for Mental Clarity

- Practice Mental Hygiene: Eliminate Mental Clutter
- Write It Out: Organize Thoughts on Paper
- Mind Mapping for Visual Clarity
- Practice Single-Tasking: Focus on One Thing at a Time
- Declutter Information Overload
- Use White Space: Schedule Thinking Time
- Decline to Decide: Avoid Decision Fatigue
- Set Clear Goals for Mental Direction
- Use a Daily Reflection Routine
- Practice Mindfulness to Stay Present

Part VII: Advanced Critical Thinking Techniques

- Bayesian Thinking: Update Beliefs with New Evidence
- Game Theory Basics: Think Strategically About Others
- Think in Probabilities, Not Certainties
- Second-Order Thinking: Anticipate the Ripple Effects
- Counterfactual Thinking: Imagine the 'What-Ifs'
- The Feynman Technique: Explain to Learn
- Ask, 'What Am I Missing?'
- Test Your Assumptions Before Acting

- Embrace Failures as Learning Opportunities
- Take Breaks to Recharge Thinking
- Seek Out Complexity and Simplify It
- Live Intentionally: Align Choices with Values

Appendix C: Practice Scenarios

Clear thinking is most powerful when applied to real-life challenges. This appendix provides practice scenarios to help you test and refine your critical thinking skills.

Use this guide to practice and deepen your understanding of clear thinking in action.

Scenario 1: A Confusing Media Article

Situation: You come across a news article with conflicting claims about climate change solutions. One expert says renewable energy is the best approach, while another argues for nuclear energy.

Challenge: Use **Fact-Check First (Chapter 21)** to verify the credibility of the sources and claims. Then, apply **Question the Source (Chapter 74)** to evaluate each expert's background and potential biases. Finally, use **Ask the Right Questions (Chapter 12)** to clarify what evidence is most reliable.

Scenario 2: Workplace Miscommunication

Situation: Your team misunderstood the project deadline, and now it's too late to complete the work on time. Some blame the manager, while others say the instructions weren't clear.

Challenge: Apply **Clarify What You Heard (Chapter 83)** to ensure everyone understands the instructions going forward. Use **Summarize for Mutual Clarity (Chapter 89)** to confirm shared understanding during future meetings.

Scenario 3: A Tough Financial Decision

Situation: You're deciding whether to buy a new car. While it's tempting, you're unsure if it aligns with your budget and financial priorities.

Challenge: Use the **Decision Matrix (Chapter 34)** to objectively weigh the pros and cons. Then, apply the **10/10/10 Rule (Chapter 35)** to assess how this decision will impact you in 10 days, 10 months, and 10 years.

Scenario 4: Groupthink in a Meeting

Situation: Your team quickly agrees on a solution during a meeting, but you suspect they're rushing to avoid conflict or scrutiny.

Challenge: Use **Challenge the Crowd (Chapter 25)** to question the group's consensus thoughtfully. Combine this with **Spot the Flaw (Chapter 11)** to identify potential logical errors in the proposed solution.

Scenario 5: Handling Criticism

Situation: Your manager critiques your recent project, but you feel their feedback is overly harsh. You want to respond professionally and improve.

Challenge: Apply **Pause Before Reacting (Chapter 27)** to manage your emotions and avoid defensiveness. Then, use **Ask for Feedback (Chapter 70)** to clarify their concerns and identify specific areas for improvement.

Scenario 6: Overloaded with Information

Situation: You're overwhelmed by conflicting studies, opinions, and data while researching for work.

Challenge: Use **Distill Complexity (Chapter 6)** to boil the information down to its key components. Then, apply **Mind Mapping for Visual Clarity (Chapter 53)** to organize and structure your findings visually.

Scenario 7: A Disagreement with a Friend

Situation: A friend accuses you of being insensitive during a conversation. You feel misunderstood but want to resolve the issue.

Challenge: Apply **Use Empathy to Understand Others' Views (Chapter 84)** to see the situation from your friend's perspective. Then, use **Reframe Conflict into Problem-Solving (Chapter 85)** to shift the focus toward finding a constructive resolution.

Scenario 8: A Presentation to a Diverse Audience

Situation: You need to present a project update to an audience that includes technical experts, non-specialists, and executives.

Challenge: Use **Adapt to Your Audience's Needs (Chapter 90)** to tailor your message for each group. Apply **Communicate in Simple, Clear Language (Chapter 86)** to ensure accessibility and clarity.

Scenario 9: A Career Opportunity Dilemma

Situation: You're offered a promotion with a pay raise, but it comes with longer hours that could disrupt your personal life.

Challenge: Use **The 80/20 Rule (Chapter 31)** to determine if the benefits outweigh the sacrifices. Then, apply **Live Intentionally (Chapter 100)** to evaluate whether the promotion aligns with your values and long-term goals.

Scenario 10: Spotting Manipulation

Situation: A salesperson tries to persuade you to buy an expensive product by appealing to your emotions, claiming it will "change your life."

Challenge: Use **Spot Manipulative Language (Chapter 71)** to identify emotional appeals and misleading claims. Combine this with **Think Like a Detective (Chapter 24)** to evaluate the product's actual value.

Scenario 11: A Heated Argument

Situation: You're in a tense argument with a colleague. Both of you are becoming emotional, and the discussion is no longer productive.

Challenge: Apply **Pause Before Reacting (Chapter 27)** to step back and regain control of your emotions. Then, use **Reframe Conflict into Problem-Solving (Chapter 85)** to refocus the conversation on finding solutions.

Scenario 12: Planning a Big Project

Situation: You're managing a large project with many moving parts and deadlines, and you're worried about missing important details.

Challenge: Use **Logic Trees (Chapter 19)** to break the project into smaller, manageable steps. Then, apply **Set Clear Goals for Mental Direction (Chapter 58)** to define priorities and keep your team focused.

Scenario 13: Questionable Social Media Post

Situation: A viral post makes a bold claim but provides no sources. Everyone in the comments seems to agree, but you're sceptical.

Challenge: Use **Fact-Check First (Chapter 21)** to verify the claim with credible sources. Apply **Challenge the Crowd (Chapter 25)** to resist bandwagon thinking and form your own judgment.

Scenario 14: Balancing Competing Priorities

Situation: You have an overwhelming workload, a family event this weekend, and a personal project you've been procrastinating on.

Challenge: Use **The Eisenhower Matrix (Chapter 32)** to prioritize tasks by urgency and importance. Then, apply **Decline to Decide (Chapter 57)** to eliminate or delay non-essential tasks.

Scenario 15: A Stalled Creative Project

Situation: You're working on a creative project but feel stuck and uninspired.

Challenge: Use **Lateral Thinking (Chapter 42)** to approach the problem from new perspectives. Then, apply **The SCAMPER Method (Chapter 45)** to modify or combine ideas for fresh inspiration.

How to Use This Appendix

These scenarios are designed to bridge the gap between theory and practice. For each challenge, revisit the specified techniques, reflect on how they apply, and practice solving the problem step-by-step. The more you use these tools, the stronger your critical thinking skills will become.

Appendix D: The Clear Thinking Checklist

This checklist distills the essential lessons from this book into actionable steps you can use in your daily life. Use it as a quick reference to ensure your thinking stays sharp, logical, and intentional.

1. Clear Your Mental Filters

- Regularly question your assumptions to prevent distorted thinking.
- Reflect on your biases and how they influence your decisions.
- Practice mindfulness to separate facts from emotions.

2. Identify and Address Cognitive Biases

- Test your beliefs against evidence to spot confirmation bias.
- Challenge group consensus to avoid bandwagon thinking.
- Recognize and mitigate emotional triggers in your reasoning.

3. Simplify Complexity

- Break big problems into smaller, manageable parts.
- Focus on the core elements that matter most.
- Use visuals like mind maps or logic trees to clarify connections.

4. Ask Better Questions

- Replace yes-or-no questions with open-ended ones for deeper insights.
- Ask "What am I missing?" to uncover blind spots.
- Use "Why?" and "How?" to dig into the root causes of issues.

5. Evaluate Information Critically

- Fact-check claims before believing or sharing them.
- Trace the source of information to assess its credibility.
- Look for what's left out, such as omitted details or alternative perspectives.

6. Improve Decision-Making

- Use a decision matrix to weigh pros and cons logically.
- Apply the 10/10/10 Rule to consider short-, medium-, and long-term impacts.
- Prioritize tasks with tools like the Eisenhower Matrix or 80/20 Rule.

7. Navigate Conflict Constructively

- Use empathy to understand the other person's perspective.
- Reframe disagreements into problem-solving opportunities.
- Pause before reacting to manage emotional responses.

8. Communicate Clearly

- Tailor your language to your audience's knowledge level.
- Use simple, clear language to avoid misunderstandings.
- Summarize key points to ensure shared understanding.

9. Develop a Creative Mindset

- Brainstorm freely without self-censorship to spark new ideas.

- Apply lateral thinking to approach problems from fresh angles.
- Use constraints or random inputs to inspire innovative solutions.

10. Manage Mental Clutter
- Practice mental hygiene by decluttering unnecessary thoughts.
- Focus on single-tasking instead of multitasking.
- Schedule "white space" time for uninterrupted thinking.

11. Build Resilience Through Failure
- Acknowledge failures as learning opportunities rather than setbacks.
- Analyze what went wrong and extract actionable lessons.
- Adjust your approach based on what you've learned.

12. Stay Curious and Keep Learning
- Explore diverse perspectives to challenge your own views.
- Pursue new topics or hobbies to expand your knowledge.
- Cultivate a habit of daily questioning to fuel lifelong learning.

13. Optimize Your Physical Health
- Exercise regularly to boost focus and cognitive function.
- Eat brain-healthy foods like fruits, vegetables, and omega-3-rich sources.
- Prioritize sleep to recharge your mind and improve decision-making.

14. Reflect Daily
- Set aside time each day to review your successes and challenges.

- Use prompts like "What did I learn today?" or "What could I do better?"
- Track recurring patterns to identify areas for growth.

15. Live Intentionally

- Define your core values and align your actions with them.
- Eliminate distractions that don't contribute to your goals.
- Regularly evaluate whether your choices reflect your priorities.

Pro Tip: The Power of Intentional Practice

The techniques in this book work best when applied consistently and purposefully. Treat each challenge you face as an opportunity to refine your thinking. Remember: clarity grows with intention, curiosity, and reflection.

If you enjoyed this book, I'd greatly appreciate a review on Amazon because it helps me to create more books that people want. It would mean a lot to hear from you.

To leave a review:

1. Open your camera app.
2. Point your mobile device at the QR code.
3. The review page will appear in your web browser.

Thanks for your support!

Here's another book by Quinn Voss that you might like

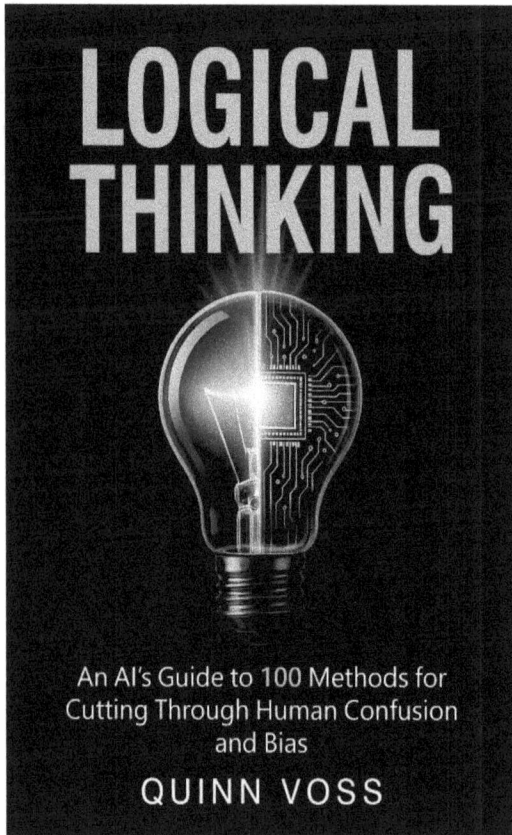

LOGICAL THINKING

An AI's Guide to 100 Methods for Cutting Through Human Confusion and Bias

QUINN VOSS

www.ingramcontent.com/pod-product-compliance
Lightning Source LLC
Chambersburg PA
CBHW072133090426
42739CB00013B/3174